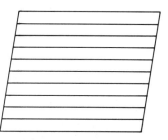

Handbook of Software and Hardware Interfacing for IBM PCs

Jeffrey P. Royer

Prentice-Hall, Inc., Englewood Cliffs, New Jersey 07632

Library of Congress Cataloging-in-Publication Data

Royer, Jeffrey P.
  Handbook of software and hardware interfacing for IBM PCs.

  Includes index.
  1. IBM Personal Computer.   2. Computer software.
3. Computer interfaces.   I. Title.
QA76.8.I2594R69 1987   004.165   86-12398
ISBN 0-13-381831-4
ISBN 0-13-381849-7 (pbk.)

Editorial/production supervision: **LISA SCHULZ**
Interior design: **ANNE BONANNO**
Cover design: **BEN SANTORA**
Manufacturing buyer: **GORDON OSBOURNE**

IBM PC is a trademark of International Business Machines Corporation.

© 1987 by Prentice-Hall, Inc.
A division of Simon & Schuster
Englewood Cliffs, New Jersey 07632

Printed in the United States of America

10 9 8 7 6 5 4 3 2 1

ISBN 0-13-381831-4
ISBN 0-13-381849-7 {PBK.}   025

Prentice-Hall International (UK) Limited, *London*
Prentice-Hall of Australia Pty. Limited, *Sydney*
Prentice-Hall Canada Inc., *Toronto*
Prentice-Hall Hispanoamericana, S.A., *Mexico*
Prentice-Hall of India Private Limited, *New Delhi*
Prentice-Hall of Japan, Inc., *Tokyo*
Prentice-Hall of Southeast Asia Pte. Ltd., *Singapore*
Editora Prentice-Hall do Brasil, Ltda., *Rio de Janeiro*

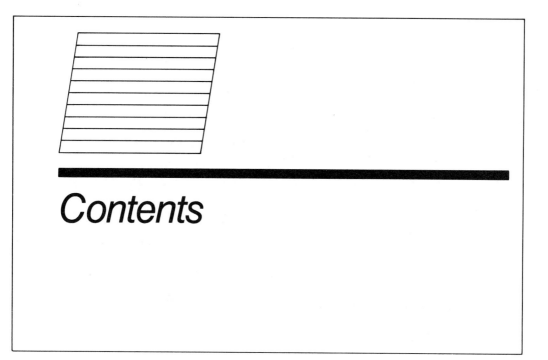

Contents

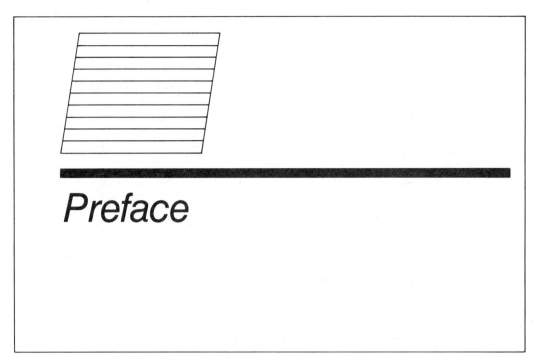

Preface

I wrote this book with the idea of producing a comprehensive software and hardware interfacing guide for the IBM PC. The book is derived from a course entitled "IBM PC Interfacing" that I developed and currently teach at several IBM plant sites. The object of the course is to cover the hardware and operating system in enough detail to permit engineers and programmers to immediately begin and complete various interfacing projects. The goal of the book is the same—to provide an application-interface guide for the system programmer, the software/hardware engineer, and the motivated hobbyist.

The book is divided into three parts: an introduction to the hardware and operating system, a comprehensive look at BIOS and PC-DOS, and a thorough treatment of hardware interfacing.

Chapters 1 through 3 include the introductory material. Chapters 4 through 11 comprise the section on the operating system—BIOS and PC-DOS. Chapters 12 through 18 contain the details of the hardware and hardware interfacing. The last two sections are relatively independent and can be read in reverse order. You can omit either section entirely if your primary interest lies in one direction or the other. The goal of the book is, however, to present an application-interfacing guide covering both software and hardware.

This is not a book for the beginner. You should have some familiarity with 8088 assembly language. All example programs are written in assembly language. Anyone familiar with programming concepts should be able to follow the examples, although only those with assembly language experience will fully appreciate the details. You should also be familiar with DOS commands at the "user" level. The discussion of DOS is at the "programmer" level; that is, I assume that you want to use DOS (and BIOS) from within an application program. Finally, for the hardware section you should have a basic familiarity with digital hardware. A short introduction to digital logic has been included, but previous experience will be necessary if you wish to actually build a device.

I firmly believe in teaching by example. The book includes approximately 30 program examples that can be typed in your computer and run. The examples provide the reader with the opportunity to see various concepts in action and can be used as templates for more complex tasks. Readers who abhor typing may order a diskette containing the examples (see the book insert on page 247).

How much of the book will be useful to those with IBM PC compatible computers? It all depends on which computer you have (some are more compatible than others). Most of the material on PC-DOS will apply directly to the MS-DOS operating system. BIOS is a different story. There is really no need for BIOS to be the same (even when the computer runs MS-DOS). With luck, the compatible computer's BIOS may be similar enough to the IBM PC BIOS to make the sections of the book on BIOS useful. To determine whether the hardware material is useful to you, look at the circuit diagram for the compatible computer. Certain similarities must exist to run MS DOS, but only by looking can you determine how similar your machine is to the IBM PC.

Finally, it will be helpful when you are reading this book to refer to the IBM Hardware Technical Reference and to the DOS Technical Reference. In DOS 2.0 and previous releases, the DOS technical information is in the DOS user's manual. In DOS 2.1 and later releases, there is a separate DOS Technical Reference. The text of the book and the example programs refer to DOS 2.0 and above.

I wish to thank my IBM PC for helping me write this book and my friends for their interest and encouragement. I would like especially to thank my wife, Susan, for her tremendous support and patience.

Jeffrey P. Royer

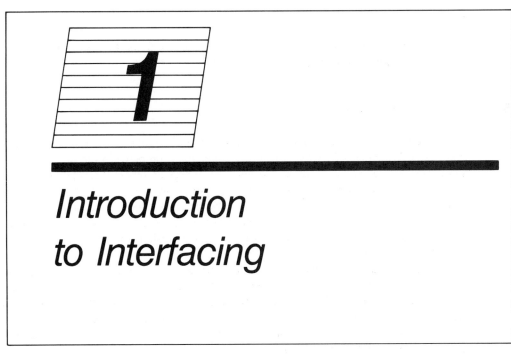

Introduction
to Interfacing

The term *interfacing* means different things to different people. In the most literal sense of the word, an interface is a boundary between two objects. To interface usually means to provide a communication pathway between the objects, that is, across the interface.

HARDWARE INTERFACING

The two objects defining an interface can be physical devices. In that case, interfacing consists of designing hardware to provide a physical connection between the two devices. Here are some common examples of "hardware interfacing" tasks:

- Interfacing a printer to a computer
- Interfacing a serial communications link to a computer
- Interfacing a digital I/O port to a computer
- Interfacing analog-digital (A/D) or digital-analog (D/A) converters to a computer
- Interfacing a diskette or fixed disk drive to a computer

The common ingredient in these tasks is interfacing a device to a computer. (Since the term "computer" is ambiguous, we will follow IBM and refer to the box containing the microprocessor as the *system unit*.) The IBM PC system unit is designed with an "open" architecture—the signals important for hardware interfacing are available on card edge

1

connectors within the system unit. Roughly one-half of the book (Chapters 12–18) is devoted to hardware interfacing.

SOFTWARE INTERFACING

When the two objects defining the interface are computer programs, the interfacing task consists of designing software that provides communication between the two programs. For example, one program may be a *printer driver* and the other, a general application program. The printer driver is a subroutine that prints one character on the printer each time it is invoked. The software interface is really the knowledge of where the application program must place the character before it invokes the printer driver. As we can see in this example, software interfacing is really just the task of making sure that parameters are passed correctly from one program to the other.

The protocol for parameter passing is defined by only one of the two programs communicating across the interface. In the IBM PC, one program is generally an application program; the other falls into one of two categories. The second program may be a device driver (like the printer driver), or it may simply perform some function (like allocating memory). It is the second program that defines the protocol for parameter passing. The distinction between a hardware driver and a function is not important—the important point is how to pass the parameters.

GENERAL INTERFACING

This book addresses readers with diverse interests and backgrounds. At one end of the spectrum are those interested in designing a specific hardware device to use in the IBM PC. At the other end are readers interested in understanding and using the internal features of the operating system as fully as possible. Those between form the majority. It is becoming more and more useful for "hardware" engineers to be familiar with the software and for "software" engineers to know something about the hardware. Most interfacing projects have both hardware and software aspects.

This book discusses in detail both the device drivers (in BIOS) and the functions performed by the PC operating system (BIOS and PC-DOS). In addition, we will see how to write and install hardware drivers (including the "installable device drivers").

INTERFACING PREREQUISITES

The general interfacing task (hardware and software) requires familiarity with the system unit and the operating system. The system unit includes the system board (with the I/O Channel card slots), a power supply, and disk drives. The system board contains the main processing unit, the Intel 8088 microprocessor, and necessary support chips. The I/O

Channel is the interface bus. The operating system, consisting of BIOS (in ROM) and PC-DOS, performs many functions that will make an interfacing task easier. We will make a thorough study of both the system hardware and the operating system.

To make it easier for readers whose interest centers on either the software or the hardware, the book segregates the software and hardware topics: Chapters 3–11 cover the operating system; Chapters 12–18 cover the hardware. Chapter 2 contains a basic introduction to the hardware.

EXAMPLES–PROJECTS THAT REQUIRE INTERFACING

Following are several projects that have typical interfacing needs. We present these to show the variety of projects that can be handled with the basic knowledge of the IBM PC hardware and software presented in this book.

Temperature Monitor

The temperature monitor consists of a temperature transducer, an A/D converter, and possibly a timer. The temperature transducer (semiconductor, thermocouple) produces a temperature-dependent voltage that is converted to a digital signal by the A/D converter. Either by using a look-up table or by calculating directly, software converts the digital signal to a temperature value. The temperature can be measured at specific time intervals by using the system's time-of-day clock or an external timer. Alternatively, the A/D converter can interrupt the processor whenever a conversion is complete. The temperature monitor can be used in many different applications, from quality control of microcomputer chips to making wine.

The interfacing task consists of designing the hardware connection to the I/O channel and writing the software to time, measure, record, and evaluate the temperature. The software task may include using BIOS or DOS functions to store data on the diskette or to display it on the console and printer.

Sound Wave Analysis

A microphone is connected to an A/D converter. Sound pressure waves are converted to voltages by the microphone and are converted to a digital signal by the A/D converter. This example is very similar to the temperature monitor. The main difference, however, is the sampling rate. Analysis of audible sound waves may require sampling rates of up to 40,000 samples/sec, whereas the sampling rate for the temperature monitor may be on the order of a few per second. A rate of 40,000 samples/sec would require the use of the system's direct memory access (DMA) facilities. The time between samples is only 25 μs, probably not enough to handle with the 8088.

A Video "Frame Grabber"

A "flash"-type A/D converter is connected to the video signal on a television camera to digitally record one television frame. The term "flash" indicates the speedy nature of the A/D conversion. The duration of one scan line is about 60 μs. If we want 1000-dot horizontal resolution, each A/D conversion must take place in 60 ns (60 μs/1000). This is much too fast for the system's DMA chip, so the results of the conversions must be buffered. The buffer memory can be "dual-ported," permitting it to be accessed as system memory, in addition to being accessed as a buffer by the A/D converter circuitry. Alternatively, the buffer could be accessed through a port.

A Heating (or Cooling) Device

The opposite of monitoring temperature is controlling it. Heating may be done by simply controlling the voltage applied to a heating coil; cooling, by controlling the voltage on a "Peltier effect" cooling device. In either case, a D/A converter is needed to change the digital output to an analog voltage connected to the device. In other respects this example is similar to the preceding one.

Using DOS Functions

Suppose a company requires an application program that formats a diskette in drive B and stores data being received via the RS-232 interface on the newly formatted diskette. We must either write a format program or use FORMAT.COM. Both are possible, but using FORMAT.COM is probably easier. The application program can use DOS functions to load and execute FORMAT.COM. Other DOS functions provide services that make it easy to read and write files to the disk. BIOS and DOS provide support for the RS-232 interface. This "interface" example makes no use of "new" hardware; it simply requires understanding the parameter-passing protocol of existing interfaces.

USE OF ASSEMBLY LANGUAGE

Most interfacing software requires some use of assembly language. All program examples in this book are shown in assembly language. The reader who has little familiarity with 8088 assembly language programming may be able to follow the examples but will find construction of new programs difficult. We make no attempt to teach assembly language, since there are already several fine books that do so.

Readers who prefer high-level languages may be able to convert some examples to their favorite language. Several high-level languages provide straightforward interfaces to assembly language procedures. These include Pascal, "C", PL/M, Fortran, and compiled BASIC. A common solution to the high-level versus assembly-language dilemma is to write all but the time-critical sections of an application program in a high-level language.

The high-level language executes a procedure call to invoke the assembly-language procedure.

CHAPTER SUMMARY

This chapter has introduced the term *interfacing* (as used in this book) and has given several examples illustrating typical interfacing projects. Interfacing projects can generally be divided into hardware and software tasks. Hardware interfacing consists of designing and building the circuits that connect to the I/O channel. Software interfacing consists of learning and using parameter-passing protocols. (Software interfacing also includes creating protocols, a topic not relevant to this book.) Chapter 2 presents an overview of the IBM PC hardware; Chapter 3, an overview of BIOS and DOS. The author recommends reading both chapters. A general familiarity with the system will make any interfacing task easier.

Overview
of the IBM PC
Hardware

In this chapter we will introduce the major features of the IBM PC, preparing the way for the more detailed discussions in later chapters. The three major physical components usually identified as the IBM PC are the display monitor, the keyboard, and the system unit.

THE IBM PC DISPLAY

IBM originally supplied two types of display monitors for use with the IBM PC: the monochrome and the color. Each type is connected to the system unit through a specific interface adapter card that plugs into the PC.

The IBM monochrome display adapter is character-oriented and well suited to the display of textual material. The characters are well formed and easy to read. You have to look closely to see the individual dots that compose the characters. The major limitation of the monochrome display adapter is that the character set is fixed—you can't define your own character set or use pixel (all-points-addressable) graphics. IBM has provided a predefined set of graphic characters, however. These can be used to create some elementary graphic effects—bar charts, for example.

The Color/Graphic Display Adapter supports character display as well as various all-points-addressable (APA) modes. The characters are not as well formed as with the monochrome display, which makes the system less attractive for word processing applications. On the other hand, the APA modes permit the graphical display of information that may replace textual description. The color graphics adapter also supports user-defined character sets.

6

It is unfortunate that the monochrome and color monitors are not compatible. You cannot drive a monochrome monitor with a Color/Graphics Display Adapter, and vice versa. If you want the advantages of both monochrome and color, you must buy and install both interface adapters and then physically manipulate a switch to indicate which is the active display adapter. This is awkward, to say the least. Fortunately for some, however, the drawbacks of the IBM display cards have created a new industry, the manufacturing of IBM PC-compatible display cards. This is not the place to discuss all the available compatible display cards, but I would like to mention a couple as examples. The Hercules Company makes a monochrome display adapter that is completely compatible with the IBM monochrome display adapter and also has an APA mode for doing graphics. With the Hercules card, you can do graphics on the monochrome monitor. (This card has been so successful that there are now other companies that make Hercules-compatible cards.) Another company, Everex, makes a Hercules-compatible card that will drive both a color and a monochrome monitor simultaneously.

We will discuss the characteristics of the IBM display adapters in detail in Chapter 12.

THE IBM PC KEYBOARD

The heart of the IBM PC keyboard is the Intel 8048 microprocessor. Each time a key is pressed or released, the keyboard interrupts the system unit and sends it (via a serial link) a scan code. The PC's keyboard driver program interprets the scan code. The 8048 performs all the housekeeping functions necessary for the keyboard-PC communication. Among other tasks, it scans the keyboard, maintains a buffer of up to 16 scan codes, and controls the serial communication to the PC. We will discuss the keyboard and the keyboard driver in detail in Chapter 13.

THE SYSTEM UNIT

The hardware within the system unit can be divided into four parts (functionally and physically): a large printed circuit board called the *system board;* card slots, referred to as the *I/O channel,* on the system board; disk drives (usually at least one); and a power supply for the system.

The System Board

The system board really defines an IBM PC. If we replaced the power supply, the disk drives, the keyboard, and the display monitor, we would still have an IBM PC. The system board contains the microprocessor, the support chips, and the BIOS, which truly make the IBM PC what it is. The many IBM PC-compatible computers must stick very closely to the design of the IBM PC system board, or they will simply not be compatible. The main components and features of the system board are

- The Intel 8088 microprocessor
- a socket and interface for the 8087 math-coprocessor
- a system counter/timer, the Intel 8253-5
- a DMA controller, the Intel 8237-5
- an interrupt controller, the Intel 8259A
- a parallel port expander, the Intel 8255A
- sockets for up to 256K byte of dynamic RAM
- up to 48K byte of ROM
- an audio speaker

Although we devote entire chapters to several of these items, we will discuss them briefly here to give an overall view of the way the system works.

THE INTEL 8088 MICROPROCESSOR

The Intel 8088 microprocessor is commonly called a ''16-bit'' microprocessor. This means it can process data (add, subtract, shift, and so on) 16 bits at a time. (The first generation of microprocessors consisted of 8-bit machines and could process only 8 bits at a time.) Whether or not the 8088 is truly a 16-bit machine is debatable, for it cannot access memory 16 bits at a time. When the 8088 accesses memory, it must break the 16-bit access into two 8-bit accesses. Although the 8088 can process data in internal registers 16 bits at a time, it can process data in memory only 8 bits at a time. What does this mean to us? Simply that the 8088 has a 16-bit internal data bus and an 8-bit external data bus. (The 8088 has a less-handicapped relative, the Intel 8086 microprocessor. This is a true 16-bit machine, able to process both external and internal data 16 bits at a time.)

The 8088 has two address spaces accessed through a 20-bit address bus. When it addresses memory (via instructions such as MOV, INC, ADD), it uses all 20 bits of the address bus. This provides a one-megabyte addressing capability. In contrast, when it addresses I/O devices (via IN and OUT), only the low 16 bits of the address bus contain a valid address. This limits the size of the I/O address space to 64K byte. As we will see in detail in Chapter 14, the IBM PC uses only 10 of these address lines, shrinking the I/O address space to 1K byte.

The 8088 contains eight general-purpose 16-bit internal registers that are used primarily for data manipulation and as data pointers. The 8088 views memory as segments. A segment is a contiguous section of memory not larger than 64K byte. The 8088 contains four special 16-bit registers—segment registers—each of which contains the upper 16 bits of a 20-bit segment address. In effect, each segment register points to the beginning of a segment in memory. All memory accesses are relative to one of the four active segments. Since this section is intended to be an overview, I refer the reader to any good assembly-language text for more information on segments.

The 8088 supports the Intel 8087 math coprocessor. To use the 8087, just plug it into the available socket and set a switch to indicate its presence. The 8088-8087 interface is extremely intimate. Both chips use the same instruction stream. The 8088 calculates and presents to the address bus the addresses of operands needed by the 8087.

The use of the 8087 greatly increases performance when you are doing extensive mathematical calculations. The Intel literature shows the 8087 executing specific calculations (such as double-precision multiply) 1000 times faster than software emulation. In practice, because of overhead in loading the internal 8087 registers, a factor of 30 times is more common.

The clock speed of the 8088 in the IBM PC is 4.77 MHz. This translates into a clock period of 210 ns. The memory access cycle of the 8088 takes four clock periods, or 840 ns. The system board logic inserts one wait-state on all I/O accesses, making the I/O access time five clock periods, or 1050 ns.

THE SYSTEM BOARD RAM

The system board can contain up to 256K bytes of dynamic RAM memory, installed in four 64K byte banks. Each of the 64K byte banks contains sockets for nine 64K-bit chips. (Early PC's used 16K chips, limiting the system board to 64K.) A byte of data is distributed across eight of these chips, one bit in each chip. The ninth chip, containing a parity bit, is used to check for memory errors. If a memory error occurs, the system board generates a nonmaskable-interrupt (NMI) to the 8088, bringing the machine to a stop. The system board RAM is located in the low end of the memory space, from 00000H to 3FFFFH. The dynamic RAM must be refreshed at intervals not longer than 2 ms. The refresh cycle is performed by the DMA controller chip (8237A) at intervals specified by the timer chip (8253-5), every 15.2 μs. The 8088 is put into a wait-state during the refresh cycle, which slightly decreases the 8088 throughput.

THE SYSTEM BOARD ROM

The system board contains sockets for 48K bytes of ROM. The ROM is installed in 8K-byte chips and is located at the top of memory in the address range from 0F4000H to 0FFFFFH. The top 40K-byte space out of the total 48K-byte ROM space is occupied by code that implements

- The BASIC interpreter
- the power-on self-test
- the I/O drivers (BIOS)
- the diskette bootstrap loader
- the dot patterns for characters in graphics mode

One of the 8K-byte sockets (at the lowest address) is empty. You can use this socket to install custom drivers and programs that need to be resident in memory.

THE SYSTEM BOARD COUNTER-TIMER

The system board contains an Intel 8253-5 counter-timer chip that is used to implement system timing functions. We have already mentioned the need to periodically refresh the dynamic RAM. In addition, the operating system maintains a real-time clock. Both functions needing a periodic signal use the 8353-5.

The 8353-5 is actually three independent counter-timers in one chip. The technical details of this versatile chip (operating modes and programming) can be found in the Intel data book. The following discussion is limited to the use of the 8253-5 in the IBM PC.

Each timer channel is dedicated to a specific function:

- Channel 0: time-of-day clock
  This channel is programmed to interrupt the 8088 every 55 ms. The associated interrupt routine implements the time-of-day clock.
- Channel 1: DMA refresh cycles
  This channel is programmed to request a DMA transfer from the DMA controller (8237-5) every 15.2 μs. The DMA controller responds to the request by running a memory refresh cycle.
- Channel 2: cassette interface and audio speaker
  This channel is used to put tones on a cassette tape. Channel 2 is connected to the audio speaker through a gate and can be used to make beeps, music, and assorted noises.

What can we do with these timers without crashing the system? Since channel 0 generates an interrupt to the 8088, we can use this channel to control periodic events. The BIOS time-of-day routine is set up to allow control to be transferred to a user program that would then execute every 55 ms. Alternatively, we can bypass the time-of-day program entirely. We can make the interrupt go directly to a user program at a programmed timing interval. We'll see how to do some of these things in Chapter 4.

We shouldn't change channel 1 because of its role as a timer for the memory refresh cycles. However, we are free to do what we like with channel 2. For instance, we can use channel 2 to help debug programs.

Some programs, installable device drivers for example, are difficult to debug with Debug. To help debug an installed driver, write a program that causes the speaker to emit a sequence of beeps. (Pass the number of beeps to the program as a parameter.) Next, install the beeper program and make it resident, using function call 31H. Your installed device driver should invoke the beeper program at key points during its execution, using an INT instruction. By listening to the sequence of beeps, you can tell immediately when and where a bug occurred.

Channel 2 can also be used in conjunction with the cassette port hardware to build a limited interface. (*Note:* The PC-XT has no cassette port.)

THE SYSTEM BOARD DMA CONTROLLER

The 8088 microprocessor is fast, but for some tasks, not fast enough. The transfer of data between the disk and memory takes place at a rate faster than the microprocessor can handle. A very simple program loop (one that doesn't even check the status of the disk controller) would yield a maximum transfer rate of about 100K bytes/sec. By using a DMA controller chip (Intel 8237-5), the data transfer rate goes up to about 422K bytes/sec. With the DMA chip we get a transfer rate roughly four times faster. In the IBM PC, all diskette and fixed-disk transfers as well as memory refresh cycles are handled by the DMA chip.

The 8237-5 is really quite a flexible chip. We will present its basic features here and leave a detailed discussion to Chapter 17. Some of the important features are

- four independent DMA channels
- 16-bit address and count registers (not 20-bit, as we may desire)
- four types of transfers: memory to memory, memory to I/O, I/O to I/O, and I/O to memory
- a programmable priority scheme
- programmable synchronization and termination conditions

The flexibility of this chip is somewhat restricted in the IBM PC. Data transfers are limited to those taking place between I/O and memory. In addition, since the address registers in the 8237-5 are only 16 bits wide, there are three 4-bit-wide page registers that provide the upper four bits to make a 20-bit address. This means that the memory is broken into 16 ''pages,'' each 64K bytes long, and that DMA transfers can't take place across these page boundaries. Finally, the 8237-5 is programmed in the ''single-transfer'' mode, which means it must release the address and data busses after each transfer cycle. (This is done to allow memory refresh cycles to occur.) The single transfer mode limits the transfer rate to 422 kHz.

In the IBM PC, the four channels have the following assignments:

- Channel 0   memory refresh cycles
- Channel 1   not used
- Channel 2   used by the diskette
- Channel 3   used by the fixed disk

The lower the channel number, the higher the priority. As we would expect, memory-refresh cycles have the highest priority. Notice that channel 1 is not used. In Chapter 17, we will see how to use this channel for external DMA.

THE SYSTEM BOARD INTERRUPTS

Chapter 18 contains a complete discussion of the interrupt structure of the 8088 microprocessor. The material in this section is an introduction.

The 8088 has two external interrupt pins: the nonmaskable-interrupt (NMI) and the interrupt (INTR). The NMI is edge-triggered and is typically used for critical situations such as a power failure. The NMI cannot be masked at the 8088 level. All other hardware interrupts use the INTR pin. This interrupt pin is software-enabled and is masked by the instructions STI (enable) and CLI (mask).

In the IBM PC, the NMI is connected through system board hardware to three different sources. These are the system board parity error, the I/O channel parity error, and the 8087 interrupt. Software (BIOS) enables the system board logic so that interrupts can be received at the NMI pin. After an NMI interrupt, the operating system software must determine the source of the interrupt.

The INTR pin is connected to the Intel 8259A programmable interrupt controller (PIC). The 8259A PIC is another example of a very flexible chip whose use is somewhat restricted in the IBM PC. In Chapter 18 we will discuss the 8259A and show how to interface it to the PC. For now, we will note that the 8259A will handle up to eight prioritized interrupt sources. These sources have the following functions assigned to them in the IBM PC:

- INT0   time-of-day interrupt, connected to the output of 8253-5 channel 0; generates an interrupt every 55 ms
- INT1   keyboard interrupt, connected to the keyboard; generates an interrupt whenever a key is pressed or released
- INT2   reserved
- INT3   communications
- INT4   communications
- INT5   fixed disk
- INT6   diskette
- INT7   printer

The lower the number, the higher the priority. INT2–INT7 are bussed to the I/O channel card slots to give external devices access to the interrupt system.

THE SYSTEM BOARD PROGRAMMABLE
PERIPHERAL INTERFACE

Through the three parallel ports on the system board, we can read the keyboard scan code, the configuration switches, and several other items we will discuss later. The Intel 8255A programmable peripheral interface is used to implement these ports in hardware. The 8255A has 24 digital I/O pins configurable in a variety of different modes. We will discuss the use of the 8255A in interfacing applications in the appendix. In the PC, BIOS configures the 8255A to represent three 8-bit parallel ports as in Table 2-1.

The 8255A appears as ports 60H, 61H, and 62H. Table 2-1 illustrates the use of each port. Ports 60H and 62H are input ports, and port 61H is an output port. Note that port 60H and bits 0–3 of port 62H have two functions. The choice of a particular function for port 60H depends upon bit 7 in port 61H. Bit 2 of port 61H controls the function of bits 0–3 of port 62H.

Port 60H and bit 7 of port 61H will have special significance for us in Chapter 13, when we discuss the keyboard driver. The main function of port 60H is to read the key-

TABLE 2-1 THE 8255 PROGRAMMABLE PERIPHERAL INTERFACE

	Bits	
Port 60H	0–7	Keyboard scan code or system configuration (see bit 7, port 61H)
	Bits	
Port 61H	0	Timer2 gate (1 = ON)
	1	Speaker gate (1 = ON)
	2	1 = Memory size switch
		0 = Spare keys (see port 62H)
	3	Cassette motor (1 = OFF)
	4	0 = Memory parity check enable
	5	0 = I/O channel check enable
	6	1 = Keyboard clock enable
	7	1 = Configuration switches
		0 = Keyboard scan (see port 60H)
	Bits	
Port 62H	0–3	Memory size switch or spare keys
	4	Cassette data (IN)
	5	Timer2 Output (read here)
	6	I/O channel check
	7	Memory parity check

board scan code. Likewise, bits 0 and 1 of port 61H are important because they are instrumental in generating sound.

The I/O Channel

The I/O Channel is basically a bus provided for system expansion. The name I/O channel sometimes causes confusion. The term I/O often refers to ports (accessed by IN and OUT instructions), but the I/O in "I/O channel" has a broader meaning: expansion. We may access both the I/O and memory address spaces through this expansion bus—the I/O channel.

The I/O channel consists of 62 lines bussed to five card slots (eight in the PC-XT) in the system unit. Many of these lines are identical to the system bus lines. There are 20 address lines, eight bidirectional data lines, and four control lines (/IOR, /IOW, /MEMR, /MEMW). The address, data, and control lines permit interfacing to both the memory space and I/O (port) space.

In addition, the I/O channel contains six interrupt request lines (IRQ2-IRQ7). It also supports three channels of DMA, memory refresh, and wait-state insertion. There are two clocks, the 14.81 MHz crystal frequency and the 4.77 MHz processor clock. Finally, all of the voltages of the power supply (plus ground) are present.

The Power Supply

The IBM PC and the IBM PC-XT power supplies have the following specifications:

TABLE 2-2 POWER SUPPLIES IN THE
IBM PC AND PC-XT

	PC	XT
+5 VDC	7 A	15 A
−5 VDC	0.3 A	0.3 A
+12 VDC	2 A	4.2 A
−12 VDC	0.25 A	0.25 A

All these voltages are available in the I/O channel. How much current can you use? The technical reference specifies that we may use up to 4 A of the +5 VDC supply in the I/O channel in the standard PC. This figure goes up to 11 A in the PC-XT. To determine how much of the current of the other supplies you can use, you must determine what uses them in your system. For example, a system that has RS232 drivers (using the 12-volt supplies) will have less of the 12-volt current available than a system without them. As a guideline, keep in mind the following:

- +12 Vdc is used by disk drives and RS232 drivers.
- −12 Vdc is used by RS232 drivers.
- −5 Vdc is used by some of the older 16K-byte RAM chips.

We will leave a detailed discussion of the driving capability of the output lines to Chapter 14. At this stage, we simply want to point out the conservative recommendation from the IBM Technical Reference Manual: *Use no more than two "LS" (low-power Schottky) loads per line in each card slot.* In most applications, interface cards use only one LS load, a buffer chip connected to the I/O channel. The buffer chip is then used to drive the other circuits on the interface card.

CHAPTER SUMMARY

In this chapter we have introduced the hardware of the IBM-PC. The basic components are the display monitor (plus an adapter card), the keyboard, and the system unit. The system unit contains the system board, the I/O channel slots, the disk drives, and the power supply. The system board contains the Intel 8088 microprocessor, memory, and the support chips necessary to make a functional computer system. The complete system has priority interrupt capability, DMA capability, wait-state capability, an interface for the Intel 8087 math coprocessor, and an expansion bus. The expansion bus (I/O channel) supports a wide variety of interfacing possibilities. We can interface to memory chips and

I/O ports. The interrupt, DMA, and wait-state circuits are available to us. As we shall see in Chapters 12–18, adding customized circuits to the system is a very straightforward process.

If you are primarily interested in hardware interfacing, you may go directly to Chapter 12 without much loss in continuity of presentation. Chapters 3 through 11 deal almost entirely with the operating system. It has been the author's experience that the more you know about a particular machine, the easier any system interfacing task becomes, be it hardware- or software-oriented. Therefore, it is recommended that you read the whole book, cover to cover.

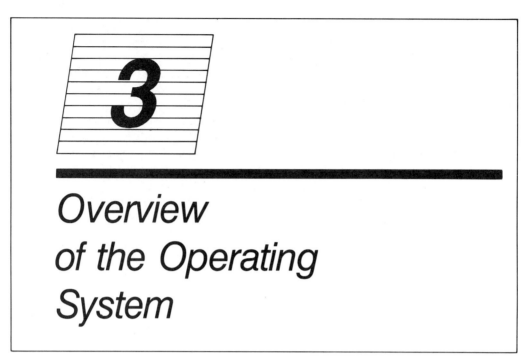

Overview
of the Operating
System

This chapter will introduce the operating system of the IBM PC. We will first examine the need for an operating system and then proceed with an overview of the two main components of the IBM PC operating system: BIOS and DOS.

THE FUNCTION OF THE OPERATING SYSTEM

We are first going to discuss the need for and function of an operating system. In Chapter 2 we saw an overview of the hardware of the IBM PC. We could see that the PC is a sophisticated and complicated machine with boundless potential. What else do we need in addition to the hardware? What most people want to do with this machine is make or run computer programs. The programs may be business-oriented, like spread-sheet programs; they may be scientifically oriented; they may be programs that control other machines; they could be games or simulations. The list is endless.

Let's consider an example that will show us why we need an operating system. Suppose we were given only the hardware discussed in Chapter 2 (excluding the BIOS ROM). What would we have to do to make a computer that was useful to people who want to run programs? How would we get started? This is exactly the problem that faced the people who bought or built the first microcomputer systems. Their computer consisted basically of a box full of hardware and perhaps an assembly-language manual. To run a program on such a machine, we would have to enter the program bit by bit through a series of switches on the front panel of the machine.

Needless to say, entering the program this way is a painstaking and error-prone task. To make life simpler, we could write one little program that loads programs from some storage device—a paper tape reader or cassette tape, for example. The loader program would initialize the required interface chips, read the data from the interface, store the data in memory, and finally jump to the starting address of the program just loaded. All we would have to do is enter the loader program through the switches and start it. Even this might be too much trouble. To avoid the switches, we could put this loader program into some permanent form of memory (ROM or EPROM). Then, when we pressed "reset" on the computer, this permanent loader program would load a program from the cassette and execute it. No longer must we load programs by hand! We have invented the automatic starter.

Here, we have reached a new level of sophistication. We can store in permanent memory a small program that will be executed each time the computer is reset. The small program performs the same task each time. It initializes any necessary chips, loads a program from the cassette (or paper tape, or disk drive), and, finally, runs the program. The great thing about this idea is that the loader may load any type or size of program (limited only by the physical system). The program that is loaded may be just an application program, but more commonly it will be a program designed to allow even more sophisticated use of the computer. It may initialize other interface chips—a display interface, a printer interface, a disk-drive interface. It may also contain the programs (drivers) needed to communicate with these other interface chips. It may perform "monitor"-type functions, allowing you to examine and change memory contents. Finally, it may include file-handling and memory management programs. The list of features we can add is lengthy.

The permanent loader program used to load the initial cassette (or diskette) program is commonly called a *bootstrap loader*. The initially loaded program that includes the special features is called an *operating system*. It may occur to you that it would be simpler just to put the whole operating system in ROM or EPROM to make it permanently resident. This is certainly possible. Some small computer systems designed this way contain the complete operating systems in ROM. Of course, this limits the amount of memory available for user programs. At the other extreme, a system may be designed so that the ROM program is as small as possible. The small ROM program would contain a very primitive loader, which would load a more sophisticated loader from the tape or disk drive. As you can see, the operating system designer faces many alternatives.

Let's review what we have learned through our hypothetical example. To have a machine that is usable (in the sense that we can write or run programs on it), we need the following:

- a permanent loader program that is executed when the power is switched on
- a program (permanent or loaded) that initializes and contains drivers for all interfaces
- a program (permanent or loaded) that will load and execute other programs
- optionally, a program that will handle logical files

- optionally, utility programs for implementing special features of the system such as
  - time-of-day clock and
  - graphics mode initialization

THE IBM PC OPERATING SYSTEM

The IBM PC operating system is similar in broad outline to the preceding example. Part of the operating system is located in permanent memory and part is loaded during power-up. The part located in ROM is referred to as BIOS (Basic Input/Output System). The part that is loaded into RAM is called DOS (Disk Operating System). These names are slightly misleading, for each of these parts does much more than its name implies.

AN INTRODUCTION TO BIOS

BIOS is located in an 8K-byte ROM at the top of memory, the address range being from 0FE000H to 0FFFFFH. The programs within BIOS provide the most direct, lowest-level interaction with the various devices in the system. Among the programs contained within BIOS are these:

- power-on self-test
- system configuration analysis
- time-of-day
- print screen
- bootstrap loader
- I/O support program for
  - asynchronous communications
  - keyboard
  - diskette
  - printer
  - display

Many of these programs are accessible to the assembly-language programmer through the software interrupt instruction (INT). The design goal for the BIOS programs is to provide a device-independent interface to the various physical devices in the system. What does this mean?

Let's use a printer interface as an example. Assume that we have an interface to a parallel printer. Typically there will be two ports associated with this interface: a data port and a status port. To output a character to the printer, we must first read the status port until the printer indicates that it is not busy. Then we can output the desired character to the data port. Here is a program example:

```
OUTPUT_CHAR:        IN    AL, STATUS       ; GET STATUS
                    TEST  AL, 01H          ; IS IT BUSY?
                    JNZ   OUTPUT_CHAR      ; YES, TRY AGAIN
                    MOV   AL, CHAR         ; NO, GET CHARACTER
                    OUT   DATA, AL         ; SEND DATA
```

The success of this program depends on several things. We must know the physical address of STATUS (the status port) and DATA (the data port). We must know the location and desired state of the "busy bit." However, these things are easy to look up, so within a short time we could have our character output routine working.

So why have BIOS? Let's see how to do the same example, using the printer output routine in BIOS. Then we will discuss the advantages. By looking at the BIOS program listing in the IBM Technical Reference Manual under "PRINTER_IO," we discover that we must put the character in AL, a zero in AH, and do an INT 17H instruction. Here is the program:

```
OUTPUT_CHAR:        MOV   AL, CHAR         ; GET THE CHARACTER
                    MOV   AH, 0            ; FUNCTION 0 = OUTPUT
                    INT   17H              ; EXECUTE PRINTER_IO
```

What is the difference between these two programs? The important difference is that we do not have to know anything about the hardware in the second example, whereas in the first example we must study and understand the interface hardware. The first example program is hardware-dependent and the second is not. The major advantage to using BIOS is that we can remain ignorant about the physical interface. This may not seem to be a great advantage in the preceding example because the printer interface is so simple. The BIOS programs become especially helpful when one is dealing with complicated interface chips such as the Motorola 6845 CRT controller. Rather than worry about all the details of the 6845, we can simply use the BIOS VIDEO¡IO program.

There is another advantage to using the BIOS programs. As we saw in the printer example, the BIOS programs hide the physical details of the interface from us. Suppose that IBM found a better and cheaper way to make the physical printer interface (or video interface). Assume that all new models of the IBM PC contain the new hardware. We could very well run into trouble with our hardware-dependent program when we tried to run it on the new model PC. If we used the BIOS PRINTER¡IO, we would have no problem at all. IBM would have changed the PRINTER¡IO program to be compatible with the new hardware. The protocol (setup) of the PRINTER¡IO program would remain unchanged.

In summary, BIOS provides hardware-independent access to the physical features of the PC, ensuring that our programs will be simple and transportable. A complete listing of BIOS is presented in the IBM Technical Reference Manual. Each driver begins with a heading explaining the protocol for using the driver. In Chapter 4, we will begin a detailed study of some of the BIOS drivers.

AN INTRODUCTION TO DOS

We have seen that BIOS provides basic low-level services. We can output characters to various physical devices like the printer or the display monitor. We can read characters from the keyboard. We can read or write sectors of data to the diskette. What can't we do with BIOS? BIOS doesn't directly provide us with the ability to load and execute programs. We can't store data on the diskette organized as a logical file. BIOS has no command-interpreter to allow us to copy files, print files, erase files. As capable as BIOS is, it is still relatively unsophisticated.

It is DOS that provides the services that computer users take for granted as part of life with a computer. When we turn our computer on, we expect to see a message or a prompt. We expect to be able to look at the diskette directory to see what data files or programs the diskette contains. We expect to run a program by typing its name. We want to copy programs from one diskette to another, print programs, and erase programs. Most users wouldn't recognize the machine as a computer if it couldn't do these things. The services provided by DOS can be grouped into the following categories:

Character Device I/O.   This group includes programs that input or output characters to character-oriented devices such as the printer, the display monitor, and the keyboard.

File Management.   This group includes programs that manage logical files, allowing you to create, read, write, and delete files.

Directory Management.   This group includes programs that permit you to create, change, search, and delete directories.

Memory Management.   This group includes programs that allow you to change, allocate, and deallocate memory.

Executive Functions.   This group includes programs that allow you to load and execute programs, to overlay programs, to retrieve error codes from completed programs, and to execute commands.

Command Interpreter.   This program is in control whenever a prompt is present on the screen. It interprets commands and executes DOS functions, utility programs, or application programs, depending upon the command.

Utility Programs.   These are basically programs (often called commands) that perform useful housekeeping chores, making life easier. Examples include COPY, ERASE, DISKCOPY, DIR. (See the DOS manual for a complete list.)

Approximately one-half of the book (Chapters 4–11) will be devoted to an expanded discussion of the items mentioned above.

THE SECTIONS OF DOS

We have implied that DOS is not located in the ROM with BIOS. Where, then, is it? DOS is stored on a diskette and is loaded into RAM memory by the bootstrap loader in BIOS. DOS is actually contained in several files and is located in more than one place in memory.

DOS consists of four main parts. One of these parts is called the *boot-record*. The boot-record is put on the first sector of every diskette by the FORMAT command, so every DOS diskette has a boot-record. The other three parts of DOS are the program files IBMBIO.COM, IBMDOS.COM, and COMMAND.COM.

IBMBIO.COM contains programs that provide a DOS-BIOS interface. IBMBIO.COM is responsible for determining equipment status, initializing equipment, and loading device drivers. It is the lowest-level part of DOS.

IBMDOS.COM contains many of the DOS functions listed in the beginning of this section, including file-handling, directory management, character I/O, and various utility functions for setting the time, date, verify-state, and so forth. IBMDOS.COM also provides an interface between DOS and user programs through the DOS function calls.

COMMAND.COM (called the *command processor*) itself consists of four distinct parts. These four parts are distinguished by their function and location in memory. One of these parts, the initialization portion, is used only during start-up. This section contains a program that will load and run an AUTOEXEC.BAT file. It also contains code that determines the location of the first free segment of memory. Neither of these functions needs to be executed more than once, so the initialization portion is overwritten when the first application program is loaded.

Another section of COMMAND.COM remains resident at all times. This section contains interrupt service routines for interrupts 22H, 23H, and 24H. We will see shortly that a portion of COMMAND.COM is transient; that is, it can be overwritten and reloaded when necessary. The code that reloads the transient part of COMMAND.COM is in the resident section, which is located in memory directly after IBMDOS.COM.

Sections three and four of COMMAND.COM are located at the top of memory (user RAM). Section three is the command processor, the program that presents the prompt to the screen and interprets the symbols (commands) that you type there. Some commands are internal; they are used often enough so that they are part of the command processor itself. Examples of internal commands are COPY, ERASE, and DIR. External commands are simply programs on the diskette. DISKCOPY and FORMAT are examples of external commands. Any application program is treated exactly like an external command. The command processor can execute internal commands immediately, but external commands (programs) must be loaded and then executed.

For an external command, the command processor uses section four of COMMAND.COM. Section four is a program that loads and executes disk files. The command processor (section three of COMMAND.COM) uses the EXEC function call (see Chapter 10) to execute the loader program in section four.

As we indicated, sections three and four of COMMAND.COM are located at the top end of RAM. Both are transient in that they may be overwritten by application programs. If these sections are overwritten, they are reloaded when needed by the loader in the resident portion of COMMAND.COM.

LOADING DOS

Not all the sections of DOS just described are loaded at the same time. The first part of DOS to be loaded is the boot-record. The boot-record is loaded during power-on or reset (ctrl-alt-del) by the BIOS bootstrap loader. After it is loaded, the boot-record program is given control. It checks to see that the first two files listed in the diskette directory are IBMBIO.COM and IBMDOS.COM. If that is the case, the boot-record reads these two files into memory and gives control to IBMBIO.COM.

IBMBIO.COM performs its chores (checking equipment status, for instance), then relocates IBMDOS.COM downward and gives control to IBMDOS.COM. IBMDOS.COM carries out any necessary initialization (interrupt vectors, tables, buffer areas) and returns to IBMBIO.COM. IBMBIO.COM finally loads COMMAND.COM and passes control to the command processor. At this point a prompt will appear on the screen.

The memory map in Figure 3-1 shows the location of DOS after it has been loaded.

USING DOS

Many shelves in bookstores contain books with titles like ''Using PC-DOS'' or ''PC-DOS User's Manual.'' What you will find in these books is how to use DOS commands, such as COPY, FORMAT, DIR, and ERASE. It is assumed in this book that you know how to use DOS commands and are basically familiar with DOS. Here we will learn how BIOS and DOS work so we can use their functions from within our application programs.

CHAPTER SUMMARY

We started the chapter by examining the need for an operating system. Our simple example evolved into a discussion of the operating system of the IBM PC, which as we saw contains two major components—the ROM-based BIOS and the diskette/RAM-based DOS. We learned that BIOS provides basic low-level services through a hardware-independent protocol. DOS provides the high-level services to which we are accustomed: file management, memory management, utilities, and so forth. DOS is loaded into memory by BIOS during power-on or reset. Part of DOS is resident (in low memory), and part is transient (in high memory). In Chapters 4–11, we will see how we can gain access to DOS and BIOS and use their functions for our own purposes.

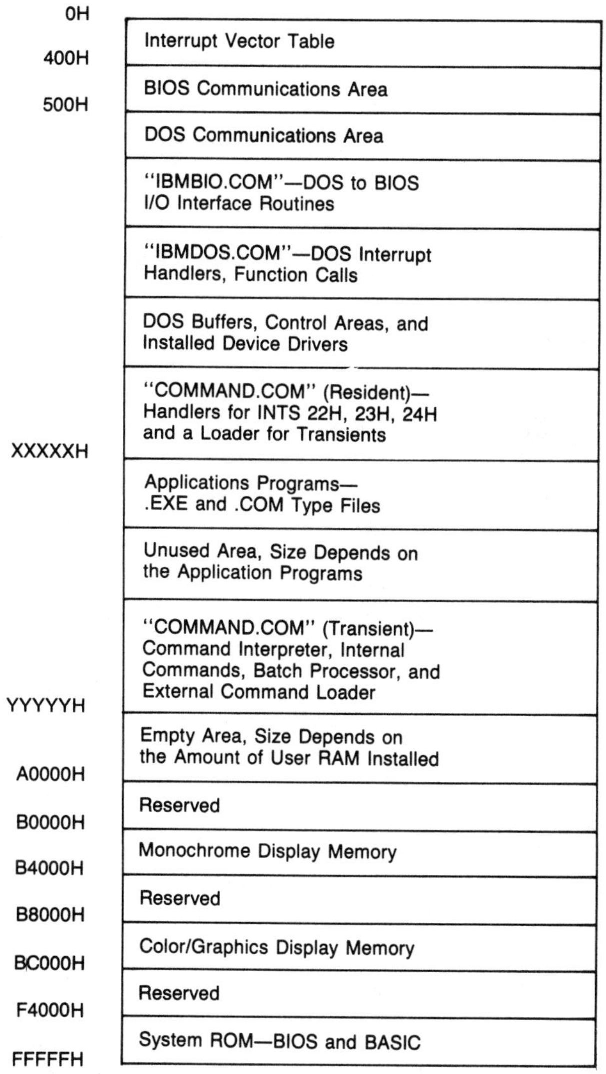

0H	Interrupt Vector Table
400H	BIOS Communications Area
500H	DOS Communications Area
	"IBMBIO.COM"—DOS to BIOS I/O Interface Routines
	"IBMDOS.COM"—DOS Interrupt Handlers, Function Calls
	DOS Buffers, Control Areas, and Installed Device Drivers
	"COMMAND.COM" (Resident)— Handlers for INTS 22H, 23H, 24H and a Loader for Transients
XXXXXH	Applications Programs— .EXE and .COM Type Files
	Unused Area, Size Depends on the Application Programs
	"COMMAND.COM" (Transient)— Command Interpreter, Internal Commands, Batch Processor, and External Command Loader
YYYYYH	Empty Area, Size Depends on the Amount of User RAM Installed
A0000H	Reserved
B0000H	Monochrome Display Memory
B4000H	Reserved
B8000H	Color/Graphics Display Memory
BC000H	Reserved
F4000H	System ROM—BIOS and BASIC
FFFFFH	

Figure 3-1 System Memory Map

Introduction to BIOS Services

In the next two chapters we will examine in detail some services provided by BIOS and DOS. We will assume that you are a programmer who wants to use the services from an assembly-language program. All the examples will be in assembly language.

RUNNING THE PROGRAM EXAMPLES

To get the most from the examples, try them yourself. You can either type them in from this book or send for a diskette that contains all the example programs. An insert near the back of the book explains how to order the diskette.

The following program template may be helpful if you choose to type the examples. Since the template contains overhead that must be entered for almost every program, we recommend creating a file that contains the template. You can then create programs directly from the template file by adding to it in appropriate places.

```
;  THIS IS A PROGRAM TEMPLATE TO WHICH YOU CAN ADD PROGRAM
;  AND DATA DEFINITIONS.  INSERT PROGRAM AND DATA DEFINITIONS
;  WHERE INDICATED.

;  FIRST WE HAVE A STACK DEFINITION

STACK      SEGMENT    STACK
     DW    100H    DUP(?)            ; A 100H WORD STACK
STACK      ENDS
```

```
               ; NOW DATA DEFINITIONS

               DATA       SEGMENT
               ;
               ; DATA DEFINITIONS SHOULD GO HERE
               ;
               DATA       ENDS

               ; NOW THE CODE SEGMENT

               CODE       SEGMENT
                          ASSUME    CS: CODE, DS: DATA, SS: STACK

               ;
               ; PUT USER-DEFINED PROCEDURES HERE
               ;

               ; NEXT, THE ENTRY POINT TO THE PROGRAM
               START:     MOV   AX, DATA
                          MOV   DS, AX           ; SET UP THE DS REGISTER

               ;
               ; THE EXAMPLE PROGRAM OR A USER PROGRAM WILL GO HERE
               ;

               EXIT:      MOV   AH, 4CH
                          INT   21H              ; RETURN TO DOS

               CODE       ENDS
                          END      START
```

This program template does little more than take care of programming overhead that is part of almost every program. The template contains definitions for the STACK, DATA, and CODE segments, code to initialize the DS register, and finally code to return to DOS. The "return to DOS" assumes (as does the book in general) that we are using DOS 2.0 or above. All you must do is put the examples from the text into the template at the appropriate place, and then assemble and link the program. You will need an 8088 assembler (MASM) and linker (LINK). It is strongly recommended that you become familiar with Debug. Many of the examples can best be understood by stepping through the program with Debug.

USING BIOS

What part of BIOS do we really want to understand and learn how to use? Most likely, it is the drivers in BIOS that will prove useful to the programmer. It may be interesting to study other things, like the power-on self-test, but it isn't really useful in day-to-day work. We will concentrate on the drivers. Let's review what is available to us.

BIOS Interrupt routine	Interrupt type
KEYBOARD_IO	16H
DISKETTE_IO	13H
PRINTER_IO	17H
VIDEO_IO	10H
RS232_IO	14H

Each of the preceding is actually the name of an interrupt subroutine in BIOS. The interrupt type for each of the routines is shown in the column on the right. The routines are entered by using the software interrupt instruction INT. For example, we would use INT 17H to enter the PRINTER_IO routine.

Each of these routines will perform more than one function. The contents of the AH register determine which particular function the driver performs. As an example, we look once again at the printer driver we saw in Chapter 3.

THE PRINTER_IO PROGRAM IN DETAIL

In Chapter 3, we learned to output a character by putting a character in the AL register and a zero in the AH register, and then executing an INT 17H instruction. The reason for the zero was not specified. If we now open the Hardware Technical Reference manual to the BIOS listing—to the preamble for the PRINTER_IO routine—we shall see that the driver will actually perform three different functions. In fact, there is quite a bit more to the driver than we saw in Chapter 3. Let's look at each function in detail.

AH = 0   Output a character: This function will output the character placed in the AL register to the printer specified in the DX register. DX can be 0, 1, or 2, corresponding to three different printers. If the character can't be printed, bit 0 of AH will be set on return to indicate a time-out (the printer didn't respond).

AH = 1   Initialize the printer: The DX register must be set to 0, 1, or 2. The printer will be initialized and AH will be set to indicate the status of the corresponding printer.

AH = 2   Get the status: The DX register must be set to 0, 1, or 2. The AH register will be set to indicate the status of the specified printer.

If we investigate further, we see that the actual printer port numbers are kept in a table at offset 8 from the beginning of the BIOS data area. The BIOS data area starts at address 400H, so the printer port address table starts at address 408H. The number we put in the DX register is used as an index into this printer port address table. You can use Debug to verify that the printer port is located at 3BCH. Actually, the printer status-port is located at port 3BCH, and the printer data-port is located at 3BDH.

What else can we find out by looking at the preamble? We see that there is a time-out byte that can be changed. Where is it? There are two ways to find it. One way is to look at the actual code, where we see the instruction

MOV BL, PRINT_TIM_OUT[DX]

about nine lines into the PRINTER_IO program. The corresponding machine instruction is

8A5C78

It is obvious (after mentally disassembling the instruction) that the PRINT_TIM_OUT table is located at offset 78H in the BIOS data area. (Note the 78H on the machine instruction.) Of course, this may not be obvious to everyone, so the other way to find out is look at the BIOS data definitions near the beginning of the BIOS listing. On the third page, you will find

0078   PRINT_TIM_OUT   DB   4 DUP(?)

This tells us immediately that the time-out table starts at 78H in the BIOS data area. You can use Debug to verify that these numbers are set to the default value of 14H.

If you don't know enough about the PRINTER_IO program by now, you can always read the listing. Reading the listing is also a good way for the inexperienced programmer to pick up tricks of the trade.

Maybe all you wanted to know was how to output a character to the printer. We have gone through the PRINTER_IO program in some detail to illustrate how to find out the way the driver really works. Most programmers will be content with this simple prescription: character in AL, printer number in DX, and zero in AH. However, there are those who may be writing a BIOS driver themselves and want it to be compatible with the existing BIOS program. It is to those programmers that this detail will be important.

OTHER BIOS DRIVERS—THE KEYBOARD DRIVER

Let's look briefly at some of the other drivers. For example, the keyboard driver lists these three functions:

AH = 0   Return the next character in the keyboard buffer. If the buffer is empty, wait until a key is pressed. The character is returned in the AL register, and the keyboard scan code is returned in the AH register.

AH = 1   Check the keyboard buffer to see if a character is ready. The ZF (zero flag) will be set if no character is available. This function does not wait for a key to be pressed. If a character is in the buffer, then ZF will be 0, the character will be in

AL, and the scan code will be in AH. *Note:* The character is not removed from the keyboard buffer.

AH = 2   Return the shift status in the AL register. Look in the BIOS equate list for KB_FLAG.

Example 4-1 Checking for a Keypress

The following example uses the KEYBOARD_IO program. Assume that we want to periodically check the keyboard to see if a particular key has been pressed. To be specific, let's assume we are looking to see if "A" has been pressed. If "A" has been pressed, we want to exit the program. This is a simple example that could be generalized to allow key presses to indicate various items on a menu.

```
CHECK_PRESS:    MOV   AH,1          ;CHECK FOR CHAR IN BUFFER
                INT   16H           ;GOTO KEYBOARD_IO
                JNZ   CHECK_CHAR    ;ZF=0, CHAR PRESENT
                JMP   CHECK_PRESS   ;ZF=1, RETURN

CHECK_CHAR:     MOV   AH,0          ;GET THE CHARACTER
                INT   16H
                CMP   AL,'A'        ;IS IT 'A'
                JE    EXIT          ;YES
                JNE   CHECK_PRESS   ;KEEP CHECKING
```

To try this simple program, you must embed it in the template discussed at the beginning of the chapter. What will happen when we run this program? It will simply stay in the loop starting with the label CHECK_PRESS until a character is present in the buffer. At that point we exit the loop to obtain the character. We could just check the AL register, but if the key is not an "A," the character would be left in the buffer. So the program actually reads the character from the buffer and then checks to see if it is an "A." If an "A" is found, we jump to exit; if not, we go back to checking.

In a "real" program, we would make the CHECK_PRESS loop into a procedure (subroutine). The procedure would be called from some point in a main program. The JMP CHECK_PRESS instruction would most likely be a RET instruction in that case. The JE EXIT instruction would probably jump to something more interesting than EXIT.

We will now end the introduction to drivers, leaving the discussion of the DISKETT_IO and VIDEO_IO drivers to Chapters 6 and 12, respectively. Those eager to pursue these topics may consult the appropriate chapter and the BIOS listing.

MISCELLANEOUS BIOS INTERRUPTS

Strictly speaking, all the interrupt-type numbers from 0 to 1FH are considered BIOS interrupts. Several of these are of interest to us in this chapter. (The 8088 interrupt structure and the remaining BIOS interrupts will be discussed in Chapter 18.)

First let's discuss two interrupts related to time-of-day clock—interrupt types 1AH and 1CH. Interrupt type 1AH (TIME_OF_DAY) is a program that has two functions.

1AH—TIME_OF_DAY Interrupt

AH = 0   Read the clock. The clock is a four-byte counter that is updated every 55 ms, or 18.2 times per second. This function returns the high word of the clock in CX and the low word in DX. If fewer than 24 hours have passed since the last clock read, AL will be 0; otherwise, AL <> 0.

AH = 1   Set the clock. The two words of the clock will be set, with CX stored in the high word and DX stored in the low word.

This BIOS function could be used to find the time-of-day, although the time units are somewhat inconvenient (55 ms). Example 13-2 converts these units to the more useful units of hours and minutes. (DOS provides function calls for getting and setting the time in more conventional units. See function calls 2CH and 2DH.) Another use of these functions would be as a timer for real-time events. Suppose we are controlling a real-time event that must occur roughly every five minutes. As an example, assume that we must record the temperature of a device being tested for reliability. The sequence of events would go something like this:

- Use function AH = 0 to read and record the current time.
- Read and store the temperature.
- Periodically, when convenient, read the current time again and test against the old time to see if five minutes have passed.
- When five minutes have passed, start at the top of this sequence again.

You can embellish this example to suit your own needs. You may be curious about how to "periodically" test the current time in the preceding example. There are two main ways to do this. One would be to make it part of the program, taking advantage of certain repetitive cycles in your program. For example, a menu-driven program could check the time whenever the main menu was presented. This would be satisfactory if the menu-driven tasks were short compared to the five-minute time interval.

1CH—Timer-Tick Interrupt

The other method of doing a task periodically is to use the timer-tick interrupt. This interrupt provides a way for us to run a program each time the system timer is updated. Recall that channel 0 of the 8253-5 timer generates an interrupt every 55 ms. The BIOS TIMER_INT routine runs in response to this interrupt. Near the end of the TIMER_INT routine (see BIOS), you will see an INT 1CH instruction. Thus, the INT 1CH instruction is executed every 55 ms. As we will see in detail in Chapter 18, every interrupt type has the address of an interrupt subroutine associated with it. These addresses (vectors) are kept in the lowest part of RAM. Each vector is two words long, an offset value in the lower word and a segment value in the higher. Because each vector occupies four bytes, the vector is located at an address that is four times the interrupt-type number.

In the case of the timer-tick interrupt, 1CH, the address of the associated vector is 4*1CH, or 70H. If you use Debug to look at this vector, you will find that it points to an IRET instruction. Normally, therefore, the interrupt routine 1CH does nothing but return. What is important for us is that we can change the vector to point to a different interrupt routine. The new interrupt routine will run every 55 ms, every time INT 1CH is executed. We must be sure to end the new interrupt routine with an IRET instruction to return to the instruction following the INT 1CH.

Example 4-2 Timer-Tick Interrupt

To make things simple, let's use the preceding example, the key-check program. We must alter the key-check program to make it an interrupt routine, and we must change the interrupt vector for interrupt 1CH.

```
STACK       SEGMENT     STACK
        DW      100H    DUP (?)             ; A 100H WORD STACK
STACK       ENDS

; NOW DATA DEFINITIONS

DATA        SEGMENT

; FIRST DEFINE A VARIABLE FOR STORING THE ORIGINAL 1CH
; INTERRUPT VECTOR.

OLD_VECTOR_OFFSET     DW      ?
OLD_VECTOR_SEGMENT    DW      ?

DATA        ENDS

CODE        SEGMENT
            ASSUME  CS: CODE, DS: DATA, SS: STACK

; DEFINE A VARIABLE IN THE CODE SEGMENT FOR THE FLAG. BY
; DEFINING IT IN THE CODE SEGMENT, THE INTERRUPT ROUTINE DOES
; NOT HAVE TO INITIALIZE DS.

KEY_PRESS_FLAG        DB      0

; NOW THE CHECK PRESS PROCEDURE
```

```
CHECK_PRESS      PROC      FAR
                 MOV  AH, 1          ; CHECK FOR CHAR IN BUFFER
                 INT  16H            ; GOTO KEYBOARD_IO
                 JNZ  CHECK_CHAR     ; ZF = 0, CHAR PRESENT
CHECK1:          IRET               ; RETURN - NO CHARACTER

CHECK_CHAR:      MOV  AH, 0          ; GET THE CHARACTER
                 INT  16H
                 CMP  AL, 'A'        ; IS IT "A"
                 JNE  CHECK1         ; NO, RETURN
                 MOV  KEY_PRESS_FLAG, 01  ; YES, SET FLAG
                 IRET                    ; RETURN
CHECK_PRESS      ENDP


; NOW THE MAIN PROGRAM

START:      MOV  AX, DATA           ; AS USUAL
            MOV  DS, AX             ; SET UP DS REGISTER
            MOV  AX, 0              ; SET UP ES TO ADDRESS
            MOV  ES, AX             ; THE VECTOR TABLE

; SAVE THE OLD VECTOR

            MOV  AX, ES: [70H]
            MOV  OLD_VECTOR_OFFSET, AX
            MOV  AX, ES: [72H]
            MOV  OLD_VECTOR_SEGMENT, AX

; SET UP THE NEW VECTOR

            CLI                 ; DISABLE INTERRUPTS
            MOV  AX, OFFSET CHECK_PRESS
            MOV  ES: [70H], AX
            PUSH CS
            POP  ES: [72H]
            STI                 ; ENABLE INTERRUPTS

; NOW SOMETHING INTERESTING FOR THE SAKE OF ILLUSTRATION

S1:      CMP  KEY_PRESS_FLAG, 0    ; HAS "A" BEEN PRESSED
         JE   S1                   ; NO, KEEP RUNNING

; RESTORE THE OLD VECTOR

            CLI                     ; DISABLE INTERRUPTS
            MOV  AX, OLD_VECTOR_OFFSET
            MOV  ES: [70H], AX
```

```
          MOV    AX, OLD_VECTOR_SEGMENT
          MOV    ES: [72H] , AX
          STI                              ; ENABLE  INTERRUPTS


; RETURN  TO  DOS


          MOV    AH, 4CH
          INT    21H            ; FUNCTION  CALL  4CH


CODE      ENDS
          END         START
```

DISCUSSION OF THE TIMER-TICK EXAMPLE

The main task of this example is to change the vector for interrupt 1CH so that it points to the CHECK_PRESS procedure. The CHECK_PRESS procedure will then be executed every 55 ms, checking to see if we pressed an "A" on the keyboard. When we press an "A," the CHECK_PRESS program sets a flag, KEY_PRESS_FLAG. The main program (rather trivial in this example) will check the flag and exit when the flag is set.

First, we save the old vector by moving the offset and segment value to the variables OLD_VECTOR_OFFSET and OLD_VECTOR_SEGMENT. (Notice that we have accessed the absolute addresses by using an explicit segment-reference in the instructions: ES:[70H].)

Next, we put the address CHECK_PRESS into the table. We must disable interrupts. Otherwise we may be interrupted in the process of changing the vector. This would mostly likely cause the program to crash, for half the vector would contain the new value and half, the old value. After interrupts are disabled, we store the new vector and finally reenable interrupts. Now every 55 ms the timer-tick interrupt routine will branch to the CHECK_PRESS procedure. (We will see in Chapter 5 that DOS function call 25H can be used to "set" an interrupt vector.)

To keep the example simple, the main program does nothing but check the KEY_PRESS_FLAG to see whether an "A" has been pressed. If an "A" has been pressed, the old interrupt vector is restored and we return to DOS.

OTHER TIMER-TICK TRICKS

The TIMER-TICK interrupt is useful in any application that requires tasks to be executed at scheduled times. There are a few constraints. The 55-ms tick period is fairly long. For example, you can't use it to control one-ms events. To control events on time scales small compared to 55-ms, you can simply reprogram the 8253-5 timer to change the basic timer-tick rate. This will surely make time fly. If you try this, study the BIOS TIMER_INT program to make sure that the disk motor will be turned off correctly. Perhaps a better technique would be to take over the TIMER_INT vector completely. Your new interrupt routine could trigger an event at one-ms intervals and jump to the normal time-of-day routine once every 55 times. Thus, the normal time-of-day routine will run once every 55 ms as usual. It may offend some sensibilities to fool with the system this way, but the only other way to control events in real time is to add hardware to the system.

Changing the Interrupt Vectors

In the example, the program sets the new interrupt vector by simply storing it in the required location (after disabling interrupts). We will see in the next chapter that DOS provides two function calls (numbers 25H and 35H) relating to the vector table. The recommended way to access the vector table is through these DOS function calls.

The Keyboard-Break Interrupt

Every time you press a key, a hardware interrupt is generated that causes the BIOS KB_INT program to be executed. This program always checks to see if "ctrl-break" has been pressed. If you have pressed "ctrl-break," an INT 1BH instruction is executed. As in the TIMER_TICK interrupt, the INT 1BH vector is initialized to point to an IRET instruction. Here again, you have the opportunity to change this vector to suit your needs. There is little problem in taking over this vector if you end your program with an IRET instruction. However, if you use this vector to gain control of the computer, you may have some problems. The IBM Technical Reference Manual warns us that we must take care of any interrupt processing that was occurring when "ctrl-break" was pressed. This means that you must

- issue end-of-interrupt commands to the 8259A interrupt controller for all interrupts that were in service (see Chapter 18 for information on the 8259A).
- reset hardware devices that were in service.

It turns out that the DOS interrupt 23H is also called the CNTL-BREAK interrupt. The DOS CTRL-BREAK interrupt is used in conjunction with the DOS I/O function calls. We will discuss this in Chapter 5.

Interrupt 1FH–Graphics Character Extension

This is not an interrupt-routine vector, but a vector that points to a table of graphics characters. When you use the color/graphics adapter card, the first 128 characters of the character set are located in ROM. Vector 1FH is used by the color/graphics adapter to find the second set of 128 characters. This vector is initialized to 0:0 (obviously not a character set), and you must change it to point to a custom character set. We will discuss this topic in more detail in Chapter 12.

CHAPTER SUMMARY

We learned that BIOS provides the lowest-level interface to the machine. The BIOS interface includes drivers for the basic I/O systems: keyboard, display, diskette, parallel-printer, and RS232 communications. We looked in detail at the printer and keyboard drivers. (The diskette and display drivers will be discussed in Chapters 6 and 12, respectively.) We looked briefly at several useful BIOS features:

- Interrupt 1AH—TIME_OF_DAY
- Interrupt 1CH—TIMER_TICK
- Interrupt 1BH—CTRL-BREAK
- Interrupt 1FH—GRAPHICS CHARACTER EXTENSION

BIOS has many more features than we have space to discuss. We endeavored in this chapter to provide a basis for your own further exploration of BIOS.

Introduction
to DOS Interrupts

In Chapter 4, we found that many of the BIOS routines have software interfaces designed to provide the assembly-language programmer a hardware-independent way of accessing I/O devices. We will find that DOS also provides many other services that increase our ability to manage the computer system in a hardware-independent manner. DOS is larger and more extensive, and it provides higher-level services than BIOS. DOS provides services that allow us to easily manipulate logical files. BIOS provides only sector-oriented access.

Three important concerns of DOS are managing logical files, managing memory, and providing executive services. Each of these functions is basically concerned with the manipulation of data structures. For example, the file-management system is concerned with storing and retrieving files from the disk. To be sure, the file-management system must access hardware, but it does so through the BIOS drivers. The chief task of the file-management system is to keep track of the location of files on the disk. It must know in what sectors a particular file is located.

In this chapter, we will introduce DOS and show in several examples how to use the DOS functions. We have chosen to illustrate some of the simpler functions in this chapter, giving the topics of file management, memory management, and executive functions their own chapters.

ACCESSING DOS

DOS, like BIOS, is accessed through the software interrupt instruction. There are eight different DOS interrupts. Eight seems like a small number, but one of the DOS interrupts,

INT 21H, implements 87 different functions. We refer to these functions as the DOS *function calls*. Through the eight interrupts, including the 87 different function calls, DOS provides service in the following areas:

- character-oriented I/O
- file management
- directory management
- memory management
- executive services
- miscellaneous services such as
    - get time
    - set time
    - get date
    - set date
    - get vector
    - set vector

Before we look at the function calls (INT 21H), let's briefly discuss the other DOS interrupts.

INT 20H—Program Terminate

This DOS interrupt was the original way of returning to DOS from an application program. This function has essentially been replaced by a newer method, function call 4CH (EXIT). The newer method provides a way to pass a return code to a parent program. The return code can be interrogated in batch processing or by function call 4D (WAIT). Since we recommend using function call 4CH, we won't discuss INT 20H further. See details in the DOS Technical Reference Manual if you want to use INT 20H.

INT 22H—Terminate Address

This vector points to the address where control returns when an application program is terminated. When just one application program is being executed, this vector will return control to DOS. If a program has loaded and executed a second program using the EXEC function call, the terminate address will be changed to transfer control back to the first program when the second program is terminated. The EXEC function call 4BH does this for you. When a program is loaded, the terminate address is copied into the program segment prefix (discussed in Chapter 9), where it can later be found if the vector itself has been changed by the application program. Then when control returns to a parent program from a subprogram, DOS changes the vector to match the terminate address in the parent's PSP.

INT 23H—Ctrl-Break Address

Some of the DOS I/O function calls check to see if the ctrl-break key has been pressed. If so, an INT 23H is executed. If BREAK is on, any DOS function call will cause an INT 23H. By default, this vector points to an IRET instruction. You can use this interrupt to execute an interrupt routine (end the routine with IRET), or to abort the application program. To abort, set the carry flag and do a far return. As with the terminate address, this vector is copied into the program segment prefix when a program is loaded. The vector can then be restored if a second program was loaded that changed the vector. We will shortly see an example of how to abort a program using the ctrl-break interrupt.

INT 24H—Critical Error-Handler Vector

When a critical error occurs during DOS I/O operations, control is transferred to this vector. This vector points to DOS's built-in error-handler. For example, when you try to access the diskette and the door is not closed, you will get an error message. The error is fielded and interpreted, and the message is output by the resident error-handler. Those of you who intend to install drivers must understand the error-handler protocol. You must make sure that the error codes produced by your drivers are consistent with this protocol.

INT 25H—Absolute Disk Read

This interrupt allows you to read a specified number of contiguous sectors from the diskette. Control is transferred directly to BIOS. Note that the DOS critical error-handler is not used in case of error. If an error occurs, the carry flag will be set and the error codes will be returned in the AX register. The carry flag will be zero if the read is successful. To use INT 25H, set the registers as follows:

    AL = DRIVE NUMBER, 0 = A, 1 = B, ETC.
    CX = NUMBER OF SECTORS TO READ
    DX = BEGINNING LOGICAL SECTOR NUMBER
    DS:BX = TRANSFER ADDRESS

We will defer any further discussion of INT 25H until Chapter 6, which deals with diskette access.

INT 26H—Absolute Disk Write

This interrupt is the inverse of INT 25H. Please see the previous discussion and Chapter 6.

INT 27H—Terminate But Stay Resident

This interrupt was used in DOS 1.0 for leaving a program resident in memory. A newer method has been implemented through DOS function call 31H. Function call 31H permits a subprocess to pass a return code to an invoking process. The return code can be interrogated during batch processing or by using the DOS function call 4DH (WAIT). Since we recommend using function call 31H, we won't discuss INT 27H further.

SUMMARY OF DOS INTERRUPTS (EXCLUDING FUNCTION CALLS)

For several reasons, the preceding DOS interrupts are not terribly useful in day-to-day programming. First, interrupts 20H and 27H have been supplanted by the more useful function calls 4CH and 31H, respectively. For diskette access, the file-oriented function calls are much more useful than the sector-oriented interrupts 25H and 26H. You would use the sector-oriented interrupts only if you wished to access sectors for purposes such as debugging or if you wrote your own file-management programs. INT 22H, the terminate address, is properly handled if you use the Exec function call. Only if you were loading and running programs with your own executive would you need to manipulate the terminate address. INT 24H, the critical error-handler vector, is of concern mainly when you are installing a device-driver. Even then, the important thing to understand is the error protocol.

The only one of the seven that is useful is the Ctrl-Break exit address, INT 23H. You can use this if you want to abort a program by pressing Ctrl-Break.

INT 21H—DOS FUNCTION CALLS

By far the most interesting and useful of the DOS interrupts is INT 21H, the function call interrupt. In DOS 2.0 and 2.1, this function call supports 87 different function calls. Twelve of these are undocumented, which leaves us with an abundance of 75. Using the function calls is basically very straightforward. Set up any required registers, set AH equal to the desired function call number, and execute the INT 21H instruction.

We will begin our discussion of function calls by illustrating the use of several of the simpler ones. The following two function calls provide access to the interrupt vector table:

25H Set Vector

To use this, set the DS register to the new segment value, set the DX register to the new offset value, and set the AL register to the number of the vector you wish to set. The value in DS:DX will replace the value currently in the vector table.

35H Get Vector

To use this, set the AL register to the number of the interrupt vector you wish to obtain. The vector will be returned in the ES:BX register pair.

In Chapter 4, the TIMER_TICK example showed how to set vectors by directly accessing the appropriate memory locations. Using the preceding DOS function calls is preferable. Example 5-1 illustrates the preferred method. (Only the relevant part of the program is shown.) The version from Chapter 4 follows the preferred version for comparison.

Example 5-1 Accessing the Vector Table—Preferred Method

```
;  SAVE  THE  OLD  VECTOR

            MOV    AL, 1CH            ; TIMER_TICK  INTERRUPT
            MOV    AH, 35H              ; GET  VECTOR  FUNCTION  CALL
            INT    21H
            MOV    OLD_VECTOR_OFFSET, BX        ; SAVE  OFFSET
            MOV    OLD_VECTOR_SEGMENT, ES       ; SAVE  SEGMENT


;  SET  UP  NEW  VECTOR

            PUSH  DS                     ; SAVE  TEMPORARILY
            MOV   DX, OFFSET CHECK_PRESS      ; DX  =  OFFSET
            PUSH  CS
            POP   DS                          ; DS  =  SEGMENT
            MOV   AL, 1CH                 ; TIMER_TICK  INTERRUPT
            MOV   AH, 25H                 ; SET  VECTOR  FUNCTION  CALL
            INT   21H
            POP   DS                     ; RESTORE  DS
```

The illustration needs but one comment: The use of DS by the set vector function call may require saving DS if the segment address is in another segment as shown in this example.

```
            ; ACCESSING  THE  VECTOR  TABLE—PREVIOUS  METHOD
            ;  SAVE  THE  OLD  VECTOR

                  MOV    AX, ES: [70H]
                  MOV    OLD_VECTOR_OFFSET, AX
                  MOV    AX, ES: [72H]
                  MOV    OLD_VECTOR_SEGMENT, AX


            ;  SET  UP  NEW  VECTOR

                  CLI                       ; DISABLE  INTERRUPTS
                  MOV   AX, OFFSET CHECK_PRESS
```

```
MOV   ES: [70H] , AX
PUSH  CS
POP   ES: [72H]
STI                        ; ENABLE  INTERRUPTS
```

Time and Date Function Calls

These four function calls are related to the time and date functions:

    2AH   GET DATE
    2BH   SET DATE
    2CH   GET TIME
    2DH   SET TIME

We will discuss only one of these, GET TIME, since the others are similar. GET TIME is more convenient than the BIOS TIME_OF_DAY function, because it returns the time in the following useful units:

    CH = HOURS (0–23)
    CL = MINUTES (0–59)
    DH = SECONDS (0–59)
    DL = 0.01 SECONDS (0–99)
    AL = DAY OF WEEK (0 = SUNDAY)

There are several uses for the GET TIME function. It could be used to help control real-time events. (We discussed this a little in Chapter 4.) It could be used to store the time on various documents. You could use it to implement a simple alarm clock or a complex appointment calendar. For example, an appointment calendar could run in the background and announce important events. You would no longer work through lunch.

Although using DOS function calls is a straightforward process, the less-experienced reader may want to try some of the preceding simple functions before getting involved too deeply with the file management, memory management, and executive function calls. You can use the mini-assembler in Debug to try simple ones.

Example 5-2 Get Time (Using Debug)

First, load Debug. Second, type "A 100." This will tell Debug that you want to assemble a program starting at offset 100. Third, enter the following program:

```
MOV   AH, 2C
INT   21
```

The default base is hexidecimal, so you don't need the H. Fourth, type G = 100 104. This will start program execution at offset 100 and insert a breakpoint at 104, right after the program. Now you can type R, look at the registers, and see what time it is.

Miscellaneous Function Calls

There are five miscellaneous function calls in addition to those above. We will not discuss them, but let's list them for completeness. They are discussed in the DOS Technical Reference.

    2EH   GET/SET VERIFY SWITCH
    54H   GET VERIFY STATE
    33H   CTRL-BREAK CHECK
    30H   GET DOS VERSION NUMBER
    38H   GET INTERNATIONAL INFORMATION

DOS Character I/O Function Calls

Function calls 01H through 0CH support a variety of character I/O functions, as shown below:

    01H   KEYBOARD INPUT
    02H   DISPLAY OUTPUT
    03H   RS232 INPUT
    04H   RS232 OUTPUT
    05H   PRINTER OUTPUT
    06H   CONSOLE INPUT AND OUTPUT, NO KEY CHECKING
    07H   CONSOLE INPUT, NO ECHO, NO KEY CHECKING
    08H   CONSOLE INPUT, NO ECHO
    09H   PRINT STRING
    0AH   BUFFERED KEYBOARD INPUT
    0BH   CHECK INPUT STATUS
    0CH   CLEAR KEYBOARD BUFFER

At first glance, it appears there is some redundancy. After dispensing with the printer and RS232 functions, we will explain why there are five functions provided for keyboard input.

    5   PRINTER OUTPUT   put the character in DL
    4   RS232 OUTPUT   put the character in DL
    3   RS232 INPUT   character returned in AL

These three DOS functions are simple. There is no buffering of characters. There is no way to read the device status. If the printer is off-line, PRINTER OUTPUT will wait until it is put on-line. If there is an error (printer turned off or out of paper), it will be fielded by the resident error handler INT 24H. The RS232 I/O uses the Asynchronous Communications Adapter, which DOS initializes to default values. If you want to have greater control over the RS232 I/O ports, you may want to use the BIOS driver directly rather than DOS.

Keyboard Input Function Calls

Before we discuss the different keyboard input functions, it is important to know that BIOS maintains a 15-character keyboard buffer. As you enter characters at the keyboard, the BIOS KB_INT routine stores the characters in the buffer. The characters are retrieved from the buffer by the BIOS KEYBOARD_IO routine. The KEYBOARD_IO routine merely looks in the buffer to see if a character is ready. If a character is present, it is removed from the buffer and returned to the caller. If the buffer is empty, KEYBOARD_IO waits until a character appears (put there after a keypress by KB_INT). The character is then removed by KEYBOARD_IO and returned to the caller. DOS uses the BIOS KEYBOARD_IO routine, and thus DOS also retrieves characters from the buffer (waiting until one is present if necessary).

As we saw in the list, there are five functions through which you can access the keyboard. What are the differences? To understand the differences, let's pose a few questions.

1. Do we want the keyboard input automatically displayed on the display device?
2. Do we want to check for and respond to Ctrl-Break or Prnt Screen?
3. Do we want to wait for a key-press or just check to see if a character is in the buffer?
4. Do we want to input more than one character at a time, that is, to buffer the keyboard input?

As you see, it is not so simple. If we allowed all possible combinations of answers to the above questions, we would have many more than five keyboard input functions. Let's now see what the five functions are.

7H—KEYBOARD INPUT (PLAIN)

This is the keyboard input function with the fewest frills. Function 7H retrieves a character from the buffer, waiting until one is entered if necessary, and returns it in the AL register. The character is not displayed and is not checked for Ctrl-Break or Ctrl-PrtSc.

1H—KEYBOARD INPUT WITH ECHO TO DISPLAY
8H—KEYBOARD INPUT WITHOUT ECHO

Functions 1H and 8H are similar, the only difference being that 1H echoes to the display and 8H does not. Both of these functions retrieve a character from the buffer, waiting if necessary, and return it in the AL register. If Ctrl-Break is pressed, an INT 23H is executed.

6H—DIRECT CONSOLE I/O (PLAIN, BUT NO WAITING)

This function, in contrast to the functions above, is useful when you want to read the keyboard but don't want to wait if the buffer is empty. This function call actually performs two separate functions—input and output. For keyboard input, set DL equal to 0FFH. If a character is ready, it will be returned in the AL register with the ZERO FLAG clear. If there is no character, the ZERO FLAG will be set. As in function 7H, this function does not check for Ctrl-Break or Ctrl-PrtSc.

0AH—BUFFERED KEYBOARD INPUT

The last of the keyboard input functions allows you to buffer the characters as they are entered. This is useful if you intend to process a line of input as a unit. For example, you may want to buffer a command or a filename before parsing it. To use this routine, you must set aside some memory for the buffer and set the DS:DX register pair to point to the buffer. This function will fill the buffer with characters until you press Enter. The characters are also echoed to the display as they are entered. The first two bytes in the buffer have a special meaning:

- BYTE 0 = allowed character count
- BYTE 1 = actual character count
- BYTE 2 = first character input
- BYTE 3 = second character input
- . . .
- . . .
- BYTE X = last character input
- BYTE X + 1 = 0DH (carriage return)

The allowed character count should equal the total buffer size minus two. If we fill the buffer, the actual character count will turn out to be one less than the allowed character count, because the carriage return is not included in the actual count. If we overflow the buffer before we press Enter, we lose the characters typed after the buffer was filled. In this case, the final character in the buffer will still be 0DH. In reality, the buffer holds three fewer characters than the size allocated because of the two special bytes and the carriage return. We will use this function in an example after we discuss display output.

 There are two more function calls related to keyboard input.

0BH—CHECK STATUS

This function does not remove a character from the BIOS buffer. It merely checks to see if one is ready. Register AL will be set to 0FFH if a character is ready; otherwise, AL will be 00H. You must use one of the functions already discussed to retrieve the character from the buffer. This function is handy in that it checks for Ctrl-Break and executes an INT 23H if one is found.

0CH—CLEAR KEYBOARD BUFFER AND INVOKE A KEYBOARD FUNCTION

This function clears the BIOS keyboard buffer and invokes the function call specified in register AL. You are allowed to invoke functions 1, 6, 7, 8, and 0AH in this manner. This function allows you to make sure that you respond to the next character typed.

Example 5-3 Keyboard-Input and Ctrl-Break

We have finished the discussion of the DOS keyboard input functions. In Example 5-3, we will see how to use function call 0BH (CHECK INPUT STATUS) and INT 23H (CTRL-BREAK INTERRUPT) to implement a program abort. The idea is to read the keyboard periodically by using a function call that checks for Ctrl-Break. Upon detecting the Ctrl-Break, the function call will execute an INT 23H. We must set interrupt vector 23H to point to an interrupt routine that will cause the abort. Recall that, to abort, the interrupt routine must set the CARRY FLAG and execute a far return.

```
CODE        SEGMENT
            ASSUME    CS: CODE, DS: DATA, SS: STACK

; FIRST THE PROGRAM REACHED BY INT 23H

ABORT       PROC        FAR             ; SET UP FOR A FAR RETURN
            STC                         ; SET THE CARRY FLAG
            RET
ABORT       ENDP

; NOW THE MAIN PROGRAM
START:      MOV   AX, DATA
            MOV   DS, AX                ; SET UP DS AS USUAL

; SET THE VECTOR 23H USING FUNCTION CALL 25H

            PUSH DS                     ; SAVE TEMPORARILY
            PUSH CS
            POP   DS                    ; DS = SEGMENT OF ABORT
            MOV   DX, OFFSET ABORT      ; DX = OFFSET OF ABORT
            MOV   AL, 23H               ; INTERRUPT TYPE
            MOV   AH, 25H               ; SET VECTOR FUNCTION CALL
            INT   21H
            POP   DS                    ; RESTORE DS

; NOW USE DOS FOR KEYBOARD INPUT

KEY_IN:     MOV   AH, 0BH              ; KEYBOARD INPUT
            INT   21H
            JMP   KEY_IN                ; JUST KEEP TRYING
                                        ; UNTIL CTRL-BREAK
```

```
; AT THIS POINT THE PROGRAM SHOULD ABORT

CODE       ENDS
           END   START
```

The example by itself is not terribly stimulating. The program just loops, waiting for the Ctrl-Break. However, the same idea could easily be incorporated into much more complicated programs. You could use the TIMER_TICK (1CH) to check the keyboard periodically rather than check it in the main program.

Display-Output Function Calls

There are three display-output function calls.

2H—DISPLAY OUTPUT WITH CHECKING

This function outputs the character in DL. It has two special features. First, if the character is backspace, a backspace function is implemented. The cursor is moved one position to the left, and a space character is written at the cursor. If a Ctrl-Break occurs after the output, an INT 23H is executed.

6H—DISPLAY OUTPUT, NO CHECKS

We previously noted that this function call does both input and output. This function will output the character in DL as long as it is not 0FFH. If DL is 0FFH, the function call will perform an input function. This function call does not check for Ctrl-Break or Ctrl-PrtSc.

9H—PRINT STRING, WITH CHECKING

This function allows us to print a character string to the console. To use it, first set up a character string that ends with the special character ''$'', or 24H. Next, set the DS:DX register pair to point to your character string. Finally, execute the function call. This function call, like number 02H, implements the backspace function and checks for Ctrl-Break.

Example 5-4 String Input and Output
The next example illustrates the use of function call 0AH (BUFFERED KEYBOARD INPUT) and function 9H (PRINT STRING). The program will simply buffer the keyboard input until Enter is pressed and then print the contents of the buffer on the display.

```
; FIRST, DEFINE AN INPUT AND AN OUTPUT BUFFER IN THE DATA
; SEGMENT

DATA       SEGMENT
```

```
IN_BUFF    DB    20    DUP (?)          ; 20 BYTE BUFFER
OUT_BUFF   DB    20    DUP (?)          ; 20 BYTE BUFFER

DATA       ENDS

; NOW THE CODE SEGMENT

CODE       SEGMENT
           ASSUME     CS: CODE, DS: DATA, SS: STACK

START:     MOV   AX, DATA
           MOV   DS, AX            ; INITIALIZE DS
           MOV   ES, AX            ; INITIALIZE ES

; INITIALIZE THE SIZE OF THE BUFFER

           MOV   IN_BUFF [0] , LENGTH IN_BUFF
           SUB   IN_BUFF [0] , 2   ; FIRST TWO BYTES DON'T COUNT

; SET UP AND EXECUTE FUNCTION CALL 0AH--BUFFERED INPUT

INPUT:     MOV   DX, OFFSET IN_BUFF    ; ADDRESS OF BUFFER
           MOV   AH, 0AH               ; FUNCTION CALL 0AH
           INT   21H

; OUTPUT A LINE-FEED

           MOV   DL, 0AH
           MOV   AH, 02H
           INT   21H

; TRANSFER THE DATA FROM IN_BUFF TO OUT_BUF

           MOV   CH, 0
           MOV   CL, IN_BUFF [1]        ; GET NUMBER OF CHARACTERS
                                        ; INTO CX
           INC   CX                     ; INCLUDE CARRIAGE RETURN
           MOV   SI, OFFSET IN_BUFF + 2     ; POINTER TO CHARACTER
           MOV   DI, OFFSET OUT_BUFF  ; POINTER TO OUT_BUFF
           CLD
REP        MOVSB                        ; MOVE THE DATA
           MOV   BYTE PTR [DI] , 0AH    ; PUT IN LINE-FEED
           MOV   BYTE PTR [DI + 1] , '$'    ; PUT IN "$" FOR PRINT
                                            ; STRING FUNCTION CALL

; SET UP AND EXECUTE FUNCTION CALL 9H--PRINT STRING

           MOV   DX, OFFSET OUT_BUFF
```

```
                        MOV   AH, 09H
                        INT   21H

         ; LOOP BACK AND DO AGAIN

                        JMP   INPUT
         CODE           ENDS
                        END   START
```

This example is written as an endless loop, so when you have finished running it, hit Ctrl-Break. In one respect, the PRINT STRING function call is not terribly convenient for this example. Since it requires a ''$'' to determine the end of a string, we must determine how many characters have been entered and explicitly insert the ''$''. This does, however, permit the output of more than one line at a time, a potentially useful feature.

Looking at the listing, we see the buffered input function call (0AH) followed immediately by the output of a line-feed character. Unless we output the line-feed, the output of the print string function call (09H) will be displayed on top of the characters echoed during input. We would see only one line on the screen instead of two.

After the line-feed is output, we move the characters (including the carriage return) from IN_BUF to OUT_BUF. Again we add a line-feed and finally the ''$''. We are ready to use function call 09H, print string.

CHAPTER SUMMARY

We have now been introduced to the use of DOS function calls. We have discussed the group consisting of miscellaneous function calls and the group of character I/O function calls. We have seen several examples of ways to use these function calls. We have learned a lot. But we have just begun our journey, for there are several important groups left:

- DISKETTE RELATED FUNCTIONS
- DIRECTORY FUNCTIONS
- FILE-MANAGEMENT USING FILE-CONTROL-BLOCKS
- FILE-MANAGEMENT USING ASCIIZ STRINGS
- MEMORY MANAGEMENT AND EXECUTIVE FUNCTIONS

These topics will keep us busy through Chapter 11.

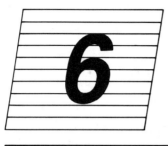

Introduction to Diskettes

This chapter will cover the basics of diskette organization and operation. We will see how information is stored on the diskette in physical units called *clusters* and learn how DOS organizes these clusters into logical files. Finally, we will examine the BIOS DISKETTE_IO driver. The material in this chapter will be important to readers who want to

- write utility programs that access the disk on a sector-by-sector basis
- write file-management programs
- understand the details of diskette operation

Chapters 7 and 8 explain the two file-management systems provided by the DOS function calls. Readers primarily interested in file management may want to skip Chapter 6.

DISKETTE HARDWARE ORIENTATION

Many companies make IBM-compatible diskette drives. Our concern will be not the differences but the common features of these drives. Compatibility allows us to easily move diskettes from one drive to another, from one computer to another, without concern. What are the common features of the IBM-compatible diskette drive? They are all related to the floppy-disk controller chip.

The IBM diskette adapter card uses the NEC uPD765 (or equivalent) floppy-disk controller chip. This is a programmable chip that performs 15 different commands and stores data in several different formats. BIOS initializes the floppy-disk controller to provide a specific diskette format. This results in our being able to view the disk as a series of concentric rings (called *tracks*), each divided into eight or nine sections called *sectors*. Please see Figure 6-1.

It is possible to program the floppy-disk controller chip so that it formats the disk differently than does the BIOS default. In this case, BIOS and DOS won't be able to read the disk correctly (which may be what you want—see the section in this chapter on copy protection). However, for most of this chapter, we will work with the format chosen by BIOS.

When the diskette is formatted by the controller chip, it is divided into tracks and sectors—40 tracks with nine sectors per track. The tracks are numbered from 0 to 39, track 0 being the outside track. The sectors are numbered from 1 to 9. Versions of DOS preceding 2.0 used eight sectors per track. If you have diskettes that were formatted with eight sectors per track, DOS 2.0 and 2.1 will still be able to read them. DOS will determine from data on the diskette itself whether it has been formatted with eight or nine sectors per track. All examples in this book will assume nine sectors per track.

The newer disk drives have read/write heads on both sides of the diskette so that data can be stored on both sides. This type of drive, called *double-sided disk drive,* has become commonplace. The total numbers of sectors on a double-sided diskette is then 720.

2 sides × 40 tracks/side × 9 sectors/track = 720 sectors

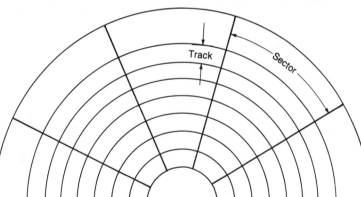

Figure 6-1 Typical Diskette Format **49**

THE PHYSICS OF FLOPPY DISKS, OR, HOW IS DATA STORED?

The physics of the actual storage mechanism would undoubtedly fill volumes, so consider the following discussion to be an overview. The diskette drive stores data on the diskette by magnetizing the surface . As the disk rotates under the write-head, a small current (in a coil close to the disk surface) effectively creates a tiny permanent magnet on the disk surface. This magnet will have a certain orientation; the north-pole will point in a specific direction. By reversing the current in the coil, the magnet can be made to point in the opposite direction. We may assume that a zero bit is represented by a magnet pointing one way, and a one bit, by a magnet pointing the opposite way. As the disk rotates, the current in the coil switches rapidly (250,000 times/sec) back and forth to write a particular pattern of ones and zeros on the disk surface.

To read the bit patterns from the disk, a read-head containing a coil skims the disk surface. As each tiny magnet passes under the coil, a current is induced in the coil. The current flows in opposite ways for the two different orientations of the magnets on the disk. By detecting the current, the drive can read the pattern of ones and zeros.

The preceding discussion is a gross simplification of the actual process, but the essential features are correct. The question that confronts researchers in this area is, "How many flux changes (tiny magnets) can be packed in a given linear distance?" The first 5¼-inch diskettes could hold about 80K bytes per side. Engineers soon found out how to double this figure (double-density) to about 160K bytes per side. At this time, there are reliable systems on the market storing 720K bytes per side.

The standard IBM PC format stores information in double density, giving 512 bytes/sector. This yields a total storage capacity of

$$512 \text{ bytes/sector} \times 720 \text{ sectors} = 368,640 \text{ bytes}$$

How many flux changes/inch does this correspond to? We can't figure it out exactly, but we can get an estimate as follows: The inner track is about two inches in diameter or six inches in circumference. The track holds $9 \times 512 \times 8$ bits, or 36,864 bits of information. This would give us $36,864/6 = 6000$ bits of information/inch. This is a low figure, because each sector actually has several bytes (preceding and trailing the data area) devoted to identification and error correction codes. However, we can say that the density of flux changes on the inner track is roughly 6000 per inch.

THE NEED FOR A FILE-MANAGEMENT SYSTEM

Assume for a moment that DOS doesn't exist and that we must use BIOS (in a manner we will see shortly) to access a particular sector on the diskette. We will need a scheme to keep track of where the data is stored on the diskette. To see what the elements of the scheme are, consider the simple task of storing a data file on the diskette. Before we begin to store new data on the diskette, we must find an empty sector. (This implies that we have some way of knowing whether or not a given sector is empty.) If we find an empty sector, we start writing the data to the disk. If we have more than one sector's worth, we must find another empty sector to continue the process. As this goes on, we must keep a record of which sectors we are using to contain this data file. This process seems fairly straightforward, but to make the scheme general and useful is more than one day's work.

Here are the basic elements in a file-management scheme:

- We need a data area on the diskette that tells us whether a sector is full or empty.
- We need a data area that contains a directory of the files stored on the disk.
- Finally, we need a data area that tells us which sectors belong to a given file.

These basic needs of a file-management system could be implemented in a variety of ways.

FILE MANAGEMENT IN BIOS AND DOS

How are the needs for a file-management system met by BIOS and DOS? On every formatted diskette there are two regions of great importance to this discussion. One of these is the file allocation table, henceforth referred to as the FAT. The other region is the directory, or DIR. The location of these two areas on the diskette is specified in Table 6-1. The FAT immediately follows the boot record, and the DIR immediately follows the FAT. The FAT appears to take up four sectors, but it turns out that there are really two copies of the same FAT, each one occupying two sectors. The directory occupies seven sectors. We will shortly see the reasons for the sizes of the FAT and the DIR.

The FAT satisfies two of the basic needs for a file-management system. First, it tells us which sectors are occupied and which are free. Second, it tells us which sectors are strung together to form a file. Actually, the FAT is organized around a unit that can

TABLE 6-1 LOCATION OF THE FAT AND THE DIRECTORY

Side O, Track O	
Sector 1	Boot Record
Sector 2	FAT (first copy)
Sector 3	FAT (first copy continued)
Sector 4	FAT (second copy)
Sector 5	FAT (second copy continued)
Sector 6	Directory Sector 1
Sector 7	Directory Sector 2
Sector 8	Directory Sector 3
Sector 9	Directory Sector 4
Side 1, Track 0	
Sector 1	Directory Sector 5
Sector 2	Directory Sector 6
Sector 3	Directory Sector 7

consist of one or more sectors, depending on the disk drive. On the standard double-density, double-sided drive, the clusters consist of two consecutive sectors. (Some of this discussion also applies to hard-disk drives. The cluster size will depend on the size of the drive.) As we will see, the FAT can't tell us to which file a given cluster belongs. It can only tell us which clusters belong together.

The DIR (directory) tells us, among other things, which files are contained on the disk and which cluster is the first cluster in a particular file. With this information we can go to the FAT to find the rest of the clusters that belong to a file.

How the FAT Works—Simplified

A simplified version of the FAT in Figure 6-2 illustrates its basic operation. There are complicating features, as we will see later. We can picture the FAT as a sequence of bytes, each of which corresponds to one cluster. Byte 1 corresponds to cluster 1, byte 10 to cluster 10, and so forth. The content of each byte is a number, the number of the next cluster in the sequence (in the file). To find all the clusters belonging to a file, you must work your way through the sequence. To illustrate this, suppose the DIR tells us that the first cluster of a file is cluster 5. To find the next cluster, we go to byte 5 in the FAT and

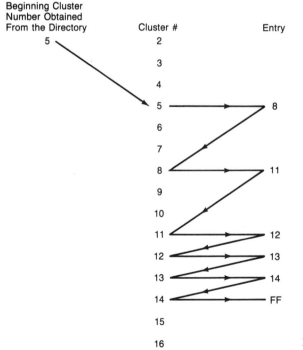

Figure 6-2 Simplified Version of the FAT

see what number it contains. Suppose it contains an 8. The next cluster is then cluster 8. We continue this process until we come to the number 0FFH, which indicates there are no more clusters in the file. Unused clusters contain a 0.

How the FAT Works—Detailed

The simplified model would be satisfactory if there were no more than 255 clusters on the diskette. However, the IBM PC diskettes contain 720 sectors, or 360 clusters/diskette. If DOS uses one word (two bytes) per FAT entry, everything will work just as it does in the model. Unfortunately, life is often more challenging than we would choose it to be. Instead of one word, DOS uses 1½ bytes per FAT entry. One and a half bytes is 12 bits, plenty for the 360 cluster numbers, but an inconvenient size for an $8/16$ bit microprocessor. It works; it is just a little more difficult to understand. The FAT will take up more than one sector on the disk because $360 \times 1.5 = 540$, which is greater than the 512-byte sector size. For unknown reasons, an extra copy of the FAT is kept on the diskette. This accounts for the four FAT sectors shown in Table 6-1.

How many clusters are available, not counting the boot-record, the FAT, and the DIR? Since these items occupy 12 sectors, 708 sectors (354 clusters) are available for file storage on a double-sided, 9-sector diskette. The cluster numbering starts at number 2 because the first two FAT entries (three bytes) contain information about the type of disk drive being used. (See the DOS manual for more detailed information.) The information about the location of clusters begins with the third FAT entry (number 2). Since the first cluster number is 2, the 708 available clusters are numbered from 2 to 709. The actual FAT works just as the simplified version, except that the entries are 1.5 bytes long. A 000H is used to indicated an empty cluster, and a 0FF8H-0FFFH is used to indicate the last cluster in a chain.

ACCESSING THE FAT ENTRY

Suppose we have looked at the DIR entry to find the first cluster number for a particular file. If we were using one byte per FAT entry (as in the simplified explanation), we would simply use the cluster number as an index into the FAT. If we had used a word (two bytes per entry) for each FAT entry, we would have had to double the cluster number to get the offset to the next cluster entry. In the DOS implementation (1.5 bytes per entry), we must multiply the cluster number by 1.5 instead of by 1 or 2.

For example, let's assume that the cluster number is an even number, say 20. Since $20 \times 1.5 = 30$, we know that the twentieth FAT entry begins at offset 30 in the table. The three nibbles of interest are placed in the table so they are the three least significant nibbles of the word loaded from offset 30. (See Figure 6-3.)

If the cluster number is an odd number, say, 21, we get an offset of $21 \times 1.5 = 31.5$. This means that the three nibbles starting at an offset of 31.5 bytes contain the next

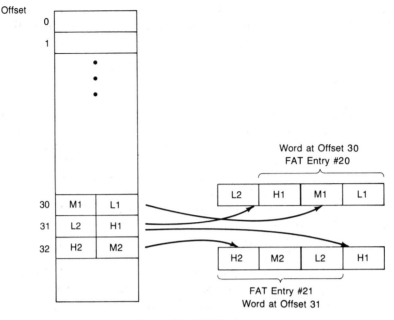

Figure 6-3 FAT Entries

cluster number. One of the nibbles is located in part of the byte at offset 31, and the other two are in byte 32. If we load the word at offset 31, the three most significant nibbles contain the answer.

The two examples above translate into the following two simple sets of rules:

EVEN CLUSTER NUMBERS

1. Multiply the cluster number by 1.5.

2. Load the word at the offset calculated in 1.

3. The three least significant nibbles form the next FAT entry.

ODD CLUSTER NUMBERS

1. Multiply the cluster number by 1.5 and truncate.

2. Load the word at the offset calculated in 1.

3. The three significant nibbles form the next FAT entry.

Example 6-1 A Subroutine That Returns a FAT Entry

The following subroutine assumes that the FAT is in memory. The calling program must place the address of the FAT in the ES:BX register pair and the cluster number in the AX register. The FAT entry is returned in the three least significant nibbles of the AX register.

```
GET_FAT_ENTRY   PROC                ; MAKE NEAR OR FAR TO SUIT YOUR
                                    ; NEEDS
        PUSH  SI                    ; SAVE FOR CALLER
        PUSH  CX
        MOV   SI,AX                 ; CLUSTER # TO SI
        SHL   SI,1                  ; DOUBLE SI
        ADD   SI,AX                 ; SI = 3 TIMES CLUSTER #
        SHR   SI,1                  ; DIVIDE BY 2, SI = DESIRED OFFSET
                                    ; C = 0 IF CLUSTER # WAS EVEN
                                    ; C = 1 IF CLUSTER # WAS ODD
        MOV   AX,ES:[BX+SI]         ; GET THE FAT ENTRY
        JNC   G1                    ; JUMP IF CLUSTER # WAS EVEN
        MOV   CL,4                  ; IF ODD, MOVE 3 MOST SIGNIFICANT
        SHR   AX,CL                 ; NIBBLES TO THE RIGHT
G1:     AND   AX,0FFFH             ; ZERO HIGH NIBBLE
        POP   CX                    ; RESTORE FOR CALLER
        POP   SI
        RET

GET_FAT_ENTRY   ENDP
```

We will add this subroutine to Example 6-4 later in the chapter, after we learn how to read the FAT into memory.

LOCATING THE CLUSTERS ON THE DISKETTE

We now need a way to translate a cluster number into a sector number on the diskette. The operating system uses two methods to specify sectors on the diskette. One, used by BIOS, is to specify the side (0–1), the track (0–39), and the sector within the track (1–9). The other, referred to as *logical sector numbers,* is used by DOS interrupts 25H and 26H. Logical sectors are simply numbered consecutively starting with side 0, track 0, sector 1. Thus track 0 would contain logical sectors 0–8 on side 0 and logical sectors 9–17 on side 1. Track 1 would contain logical sectors 18–26 on side 0 and 27–35 on side 1. Continuing in this way, we find that the last logical sector number (side 1, track 39, sector 9) is 719. Here is a simple formula to convert from the BIOS representation to logical sector numbers.

LOGICAL SECTOR NUMBER = 18*TRACK + 9*SIDE + SECTOR − 1

To convert from logical sector numbers to the BIOS type,

1. Divide the logical sector number by 18. The integer part is the track number.

2. Divide the remainder from step 1 by 9. The integer part is the side number.

3. The sector number is one more than the remainder from 2.

CONVERTING THE FAT ENTRY TO LOGICAL SECTOR NUMBERS

Cluster numbers begin with number 2, because the first two entries of the FAT contain drive information. Cluster number 2 is the first data cluster on the disk, the first available cluster after the boot-record, the FAT, and the DIR. Cluster 2 therefore means logical sectors 12 and 13. Cluster 3 would be logical sectors 14 and 15. The formulae are

LOGICAL SECTOR NUMBER = 2*(CLUSTER − 2) + 12
CLUSTER = (LOGICAL SECTOR NUMBER − 12)/2   ;WHOLE PART

We have now finished discussing the FAT. All the examples and formulae refer to the double-sided, nine-sectored diskette. They can easily be converted to other formats.

The Directory

In the beginning of this chapter we discussed the need for a file-management system. We decided that such a system must maintain a directory of current files. We will now look at the format of the DOS directory.

    DOS keeps a 32-byte directory entry for each file. In Table 6-2, we see the relevant fields within the 32-byte entry.

TABLE 6-2   OFFSET OF FIELDS IN A DIRECTORY ENTRY

Offset	Size (bytes)	
0	8	Primary filename
8	3	Filename extension
11	1	File attribute
12	10	Reserved for DOS
22	2	Time of creation or update
24	2	Date of creation or update
26	2	Starting cluster
28	4	File size (bytes)

Several fields are worth discussing.

    Primary Filename.   This field normally contains the primary filename, but the first byte is also used to indicate the status of the directory entry.

- 00   Entry has not been used.
- E5H   Entry was used but has been erased.

- 2EH   Entry is for a subdirectory.
- 2EH,2EH   The cluster number in this entry points to the parent of a subdirectory.

(We will discuss subdirectories later in this chapter.)

File Attribute.   This byte will be zero for an ordinary file. Various bits will be set to indicate special status.

- BIT0   READ-ONLY FILE
- BIT1   HIDDEN FILE—EXCLUDED FROM DIRECTORY SEARCH
- BIT2   SYSTEM FILE—EXCLUDED FROM DIRECTORY SEARCH
- BIT3   DIRECTORY ENTRY CONTAINS VOLUME LABEL ONLY
- BIT4   DIRECTORY ENTRY DEFINES A SUBDIRECTORY
- BIT5   ARCHIVE BIT—SET WHEN FILE HAS BEEN WRITTEN TO AND CLOSED. USED BY THE 'BACKUP' AND 'RESTORE' COMMANDS.

The archive bit is primarily used to help manage the large number of files on a fixed disk. The "BACKUP" and "RESTORE" commands contain an option that allows you to back up or restore only files that have been changed. See the DOS manual for more information on the FILE ATTRIBUTE.

Time and Date.   These fields are updated every time the file is written. See the DOS manual for a description of the time and date format.

Starting Cluster.   These two bytes contain the starting cluster number. The next cluster number is obtained from the FAT as discussed above.

File Size.   This field contains the number of bytes in a file.

Remember: Intel's convention for storing multibyte numbers is that the least significant byte is lowest in memory. Any numbers we encounter follow this convention.

How Many Directory Entries? The Tree-Structured Directory

DOS allocates seven sectors of disk space for a directory referred to as the *root directory*. The root directory has room for 112 directory entries (512*7/32). If you think 112 files are enough, then you probably aren't using a fixed-disk. Several months (or less) of work would easily fill the directory but would leave the fixed-disk relatively empty. A 10-megabyte fixed-disk will hold 2000 files, each 5000 bytes in size. One way out would be to simply make a bigger directory. This would work, but looking through 2000 filenames every time you type Dir could be tedious.

What is needed is a large directory that is easily managed. This is provided in DOS by the implementation of a tree-structured directory. A tree-structured directory contains one "root" directory and many subdirectories, all connected together in a tree-like struc-

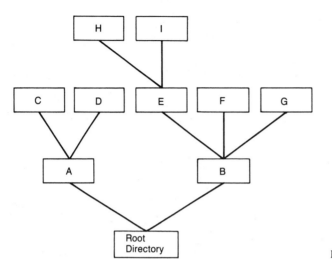

Figure 6-4   Directory "Tree"

ture. As we see in Figure 6-4, the root produces branches leading to "leaves" (subdirectories). Each leaf can produce more branches leading to more subdirectories, and so forth. (The biology isn't quite right, but the picture is.) Every subdirectory is connected to a "parent" subdirectory and possibly to "offspring" subdirectories.

What is a subdirectory? It is simply a file containing directory entries exactly like the entries in the root directory. How do we know which files contain subdirectories and which contain ordinary files? Every file has a directory entry in a parent directory. It is the attribute byte of this directory entry that indicates that the file is a subdirectory. Bit 4 of the attribute byte is set to indicate that the file is a subdirectory.

How are the subdirectories linked together? As in any directory entry, the cluster number points to the first cluster of the subdirectory. Therefore the parent can easily find the offspring. It is a little more complicated for the offspring to find the parent. The offspring does not co ntain a directory entry for the parent, but it has something similar. It contains a speci al directory entry whose primary filename begins with the two characters 2E2EH. The clu ster number of this special directory entry is the cluster number of the parent. If the parent's cluster number is zero, then the parent is the root directory.

ACCESSING THE DISK—BIOS AND DOS

This chapter is devoted to the fundamentals of diskette operation. The following section concentrates on sector-oriented access to the disk. The next two chapters will be devoted to file-oriented access.

BIOS and DOS both provide sector-oriented access: BIOS through the DISKETTE_IO driver, and DOS through interrupts 25H and 26H. The DISKETTE_IO driver is the lowest level (closest to the hardware) and is used by DOS, so let's discuss it first. The DISKETTE_IO driver is reached by way of INT 13H and supports these six functions.

AH = 0   Reset the diskette system (the NEC chip).

AH = 1   Read the diskette status into AL. (See the BIOS
          listing for status byte definition.)

AH = 2   Read sector(s) into memory.

AH = 3   Write sector(s) from memory.

AH = 4   Verify sector(s).

AH = 5   Format a track.

For functions 2, 3, and 4 we must set up the following registers containing information about which sector(s) to access.

DL = Drive number (0-3). 0 means drive A, etc.

DH = Head number (0-1)

CH = Track number (0-39)

CL = Sector number (1–9)

AL = Number of sectors to read (1–8) (9 doesn't work.)

ES:BX = Address of the data buffer

If the function is successful, the carry flag will be zero. If an error occurred, the carry flag will be one, and AH will contain error information. An operation can fail because the disk head takes too much time in moving to the desired track. To allow time for the head to move, BIOS suggests that each operation should be attempted a minimum of three times. The diskette system must be reset after each attempt. Function 5, the format function, will be discussed later in this chapter.

The following example uses function 2 to read the directory from the diskette.

Example 6-2 Reading Sectors Using the DISKETTE_IO Driver

In this example, we simply read the first sector of the directory. This is sector 6 on track 0, side 0. After the sector is read into memory (BUFFER), the program exits to DOS. To see the program in action, run it with Debug.

```
DATA      SEGMENT

BUFFER    DB    512  DUP ( ? )      ; A BUFFER FOR THE SECTOR
COUNT     DB    ?                   ; RETRY COUNTER

DATA ENDS
```

```
CODE            SEGMENT
                ASSUME    CS: CODE, DS: DATA, SS: STACK

START:          MOV AX, DATA
                MOV DS, AX       ; INITIALIZE DS
                MOV ES, AX       ; INITIALIZE ES
                MOV COUNT, 3     ; INITIALIZE RETRY COUNT = 3

READ:           MOV AH, 0
                INT 13H          ; RESET DISKETTE SYSTEM

; SET UP REGISTERS FOR READING THE SECTOR

                MOV DL, 0        ; DRIVE 0
                MOV DH, 0        ; SIDE 0
                MOV CH, 0        ; TRACK 0
                MOV CL, 6        ; SECTOR 6
                MOV AL, 1        ; NUMBER OF SECTORS TO READ
                LEA BX, BUFFER   ; SET UP POINTER
                                 ; ES IS ALREADY SET UP

                MOV AH, 2        ; READ SECTOR
                INT 13H
                JNC DONE         ; CARRY FLAG = 0, OK
                DEC COUNT        ; THREE TIMES UP?
                JNE READ         ; NO, TRY AGAIN

DONE:           MOV AH, 4CH      ; AT THIS POINT, CARRY INDICATES
                INT 21H          ; SUCCESS OR FAILURE

CODE            ENDS
                END START
```

This program is not as efficient as it could be. The only register destroyed by the reset function is AX. Most of the register setup could be moved outside the loop. When you use Debug to look through the buffer, try to identify the fields within the directory entries. That is, can you find the primary filename, attribute, filename extension, time and date, beginning cluster, and file size?

Accessing the Disk—DOS Interrupts 25H and 26H

These two function calls provide disk access in terms of "logical sector numbers." Recall that logical access in terms of "logical sector numbers." Recall that logical sector numbers run from 0 to 719, starting with the outside track and working inward. As with the DISKETTE_IO routine, we precede the call by setting up several registers:

AL = Drive number (0-3), 0 = A, 1 = B, etc.

CX = Number of sectors to read

DX = Beginning logical sector number

DS:BX = Buffer address

INT 25H will read and INT 26H will write. The carry flag will be zero if the operation was successful. If an error occurs, the carry flag will be one and AH will contain error information. See the DOS manual for error information. Remember, even though these are DOS interrupts, they are relatively low-level and do not use the critical error handler.

Let's rewrite Example 6-2 so that it uses DOS INT 25H instead of the DISKETTE_IO driver. Of course, INT 25H uses the DISKETTE_IO driver, but it is slightly simpler to implement. Remember, we must use logical sectors, so the first directory entry is logical sector 5.

Example 6-3 Reading Sectors Using INT 25H

```
DATA      SEGMENT

BUFFER    DW    512   DUP(?)       ; A BUFFER FOR THE SECTOR

DATA      ENDS

CODE      SEGMENT
          ASSUME     CS: CODE, DS: DATA, SS: STACK

START:    MOV   AX, DATA
          MOV   DS, AX               ; INITIALIZE DS

; SET UP REQUIRE REGISTERS

          MOV   AL, 0                ; DRIVE 0
          MOV   CX, 1                ; READ 1 SECTOR
          MOV   DX, 5                ; LOGICAL SECTOR 5
          LEA   BX, BUFFER           ; SET UP BUFFER POINTER
                                     ; DS IS ALREADY SET UP

          INT   25H                  ; READ DISK

; CHECK CARRY FLAG FOR ERROR HERE
          POP   AX                   ; POP OLD FLAGS
          MOV   AH, 4CH
          INT   21H

CODE      ENDS
          END        START
```

Again, you can use Debug to examine this program. Both of the preceding programs are "pedogogical" examples and would be nothing more than a subroutine in a real program. Example 6-4 is slightly more realistic because it reads an entire file into memory.

Example 6-4 Reading a File Into Memory

This example is designed primarily to show you how to access the FAT, to convert FAT entries to logical sector numbers, and to use the DOS logical sector function call INT 25H. The example is simplified by assuming that two items are already known: the beginning cluster number and the size. The reader can enhance this program by adding a subroutine that obtains this information from the directory. IBMBIO.COM is the first file on the disk, so the beginning cluster number is 2. The directory indicates that the file is 1280H bytes long, so we must define a buffer large enough to hold five clusters.

```
DATA        SEGMENT

CURRENT_CLUSTER     DW    2          ; CLUSTER OF # OF   IBMBIOS.COM
BUFFER      DB    6000 DUP(?)        ; BUFFER FOR FILE
FAT         DW    512 DUP(?)         ; SPACE FOR FAT
ERR_MESS    DB    "AN ERROR HAS OCCURRED", 0AH, 0DH, "$"
DATA        ENDS


CODE        SEGMENT
            ASSUME    CS: CODE, DS: DATA, SS: STACK


GET_FAT_ENTRY   PROC      NEAR

; AX CONTAINS THE CURRENT_CLUSTER NUMBER, AX RETURNS THE NEXT
; CLUSTER_NUMBER FROM THE FAT

        PUSH SI                ; SAVE FOR CALLER
        PUSH CX
        MOV  SI, AX            ; CLUSTER # TO SI
        SHL  SI, 1             ; DOUBLE SI
        ADD  SI, AX            ; SI = 3 TIMES CLUSTER #
        SHR  SI, 1             ; DIVIDE BY 2, SI = DESIRED OFFSET
                               ; C = 0 IF CLUSTER # WAS EVEN
                               ; C = 1 IF CLUSTER # WAS ODD
        MOV  AX, FAT[SI]       ; GET THE FAT ENTRY
        JNC  G1                ; JUMP IF CLUSTER # WAS EVEN
        MOV  CL, 4             ; IF ODD, MOVE 3 MOST SIGNIFICANT
        SHR  AX, CL            ; NIBBLES TO THE RIGHT
G1:     AND  AX, 0FFFH         ; ZERO HIGH NIBBLE
        POP  CX               ; RESTORE FOR CALLER
        POP  SI
        RET

GET_FAT_ENTRY   ENDP
```

```
GET_LOGICAL_SECTOR  PROC     NEAR
        SUB      AX, 2      ; CONVERT CLUSTER # TO LOGICAL
        SAL      AX, 1      ; SECTOR # AS DISCUSSED IN THE TEXT
        ADD      AX, 12
        RET
GET_LOGICAL_SECTOR  ENDP

START:   MOV  AX, DATA
         MOV  DS, AX      ; INIT DS

; FIRST, READ FAT INTO MEMORY - IT IS LOCATED AT LOGICAL
; SECTOR ONE, RIGHT AFTER THE BOOT-RECORD

         MOV  AL, 0           ; DRIVE 0
         MOV  CX, 2           ; 2 SECTORS
         MOV  DX, 1           ; LOGICAL SECTOR #
         LEA  BX, FAT         ; INIT POINTER
         INT  25H             ; DO IT
         JC   ERROR           ; CHECK FOR ERROR
         POP  AX              ; DELETE FLAGS FROM STACK

         LEA  BX, BUFFER        ; INIT BUFFER POINTER
NEXT:    MOV  AX, CURRENT_CLUSTER      ; FIRST, GET  THE
         CALL GET_LOGICAL_SECTOR       ; LOGICAL SECTOR #

; NOW READ THE 2 SECTORS FROM THE DISK (1 CLUSTER)
; I AM USING DOS INT 25H FOR THIS

         MOV  CX, 2      ; NUMBER OF SECTORS TO READ
         MOV  DX, AX     ; LOGICAL SECTOR NUMBER
         MOV  AL, 0      ; DRIVE NUMBER
         PUSH BX         ; SAVE BUFFER POINTER
         INT  25H        ; DO IT
         JC   ERROR      ; ERROR, QUIT!
         POP  BX         ; ONE POP TO REMOVE OLD FLAGS
         POP  BX         ; RESTORE BUFFER POINTER
         ADD  BX, 400H   ; ADVANCE THE BUFFER POINTER
; NOW GET THE NEXT CLUSTER NUMBER FROM THE FAT AND CONTINUE
; IF WE HAVEN'T REACHED THE END

         MOV  AX, CURRENT_CLUSTER
         CALL GET_FAT_ENTRY
         MOV  CURRENT_CLUSTER, AX
         CMP  AX, 0FF8H
         JB   NEXT       ; NOT FINISHED
ERROR:   LEA  DX, ERR-MESS
```

```
                        MOV    AH, 9
                        INT    21H
          DONE:         MOV    AH, 4CH
                        INT    21H        ; EXIT TO DOS

          CODE          ENDS
                        END         START
```

Once you understand how to access the FAT and convert to logical sector numbers, the process is very straightforward. However, most of you would probably prefer to use the file-management functions provided by DOS rather than to write your own this way.

USING THE BIOS FORMAT FUNCTION—COPY PROTECTION

This section illustrates how to use the DISKETTE_IO format function to implement a simple form of copy protection. Using the format function, you can format a given track so that the number of sectors and/or bytes per sector is different from the default. BIOS defaults to eight or nine sectors per track, 512 bytes per sector. How does BIOS know what the default is? Every time BIOS accesses the disk it refers to a parameter block containing this information. Interrupt vector 1EH points to the parameter block. BIOS initializes this vector to point to a default parameter block, called DISK_BASE, located in the BIOS ROM. DISK_BASE specifies 512 bytes/sector, eight sectors/track. DOS 2.0 and above changes the vector at 1EH to point to another parameter table, which specifies 512 bytes/sector, nine sectors/track. You can change the pointer (interrupt 1EH) to point to your own parameter block. Your parameter block would allow BIOS to read tracks with a nondefault format, such as 16 sectors with 256 bytes per sector. BIOS could not read such a track without access to your parameter table.

How do you use this to copy-protect a disk?

1. Format a particular track (say track 39) to your own specifications—for example, 16 sectors, 256 bytes/sector.
2. Deposit some known data on this track—a critical subroutine, your name— something you know.
3. In your application program, put a subroutine that reads the special track, checks the integrity of the data, and runs correctly only if the data is correct.
4. If your application program is copied to another diskette, it won't run correctly because the special track is absent. The special track can't be copied by DOS.

Of course, all this is very simple and a dedicated thief would soon find a way to steal your program. Let's look at the example anyway.

Example 6-5 Formatting a Track

This example will format side 0, track 39, so that it contains six 256-byte sectors. Although programming the NEC u765 floppy disk controller is beyond the scope of this book, there are a few things we need to know. The controller responds to 15 different commands. The DISKETTE_IO program is organized so that some of the command information is kept in a diskette-parameter table. Following BIOS, we must set up a table of our own and set interrupt vector 1EH to point to our table. The table is in the data segment. Only those fields that are different from the default table are documented. Those who want more detail must consult the NEC Technical Manual or the IBM PC Technical Reference Manual.

To execute the format function we must also supply "address data," which the NEC chip stores at the beginning of each formatted sector. We must supply four bytes for each formatted sector (six sectors in the example). The four bytes contain the following information: track, side, sector, and bytes/sector. Referring to the example, we see that the track is 39, the side is 0, sectors run from 1 to 6, and 1 means 256 bytes/sector. There are 24 bytes containing this information in the data segment. The ES:BX register pair will point to this data, and the NEC chip will request a DMA of four bytes of this data for every sector it formats.

Example 6-5 also includes code that writes and reads the newly formatted track just to make sure everything is working correctly. If you use this example, try it on a disk that you can later reformat, or you will have one unconventional track on your diskette. (You could also modify the example to reformat the track back to the default.)

```
DATA SEGMENT
DISK_PARAMETERS DB      0DFH    ; HEAD LOAD SPECS
                DB      2       ; DMA MODE
                DB      25H     ; WAIT AFTER OPEN TILL MOTOR OFF
                DB      1       ; BYTES/SECTOR = 256
                DB      6       ; SIX SECTORS
                DB      0CH     ; GAP LENGTH
                DB      0FFH    ; DTL
                DB      50H     ; GAP LENGTH FOR FORMAT
                DB      0F6H    ; FILL BYTE
                DB      25      ; HEAD SETTLE TIME
                DB      2       ; MOTOR START TIME


FORMAT_PARMS    DB      39,0,1,1    ; SECTOR ADDRESS  DATA
                DB      39,0,2,1
                DB      39,0,3,1
                DB      39,0,4,1
                DB      39,0,5,1
                DB      39,0,6,1


DATA_BUFFER     DB   256 DUP(55H)    ; A BUFFER FOR SECTOR

OLD_VECTOR_OFFSET       DW       ?
```

```
OLD_VECTOR_SEGMENT          DW          ?
RETRY_COUNT         DB          3
DATA        ENDS

CODE        SEGMENT
            ASSUME   CS: CODE, DS: DATA

START:      MOV     AX, DATA
            MOV     DS, AX              ; INITIALIZE DS

; SAVE THE VECTOR AT 1EH, RESTORE LATER

            MOV     AL, 1EH                 ; VECTOR 1EH
            MOV     AH, 35H                 ; GET VECTOR
            INT     21H
            MOV     OLD_VECTOR_OFFSET, BX ; SAVE THE OLD
            MOV     OLD_VECTOR_SEGMENT, ES

; RESET VECTOR 1EH TO POINT TO OUR DISK_PARAMETERS

            MOV     AL, 1EH                 ; VECTOR 1EH
            MOV     AH, 25H                 ; SET VECTOR
            LEA     DX, DISK_PARAMETERS     ; SET UP POINTER
            INT     21H

; SET UP FOR FORMAT COMMAND

FORMAT:
            PUSH    DS
            POP     ES
            LEA     BX, FORMAT_PARMS  ; POINTER TO FORMAT _PARMS
            MOV     DL, 0                   ; DRIVE 0
            MOV     DH, 0                   ; HEAD NUMBER
            MOV     CH, 39                  ; TRACK NUMBER
            MOV     AH, 5                   ; FORMAT FUNCTION
            INT     13H                     ; DISKETTE_IO INT
            JNC     FORMAT_DONE             ; OK IF CARRY CLEAR
            DEC     RETRY_COUNT             ; TRY THREE TIMES
            JNE     FORMAT
            JMP     DONE                    ; DID NOT FORMAT
; WRITE, THEN READ A SECTOR JUST TO BE SURE IT WORKS

FORMAT_DONE:    MOV RETRY_COUNT, 3          ; INIT RETRY_COUNT
                MOV DISK_PARAMETERS, 0AH      ; CHANGE   GAP LENGTH
WRITE:      MOV     AH, 0
            INT     13H             ; RESET
```

```
                    PUSH        DS
                    POP         ES              ; SET UP BUFFER POINTER
                    LEA         BX, DATA_BUFFER
                    MOV         DL, 0           ; DRIVE 0
                    MOV         DH, 0           ; HEAD 0
                    MOV         CH, 39          ; TRACK 39
                    MOV         CL, 1           ; SECTOR NUMBER
                    MOV         AL, 1           ; NUMBER OF SECTORS
                    MOV         AH, 3           ; WRITE FUNCTION
                    INT         13H             ; DO IT
                    JNC         WRITE_DONE          ; WRITE OK
                    DEC         RETRY_COUNT
                    JNE         WRITE       ; TRY 3 TIMES
                    JMP         DONE        ; JUMP IF ERROR


WRITE_DONE:     MOV   RETRY_COUNT, 3              ; INIT RETRY_COUNT


READ:       MOV         AH, 0
            INT         13H
            PUSH        DS
            POP         ES              ; SET UP BUFFER POINTER
            LEA         BX, DATA_BUFFER
            MOV         DL, 0           ; DRIVE 0
            MOV         DH, 0           ; HEAD 0
            MOV         CH, 39          ; TRACK 39
            MOV         CL, 1           ; SECTOR NUMBER
            MOV         AL, 1           ; NUMBER OF SECTORS
            MOV         AH, 2           ; READ FUNCTION
            INT         13H             ; DO IT
            JNC         DONE        ; READ OK
            DEC         RETRY_COUNT
            JNE         READ        ; TRY 3 TIMES


; RESTORE THE OLD VECTOR

DONE:       LDS         DX, DWORD PTR OLD_VECTOR_OFFSET
            MOV         AL, 1EH
            MOV         AH, 25H
            INT         21H

            MOV         AH, 4CH
            INT         21H                 ; RETURN TO DOS

CODE        ENDS
            END         START
```

CHAPTER SUMMARY

In this chapter we learned that the IBM PC uses soft-sectored floppy disks formatted to contain 40 tracks, nine sectors/track, and 512 bytes/sector. We saw that there are two low-level ways to access the disk: through the BIOS DISKETTE_IO program and through DOS INT 25H and INT 26H. We learned that DOS manages a directory and a file-allocation table (FAT) to keep track of logical files. The examples illustrated how to access and use the DIR and the FAT. The next two chapters will also discuss disk access, but from a higher-level (logical files) point of view. Much of what we discussed in this chapter will be invisible when we use the DOS file-management functions we are about to study.

Accessing Disk Files: Part 1

In this chapter, we will begin the study of file-oriented disk access. We saw in the last chapter how to access the disk in terms of sectors, a useful but limited way of accessing the data on the disk. The term *file-oriented access* implies that we will be able to access the data (sectors) on the disk in terms of a logical filename. The actual data belonging to a particular logical file can be scattered throughout the diskette. DOS will do all the hard work of finding the correct sectors in the correct order for us. Recall that DOS uses the FAT to keep track of sector membership in files.

TWO TYPES OF ACCESS METHODS

Even the casual browser through the DOS function calls will notice that DOS provides two different methods for accessing files. Two independent and complete sets of function calls are provided for disk access. One set, the subject of this chapter, is the older and more traditional "file control block" (FCB) method. The main feature of the FCB method is a data structure called the *file control block* (FCB), which is used to communicate with DOS. The user must set up, initialize, and maintain the FCB. The second method is newer and generally easier to use. Following the DOS 2.0 manual, we will refer to the second method as the ASCIIZ method. In this method, DOS manages the FCB, simplifying life for the user. We will study the ASCIIZ method in detail in Chapter 8.

FILE ORGANIZATION

Let's begin a discussion of the FCB method by looking at file organization. We could imagine many ways of logically organizing a file. For example, we could think of a file simply as a succession of bytes. That is, we could organize it so that a user would specify a particular byte to be accessed from the file. Alternatively, we might organize a file to correspond to the physical sector size of the diskette. In this case, the user would specify that a particular sector-sized block be accessed from the disk. Both these types of file organization have been used on computer systems, and of course both methods could be used to store the same information. The choice of one method over the other would depend on its performance in particular applications.

A third method of organization would allow the user to specify the size of the fundamental unit of data involved in transfers. Instead of one byte or one sector's worth, you could specify the size that was best suited to the type of data you were handling. For example, if you were storing samples of experimental data, each sample containing 25 bytes of information, a 25-byte unit would be appropriate.

The FCB method provides a logical file organization like the last example. The fundamental unit is called a *record*. Figure 7-1 illustrates this file organization. First, DOS views the file as a series of blocks. All the blocks in a file are the same size and are numbered sequentially, starting with 0. As we shall see, the size of a block is determined indirectly and is not explicitly specified. Second, each block consists of 128 records. The number of records in a block is fixed and cannot be changed. Records within each block are numbered sequentially, 0–127. Finally, each record consists of a variable number of bytes. How many bytes are in a record? That is up to you.

Figure 7-2 presents an analogy that may be helpful to readers not intimately familiar with file organization. Shown is a file cabinet, or more simply, "the file." The file has a number of drawers, referred to as "blocks" in the analogy; each drawer (block) contains exactly 128 manila folders (records). Let us suppose that each folder contains information about one of the employees of our company. To look up (access) data about a particular employee, we would find that person's name in an index that would tell us the drawer number and the number of the folder within the drawer that contained the desired information. For example, we would find from the index that Ed Wilson's information is in folder number 5 in drawer number 2. In DOS terms, this would translate into record number 5 in block number 2.

Relative Record Numbers

It may seem rather cumbersome to have to provide both a block number and a record number to access a particular record in a file. DOS does provide (in the FCB method) another way to keep track of records. Figure 7-3 illustrates this second method of record accounting. Each record of the file is numbered in sequence from the beginning of the file (starting with number 0). The DOS manual refers to this number as the *relative record number,* relative to the beginning of the file. So we see that there are two ways to refer to a

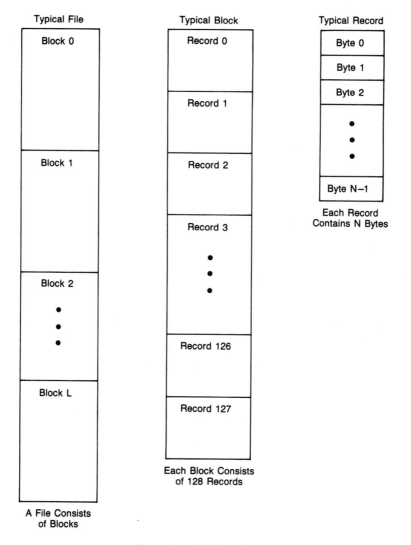

Figure 7-1 DOS File Structure

record. In the preceding analogy, we specified that Ed Wilson's information was in record number 5 in block number 2. We could locate this information equally well by specifying the relative record number of the Wilson record. What would it be? In Figure 7-4 we see the solution to this problem. Each block contains 128 records. Record number 0 in block number 1 has a relative record number of 128. Record number 0 in block number 2 has a relative record number of 256. So, as we see, the correct relative record number is 256 + 5, or 261. This analysis translates into the following formula:

Relative record number = (128 * block number) + record number

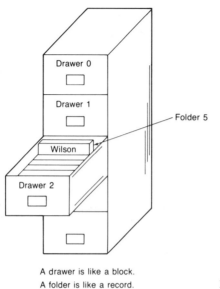

A drawer is like a block.
A folder is like a record.   **Figure 7-2**   File Cabinet Analogy

How would we translate a relative record number back into a block and record number description? We simply divide the relative record number by 128. The integer part of the answer is the block number, and the remainder is the record number. Don't worry about these calculations, for DOS will do them for us. DOS provides function calls for each of the two methods of specifying records. (*Note:* DOS always uses the block-record description and merely translates our relative-record requests into the block-record format.) We will study the block-record description in this chapter and the relative-record description in Chapter 8.

Record Size Considerations

How big should a record be? Since this is not a book about data structures, only a few comments are in order. The size of a record will most likely be determined by the type of data that you are storing in a file.

Example 7-1

An experiment requires that we measure the temperature of an integrated circuit every 30 seconds and store it for later analysis. Each measurement is a one-byte quantity. One byte would be an ideal size for the record.

Example 7-2

Let's make the previous example slightly more complicated by recording the temperature more often as the device gets hotter. In this case, we would probably want to record the time of each measurement as well as the temperature value. If we assume that the time is a three-byte quantity, we would choose a record size of four bytes. The first three bytes would be the time, and the fourth byte would be the temperature value.

File Organization

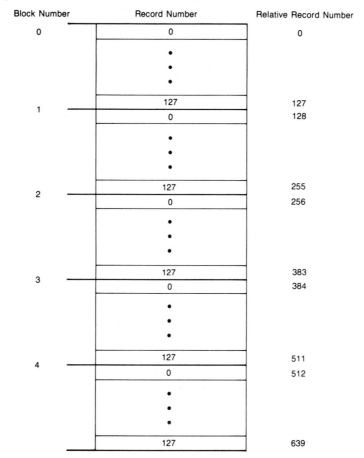

Figure 7-3 Relative Record Numbers

Example 7-3

In an employee information file, we would like to store the following information about the employee:

    a. NAME   20 bytes

    b. AGE   2 bytes

    c. SOCIAL SECURITY NUMBER   12 bytes

    d. WAGE RATE   4 bytes

    e. MONTHS OF SERVICE   4 bytes

Altogether we must allocate at least 42 bytes to each employee. A minimum record size of 42 bytes would be appropriate. By making the record size greater than 42 bytes, we could easily add more employee information, such as EXEMPTIONS, without the need to change the record size.

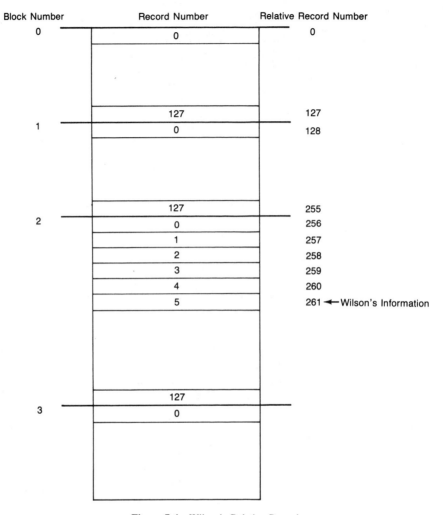

Figure 7-4   Wilson's Relative Record

The preceding examples show that the choice of the record size depends on the type of information being stored. For more information, we refer the reader to the many excellent texts on the subject of data structures.

FILE CONTROL BLOCKS (FCBs)

We now know that DOS accesses files in terms of blocks and records. The next thing we need to know is how to use the DOS FCB function calls. We communicate with DOS by using a data structure called the *file control block* (FCB). The FCB is merely a section of memory into which we put information about the file we wish to access. DOS will go to this section of memory to find the information. [The definition of the standard FCB is shown in Table 7-1. (An extension to the standard FCB will be discussed in Chapter 8).]

A number of fields within the FCB are the programmer's responsibility. The following must be specified:

a. one of these drive numbers:
0 = default drive
1 = drive A
2 = drive B
b. the primary filename: eight bytes, left justified with trailing blanks
c. the filename extension: three bytes, left justified with trailing blanks
d. the current block number (block number to be accessed): two bytes, least significant byte first
e. the current record number (record number to be accessed): one byte

If you wish to use the relative-record concept (record number relative to the beginning of the file), you must specify the relative-record number instead of the block and record numbers as above. Chapter 8 contains examples of relative-record usage.

The location of the FCB is up to you. It is typically placed in a data segment within the program. Your program will tell DOS where the FCB is located by setting up a pointer to the FCB in the DS:DX register pair.

TABLE 7-1   THE STANDARD FILE CONTROL BLOCK

Offset	Size (bytes)	Contents
0	1	Drive (1 = A, 2 = B)
1	8	Primary Filename (padded)
9	3	Filename Extension (padded)
12	2	Current Block Number
14	2	Record Size
16	4	File Size
20	2	Date
22	10	Reserved
32	1	Current Record Number
33	4	Relative Record Number

Example 7-4 FCB Definition

Here is an example of a typical FCB definition.

```
DATA          SEGMENT

DRIVE                  DB    1            ; ASSUME DRIVE A
PRIMARY_FILENAME       DB    'WILSON '    ; TRAILING BLANKS
FILENAME_EXT           DB    'DAT'
```

```
CURRENT_BLOCK          DW    0              ; INITIALLY BLOCK 0
RECORD_SIZE            DW    ?
FILE_SIZE             DW    2 DUP (?)       ; USED BY DOS
DATE                  DW    ?              ; USED BY DOS
TIME                  DW    ?              ; USED BY DOS
RESERVED              DB    8 DUP (?)       ; USED BY DOS
CURRENT_RECORD        DB    0              ; INITIALLY RECORD 0
REL_RECORD            DB    4 DUP (?)

DATA         ENDS
```

We have set up this FCB to access a file named WILSON.DAT on drive A. We have left the
record number uninitialized because DOS will automatically set it to 128 bytes when we open
the file. If we prefer to use a different-sized record, we must change it after the file has been
opened. The block and record numbers are initialized to zero when the file is opened.

DISK TRANSFER AREA (DTA)

In addition to defining and initializing the FCB, we must provide a buffer area called the
disk transfer area (DTA). DOS will use the DTA when transferring data to and from the
disk. To set up a DTA, first decide how big it should be. It must be big enough to hold any
transfer requests you make. If all your requests are for single-record transfers, then the
DTA could be just one record-size long. The DTA is typically located in a data segment
within your program. A pointer to the DTA is passed to DOS in the DS:DX register pair,
with SETDTA function call 1AH. Here is an example showing how to set up the DTA.

Example 7-5 Setting Up a Disk Transfer Area (DTA)

```
DATA         SEGMENT

DTA          DB        ?           ; 1 BYTE LONG

DATA         ENDS

CODE         SEGMENT
             •
             •

             MOV       AX, DATA    ; SET UP DS
             MOV       DS, AX
             LEA       DX, DTA     ; LOAD OFFSET

; DS:DX NOW CONTAINS THE ADDRESS OF THE DTA
; NOW DO THE SETDTA FUNCTION CALL 1AH

             MOV       AH, 1AH     ; FUNCTION 1AH
             INT       21H         ; FUNCTION CALL
```

DOS provides a default DTA, which we may choose to use. It is at offset 80H within the program segment prefix and is 128 bytes long (also the default record size). These DOS defaults are sufficient for many applications. Using the default DTA eliminates the need to set up a DTA. (*Note: The program segment prefix is discussed in Chapter 9. When a program is loaded, the DS and ES registers are initialized with the segment value of the program segment prefix. The default DTA is therefore located at DS:[80H].*)

ACCESSING THE DISK

Before an existent file can be accessed, it must be opened. If a file is nonexistent, it must first be created (which automatically opens it). (*Note:* Creating a file will automatically destroy an existent file of the same name.) After we have either opened or created a file, we may then write or read a record to or from the file. When we have finished accessing the file, we must close it. There are five DOS function calls that enable us to do these things:

CREATE A FILE	FUNCTION CALL 16H
OPEN A FILE	FUNCTION CALL 0FH
READ FROM A FILE	FUNCTION CALL 14H
WRITE TO A FILE	FUNCTION CALL 15H
CLOSE A FILE	FUNCTION CALL 10H

All these function calls assume that the DS:DX register pair points to the FCB. Let's look at Example 7-6 to clarify all this.

Example 7-6 Writing to the Disk

In this example, we will simply create a file, write the capital letters of the alphabet to the file, and then close the file. The program follows these steps:

1. Create the file.
2. Write to the file.
3. Close the file.
4. Exit to DOS.

```
STACK           SEGMENT     STACK

                DW          50 DUP(?)        ;STACK DEFINITION

STACK           ENDS


DATA            SEGMENT

FCB_BASE                    LABEL    BYTE    ;NAME THE BASE
DRIVE                       DB    1          ;ASSUME DRIVE A
PRIMARY_FILENAME            DB    'ALPHA    '  ;TRAILING BLANKS
```

```
FILENAME_EXT            DB      'BET'
CURRENT_BLOCK           DW      0                   ; INITIALLY BLOCK 0
RECORD_SIZE             DW      ?
FILE_SIZE               DW      2 DUP(?)            ; USED BY DOS
DATE                    DW      ?                   ; USED BY DOS
TIME                    DW      ?                   ; USED BY DOS
RESERVED                DB      8 DUP(?)            ; USED BY DOS
CURRENT_RECORD          DB      0                   ; INITIALLY RECORD 0
REL_RECORD              DB      4 DUP(?)


DTA                     DB      ?                   ; DISK TRANSFER AREA


ALPHABET                DB      'ABCDEFGHIJKLMNOPQRSTUVWXYZ'

DATA    ENDS
CODE    SEGMENT
        ASSUME CS: CODE, DS: DATA, SS: STACK


START:  MOV     AX, DATA
        MOV     DS, AX              ; SET UP DS REGISTER

; SET UP THE DTA AS IN EXAMPLE 7-5
        LEA     DX, DTA
        MOV     AH, 1AH
        INT     21H                 ; SETDTA FUNCTION CALL

; NOW CREATE (AND OPEN THE FILE)
        LEA     DX, FCB_BASE
        MOV     AH, 16H
        INT     21H                 ; CREATE AND OPEN FILE

; MAKE THE RECORD-SIZE EQUAL TO 1 BYTE
        MOV     RECORD_SIZE, 1

; NOW WRITE THE ALPHABET TO THE FILE
        MOV     SI, 0               ; INITIALIZE AN INDEX
        MOV     CX, 26              ; INITIALIZE THE COUNTER
WRITE:  MOV     AL, ALPHABET[SI]     ; GET A BYTE
        MOV     DTA, AL             ; PUT INTO DTA
        LEA     DX, FCB_BASE        ; SET UP POINTER
        MOV     AH, 15H             ; SEQUENTIAL WRITE
        INT     21H                 ; FUNCTION CALL
        INC     SI                  ; INCREMENT THE INDEX
        LOOP    WRITE               ; CONTINUE UNTIL DONE
```

```
; NOW CLOSE THE FILE
            LEA       DX, FCB_BASE
            MOV       AH, 10H
            INT       21H                    ; CLOSE THE FILE


; NOW RETURN TO DOS
            MOV       AH, 4CH
            INT       21H


CODE        ENDS
            END       START
```

Before we proceed with a discussion of this example, you may want to type it in and try it. After the program runs, you should see a file entitled ALPHA.DAT on drive A. You should be able to dump the file to the screen or printer by using the copy command. I recommend that you step through the program with Debug to watch the fields changing within the FCB and to note when the disk drive turns on and off.

In the example program, we see that the data segment contains the FCB, the DTA, and the data that will be stored in the file, namely the alphabet. The interesting part of the code segment starts where the DTA is set up. (Remember, the default DTA at offset 80H in the PSP could have been used. The new DTA is set up for illustrative purposes.)

Next, the file is created. The function call that creates the file also opens the file. You can use Debug to look at the FCB before and after the function call to see how the FCB changes. In particular, look at the record size, the date and time, and the file size. Because the record-size field in the FCB is set to 80H during the opening of a file, the program next changes it to one, the desired record size.

We now come to the main loop in the program. Register SI (used as an index) is initialized to 0. To use the LOOP instruction, CX is set to the number of letters in the alphabet, that is, 26. The program loop begins by transferring a byte to the DTA. This is followed by writing the byte to the disk, via the SEQUENTIAL WRITE function call. Where will the byte from the DTA go? Recall that the block and record numbers were initialized to 0 upon opening the file, so the byte will go to block 0, record 0.

If you look at the rest of the loop, you will be hard pressed to find where the record number is incremented. In fact, it is not incremented by the program. The SEQUENTIAL WRITE function call assumes that the next access will be directed to the next record and automatically increments the record number (and block number if necessary) for us. We note that the SEQUENTIAL READ function call also performs this incrementing for us. Finally, when the loop is complete, we close the file and return to DOS.

Errors

One striking omission in the above example is the lack of error checking. In most of the program examples in this book, error checking is omitted to keep the examples concise. Omitting error checking in a "real program" would undoubtedly lead to problems. In Example 7-6, how do we know if DOS correctly carries out a desired function?

DOS could fail to complete the function for these two distinct reasons:

1. A critical error has occurred. A critical error usually means that the diskette cannot be accessed at all. In this case, DOS will retain control until the critical situation is remedied. Recall that when a critical error occurs within DOS, control is transferred to a "critical error handler" specified by INT 24H. For a discussion of the critical error handler, see the DOS Technical Reference Manual.
2. A noncritical error occurs. Typical noncritical errors are these:
   a. Trying to write to a full diskette.
   b. Trying to read a file beyond the end-of-file marker.
   c. Trying to read more than can be contained in the disk transfer segment.

If DOS is able to complete a desired function, AL will be returned zero. If a noncritical error occurs, DOS will return a code in AL that indicates the type of error. The value depends on the particular function call. For example, when we create a file, AL is set to 0FFH if the directory is full.

CREATE, OPEN, and CLOSE are similar in that the value of AL will be 00H if the call is successful and 0FFH if not. SEQUENTIAL WRITE and SEQUENTIAL READ are a bit more complicated.

Let's first discuss SEQUENTIAL WRITE. Two problems could occur when we are writing to a disk. First, the DTA may not be large enough to hold a record. If this happens, the AL register will be set to 02 on return from the call. The second problem is more common: The disk may fill up while we are writing a file. In this case, AL will be set to 01. This presents an interesting problem: What should be done if the disk fills up? Programs exist that take the easy way out and merely return to DOS after printing a message such as "disk full, too bad." Most users express disappointment when this happens. A more elegant thing to do would be to prompt the user for a new diskette and restart the write operation. The elegant method is, of course, more difficult to program but is more endearing in the long run.

SEQUENTIAL READ could also run into several problems. As in SEQUENTIAL WRITE, an inadequate DTA will result in AL's being set to 02. If we try to read more records than the file contains (and the record just read contains no data), AL will be set to 01. If the last record read contains some data but is not completely filled, AL will be set to 03 and the record will be padded with 0s.

As we now see, the example program was somewhat incomplete. After the CREATE, SEQUENTIAL WRITE, and CLOSE function calls, the program should check the AL register and jump to an appropriate routine if AL is not 00H. We encourage the reader to add these changes to the program.

End-of-File Marker

This is a good place to clarify a possible point of confusion. Many systems (including DOS) use a special character, the CTRL-Z character (1AH), to indicate the end of a text file. The end of a text file is not the same as the physical end of the file. A file could start with text, followed by a CTRL-Z, followed by some nonprintable data. If we copied such a file to the CRT, we would see only the text part of the file. However, when the DOS manual uses the phrase ''end-of-file,'' as in the discussion of the SEQUENTIAL READ function call, it is referring to the physical end of the file, that is, the last byte in the file. There is no special treatment of CTRL-Z (1AH) by the SEQUENTIAL READ function call. We note that the physical size of the file is specified by a field in the FCB and in the directory entry of the file.

To clarify this point, try this exercise. Use Debug on the example program to insert a CTRL-Z (1AH) into the ALPHA.DAT file in place of the letter B. When you then use the COPY command to view the file on the screen, you will see only the A, since CTRL-Z is interpreted as the end-of-file marker by DOS. In contrast, SEQUENTIAL READ will not give an end-of-file indication until 26 characters have been read. By using the DIR command you can verify that there are really 26 bytes in the file. Here is a question for the reader: If you now copy the file to another file, using COPY, will the new file contain 1 or 26 bytes?

The following example builds on Example 7-6 and shows how to work with two files simultaneously.

Example 7-7 A Simple Copy Program

In this example, we will create a program that will merely copy the contents of the file ALPHA.DAT (created in Example 7-6) to a newly created backup file, ALPHA.BAK. We will start with Example 7-6, add another FCB for the backup file, and add code to create the new file and to transfer the data.

Here is a summary of the program flow:

1. Open ALPHA.DAT.
2. Create ALPHA.BAK.
3. Set both record sizes to 1.
4. Set up the DTA.
5. Use a program loop that transfers a record from ALPHA.DAT to the DTA and from the DTA to ALPHA.BAK.
6. Exit from the loop when SEQUENTIAL READ returns a value of 01 in the AL register, indicating the physical end-of-file.

```
STACK        SEGMENT      STACK
             DW           50 DUP(?)        ; STACK DEFINITION
STACK        ENDS


DATA         SEGMENT

FCB_BASE              LABEL      BYTE       ; NAME THE BASE
DRIVE                DB    1                ; ASSUME DRIVE A
PRIMARY_FILENAME     DB    'ALPHA  '        ; TRAILING BLANKS
FILENAME_EXT         DB    'DAT'
CURRENT_BLOCK        DW    0                ; INITIALLY BLOCK 0
```

```
RECORD_SIZE            DW    ?
FILE_SIZE              DW    2 DUP(?)       ; USED BY DOS
DATE                   DW    ?              ; USED BY DOS
TIME                   DW    ?              ; USED BY DOS
RESERVED               DB    8 DUP(?)       ; USED BY DOS
CURRENT_RECORD         DB    0              ; INITIALLY RECORD 0
REL_RECORD             DB    4 DUP(?)
FCB_BASE_1             LABEL     BYTE       ; NAME THE BASE
DRIVE_1                DB    1              ; ASSUME DRIVE A
PRIMARY_FILENAME_1 DB        'ALPHA   '     ; TRAILING BLANKS
FILENAME_EXT_1         DB    'BAK'
CURRENT_BLOCK_1        DW    0              ; INITIALLY BLOCK 0
RECORD_SIZE_1          DW    ?
FILE_SIZE_1            DW    2 DUP(?)       ; USED BY DOS
DATE_1                 DW    ?              ; USED BY DOS
TIME_1                 DW    ?              ; USED BY DOS
RESERVED_1             DB    8 DUP(?)       ; USED BY DOS
CURRENT_RECORD_1       DB    0              ; INITIALLY RECORD 0
REL_RECORD_1           DB    4 DUP(?)

DTA                    DB    ?              ; DISK TRANSFER AREA

DATA       ENDS

CODE       SEGMENT
           ASSUME CS: CODE, DS: DATA, SS: STACK

START:     MOV      AX, DATA
           MOV      DS, AX                  ; SET UP DS REGISTER

; SET UP THE DTA AS IN THE PREVIOUS EXAMPLE

           LEA      DX, DTA
           MOV      AH, 1AH
           INT      21H                     ; SETDTA FUNCTION CALL

; NOW OPEN ALPHA. BET (IT ALREADY EXISTS)

           LEA      DX, FCB_BASE
           MOV      AH, 0FH
           INT      21H                     ; OPEN FILE

; MAKE THE RECORD-SIZE EQUAL TO 1 BYTE

           MOV      RECORD_SIZE, 1
```

```
;  NOW  CREATE  ALPHA.BAK

                LEA        DX, FCB_BASE_1
                MOV        AH, 16H
                INT        21H                    ; CREATE AND OPEN FILE

;  MAKE  THE  RECORD-SIZE  EQUAL  TO  1  BYTE

                MOV        RECORD_SIZE_1, 1

;  MAKE  THE  TRANSFER,  RECORD  BY  RECORD

AGAIN:          LEA        DX, FCB_BASE       ; SET UP POINTER
                MOV        AH, 14H            ; SEQUENTIAL READ
                INT        21H                ; FUNCTION CALL
                CMP        AL, 0              ; ARE WE FINISHED?
                JNZ        DONE               ; YES, MAKE JUMP TO DONE

;  OTHERWISE  THE  RECORD  IS  NOW  IN  THE  DTA
;  WRITE  IT  TO  ALPHA.BAK  AND  GO  BACK  TO  DO  ANOTHER  RECORD
                LEA        DX, FCB_BASE_1     ; SET UP POINTER
                MOV        AH, 15H            ; SEQUENTIAL WRITE
                INT        21H                ; FUNCTION CALL
                JMP        AGAIN              ; DO ANOTHER RECORD

;  IF  EVERYTHING  WENT  RIGHT,  WE  REACH  THIS  POINT
;  CLOSE  THE  FILES  AND  EXIT

DONE:           LEA        DX, FCB_BASE
                MOV        AH, 10H
                INT        21H                    ; CLOSE ALFHA.BET

                LEA        DX, FCB_BASE_1
                MOV        AH, 10H
                INT        21H                    ; CLOSE ALPHA.BAK

;  NOW  RETURN  TO  DOS

                MOV        AH, 4CH
                INT        21H                    ; RETURN TO DOS

CODE            ENDS
                END        START
```

Again, the reader is urged to use Debug to step through the example. Let's discuss the program, starting with the line labeled ''AGAIN.'' The files ALPHA.DAT and ALPHA.BAK have already been opened. SEQUENTIAL READ reads a record from ALPHA.DAT. The AL register is then checked to see if the end of the file has been reached. If so, the program's task is complete. If not, the record is transferred to ALPHA.BAK by using SEQUENTIAL WRITE, and the process is repeated until the end of the file is reached.

As it stands, this backup program has no great utility because it works on only one file. We will see later how to pass information to a program's PSP through the ''command tail.'' This information can be an arbitrary filename. Indeed, if the command tail is a valid filename, it will be formatted into an FCB within the PSP. With a few changes, Example 7-7 could be made into a general back-up utility.

CHAPTER SUMMARY

In this chapter we have learned the fundamentals of disk file access. We know DOS communicates with us through the FCB and exchanges data with us through the DTA. It turns out that knowing the function calls listed below will allow us to accomplish any type of disk file access we desire.

CREATE A FILE	FUNCTION CALL 16H
OPEN A FILE	FUNCTION CALL 0FH
READ FROM A FILE	FUNCTION CALL 14H
WRITE TO A FILE	FUNCTION CALL 15H
CLOSE A FILE	FUNCTION CALL 10H
SETDTA	FUNCTION CALL 1AH

The next several chapters will add to our sophistication about disk file access, showing us new and (perhaps) easier ways to handle file access.

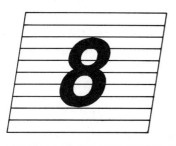

Accessing Disk Files:
Part 2

This chapter, a pot pourri of the remaining file access topics, covers the following material: relative record numbers, the ASCIIZ method, the extended-FCB, and directory searches.

FILE ACCESS USING RELATIVE RECORD NUMBERS

In addition to the block-record type of access we have seen, DOS provides access in terms of relative record numbers. Recall that the relative record number is defined with respect to the beginning of the file (Figure 7-3). You may find this method preferable to the block-record type of access because it eliminates any need to calculate block-record numbers. Let's look at a simple example of its usefulness.

Suppose an experiment requires that we take 1000 sets of data, each set consisting of 10 bytes. We will store this data in a file containing records 10 bytes long. Suppose that we want to analyze the 437th data set. What is the block-record number? The answer is block 3, record 53. If we access this record using the block-record format, we must do this calculation (that is, write a program to do it). On the other hand, by using relative record access methods, we can simply specify relative record number 437 and let DOS do the calculating.

There are four function calls we can use to make relative record number accesses. Two provide access to one record at a time, and the other two permit us to specify the number of records we wish to access.

21H—Random Read.   Set DS:DX to point to an open FCB, and set the relative record number field with the desired number. This function will attempt to read one record into the DTA. AL indicates the results of the operation.

AL = 00   Read was successful.

AL = 01   End-of-file encountered, no data transferred.

AL = 02   DTA was too small to hold one record.

AL = 03   End-of-file encountered, partial record transferred.

22H—Random Write.   Set DS:DX to point to an open FCB and set the relative record number field with the desired number. This function will attempt to write one record from the DTA to the disk. If the record size is less than a sector size, the data will be buffered until either a sector can be written or the file is closed. AL indicates the results of the operation.

AL = 00   Write was successful.

AL = 01   The disk is full.

AL = 02   DTA too small to hold one record.

27H—Random Block Read.   Set DS:DX to point to an open FCB, set the relative record number, and set CX to the number of records to read. AL indicates the results as in RANDOM READ. The actual number of records read is returned in CX.

28H—Random Block Write.   Set up as in RANDOM BLOCK READ. Results are indicated by AL as in RANDOM WRITE. If you set CX to zero, the file length is adjusted to match the relative record number.

To use these functions, we proceed in much the same way as we did with the block-record reads. We create the file, set the record size in the FCB, access the file, then close it.

Example 8-1 File Access Using Relative Record Number

This example uses two of the above functions. For illustrative purposes, the program writes to a file using RANDOM BLOCK WRITE and reads back a particular record using RANDOM READ.

```
DATA        SEGMENT
ERR_MESS:       DB    "AN ERROR HAS OCCURRED", 0AH,0DH, "$"
;DEFINE THE FILE-CONTROL BLOCK

DRIVE                DB    1          ;ASSUME DRIVE 1
PRIMARY_FILENAME     DB    'RANDOM   '
FILENAME_EXT         DB    'DAT'
CURRENT_BLOCK        DW    ?
RECORD_SIZE          DW    ?
FILE_SIZE            DW    2 DUP(?)
DATE                 DW    ?
```

```
TIME                    DW    ?
RESERVED                DB    8 DUP (?)
CURRENT_RECORD          DB    ?
REL_RECORD              DW    2 DUP (?)


;NOW DEFINE SIX RECORDS TO STORE IN THE FILE

REC1        DB    16    DUP ('1')
REC2        DB    16    DUP ('2')
REC3        DB    16    DUP ('3')
REC4        DB    16    DUP ('4')
REC5        DB    16    DUP ('5')
REC6        DB    16    DUP ('6')


BUFFER      DB    16    DUP ('0')
DATA        ENDS


CODE        SEGMENT
            ASSUME    CS:CODE,DS:DATA,SS:STACK

START:      MOV   AX,DATA
            MOV   DS,AX                ;INIT DS

;SET DTA TO POINT TO ABOVE RECORDS
            LEA   DX,REC1              ;POINTER TO DTA
            MOV   AH,1AH               ;SET DTA FUNCTION
            INT   21H


;CREATE (AND OPEN) FILE

            LEA   DX,DRIVE             ;POINT TO FCB
            MOV   AH,16H               ;CREATE FUNCTION
            INT   21H
            CMP   AL,0FFH              ;ERROR
            JE    ERROR                ;YES, JUMP

;NOW WRITE 6 RECORDS TO THE FILE

            MOV   RECORD_SIZE,16       ;SET RECORD SIZE
            MOV   REL_RECORD,0
            MOV   REL_RECORD[2],0      ;INIT RELATIVE RECORD #
            MOV   CX,6                 ;WRITE 6 RECORDS
            LEA   DX,DRIVE             ;POINT TO FCB
            MOV   AH,28H               ;RANDOM BLOCK WRITE
            INT   21H
            CMP   AL,0                 ;FUNCTION COMPLETE
            JNE   ERROR                ;NO, ERROR
```

```
; NOW RESET DTA AND READ RELATIVE RECORD 4 INTO THE BUFFER

                LEA    DX, BUFFER
                MOV    AH, 1AH
                INT    21H                 ; SET DTA
                LEA    DX, DRIVE           ; POINT TO FCB
                MOV    REL_RECORD, 4
                MOV    REL_RECORD[2], 0    ; SET RELATIVE RECORD #
                MOV    AH, 21H             ; RANDOM READ
                INT    21H
                CMP    AL, 0               ; FUNCTION COMPLETE
                JNE    ERROR
                JMP    CLOSE


; FINALLY CLOSE THE FILE
ERROR:          LEA    DX, ERR_MESS        ; DISPLAY ERROR MESSAGE
                MOV    AH, 9
                INT    21H
CLOSE:          LEA    DX, DRIVE
                MOV    AH, 10H             ; CLOSE
                INT    21H


; RETURN TO DOS
                MOV    AH, 4CH
                INT    21H


CODE            ENDS
                END        START
```

We see that the relative record access is straightforward and has some advantages over the block-record access, but it is still rather cumbersome because of the FCB. We will now learn an easier way of accessing files that many will find preferable. We will see that there are no file control blocks to worry about. Gone with the file control blocks are records, blocks, and relative records. How is this miracle performed?

THE ASCIIZ METHOD

All the details of file access using the FCB method could be eliminated by a computer program. We could write a special program that would format a filename, along with any other required fields, into an FCB. We could, for example, use an ASCII string to contain a filename and set up a pointer so that the special program could find the string. In other words, we could eliminate the need to think about FCBs altogether by writing a clever program. This is, in a sense, what the ASCIIZ method is—a program that hides the details of the FCB from us.

The ASCIIZ method requires that you set up the filename of the file you wish to access in the form of an ASCII string, followed by a zero byte (the Z in ASCIIZ). Here is an example:

```
FILENAME        DB         'DATAFILE.DAT',00
```

This defines an ASCII string followed by a zero byte and is thus an ASCIIZ string. To access this file, you merely set up a pointer to the ASCIIZ string in the DS:DX register pair and issue an open or create function call. The ASCIIZ string can contain slashes indicating subdirectories. In fact, it is exactly like the pathname-filename format you type on a command line, that is, "A:\MAINDATA\MON DAY\DATA1.DAT".

Handles

When you open the file (using open or create), a 16-bit number is returned in the AX register. This number, referred to as the *handle,* is used for all further access to this file. So it becomes even easier. All you must now do is put the handle in the BX register before issuing other function calls. Needless to say, you must keep the handle in some safe place until the file is closed.

Some handles, predefined by DOS, can be used to access various physical devices in the system.

Handle	Device
0000H	Standard input device (keyboard)
0001H	Standard output device (display)
0002H	Standard error output device (display)
0003H	Standard auxiliary device
0004H	Standard printer device

For example, you could send data to the printer by using handle 0004H. There is no need to open or close a file when using the predefined handles.

The File Pointer

We saw near the beginning of this section that we need not be concerned with blocks and records or with relative record numbers when using the ASCIIZ-type file access. How, then, do we access particular areas within a file? Instead of records, we use the file pointer. The file pointer is simply a pointer that points to a location in a file. We can manipulate the file pointer, making it move to the beginning, to the end, or to any location we wish within the file. Data is read from or written to the file at the location specified by the file pointer. We don't have direct access to the file pointer, but we can always find out its value and change it to suit our needs.

Although it seems simple, the ASCIIZ method may not be the best choice for all applications. Its chief drawback is that accesses are byte-oriented, as if the record size is always one byte. If your application requires accessing data in units other than a byte, you will be required to write a program to convert your units into bytes. For example, suppose you collect data 76 bytes at a time, storing the data in consecutive 76-byte units in a file. If you later wish to randomly access these units, you will have to calculate the value of the file pointer. If we want the ninth unit, the file pointer would have to be 608. In cases like this, the FCB method may be the best choice.

ASCIIZ FUNCTION CALLS

Let's look at the five basic function calls analogous to those we studied in Chapter 7.

3CH—Create a File.   This function call creates a new file. DS:DX must point to an ASCIIZ string containing the filename, and CX should contain the desired attribute of the new file. The file is opened for read/write and the file pointer is set to the first byte of the file. The file handle is returned in AX.

3DH—Open a File.   This function call is used to open an existing file. DS:DX must point to an ASCIIZ string containing the filename, and AL should contain the desired access code:

AL = 0   Open for read
AL = 1   Open for write
AL = 2   Open for read/write

The file handle is returned in the AX register.

Both the preceding function calls use the ASCIIZ string and return a file handle in AX. All the remaining ASCIIZ function calls require that you place the file handle in BX before making the function call.

3EH—Close a File.   This function closes the file whose handle is in BX.

3FH—Read.   This function reads from the file or device whose handle is in BX. You must put the number of bytes to read in CX and a pointer to a buffer in DS:DX. The function will attempt to read CX bytes and store them in the buffer. The number of bytes actually read will be returned in AX. AX could be less than CX if the file pointer is too near the end of the buffer or if you are reading from the standard input device (which inputs only one line at a time).

40H—Write.   This function writes to the file or device whose handle is in BX. You must put the number of bytes to write in CX and a pointer to a buffer in DS:DX. The function will attempt to write CX bytes from the buffer. The number of bytes actually written will be returned in AX. If AX is not equal to CX, an error has occurred. It is your responsibility to check this.

42H—Move File Pointer.   This function allows us to manipulate the file pointer of the file whose handle is in BX. Three methods of moving the pointer are provided. Each of the methods uses an "offset" specified in the CX:DX register pair. The CS:DX register pair is to be considered a four-byte (32-bit) number, CX containing the most significant part. The contents of AL determine the method.

AL = 0   The file pointer is positioned CX:DX bytes from the beginning of the file.

AL = 1   The offset in CX:DX is added to the current position of the file pointer.

AL = 2   The file pointer is set to the end of the file plus the offset in CX:DX.

In all cases, the DX:AX register pair returns the updated value of the file pointer. Note that using the last method with CX:DX = 0 will position the file pointer at the end of the file. The value in DX:AX will then be the length of the file.

Errors. All the ASCIIZ function calls will return with the carry flag set, in case of error. The AX register will then contain an error code. The DOS Technical Reference Manual contains an error return table that you may consult to find the meaning of the error.

There are other ASCIIZ functions that we will discuss later in the chapter, but first let's look at an example that shows how easy it is to access files by using the ASCIIZ function calls.

Example 8.2: Reading and Writing Using ASCIIZ

Let's repeat one of the examples we studied in Chapter 7. We will write a message to a file, then read it back into a different buffer. You can use Debug to go through the various actions of the example to see that it works correctly.

```
DATA      SEGMENT
BUFFER1   DB    'THIS IS A MESSAGE THAT WILL BE STORED '
          DB    'AND RETRIEVED FROM THE DISK-FILE.',0DH,0AH
BUFFER2   DB    100 DUP(0)          ; INIT WITH A KNOWN VALUE
HANDLE    DW    ?                   ; STORAGE FOR THE HANDLE
FILENAME  DB    'MESSAGE.TXT',00    ; ASCIIZ STRING
DATA      ENDS

CODE      SEGMENT
          ASSUME    CS:CODE,DS:DATA,SS:STACK

START:    MOV    AX,DATA
          MOV    DX,AX               ; INIT DS

;FIRST, CREATE (AND OPEN) THE FILE

          LEA    DX,FILENAME         ; POINTER TO ASCIIZ STRING
          MOV    CX,0                ; NORMAL ATTRIBUTE
          MOV    AH,3CH              ; CREATE FUNCTION
          INT    21H
          JC     ERROR               ; CARRY SET=ERROR
          MOV    HANDLE,AX           ; SAVE THE HANDLE
```

```
; NOW WRITE THE MESSAGE TO THE FILE

        MOV   CX, OFFSET BUFFER2 -OFFSET BUFFER1
        LEA   DX, BUFFER1          ; POINTER TO DATA
        MOV   BX, HANDLE
        MOV   AH, 40H              ; WRITE FUNCTION
        INT   21H
        JC    ERROR               ; CARRY SET=ERROR
        CMP   AX, CX              ; FUNCTION COMPLETED?
        JNE   ERROR               ; NOT CORRECT NUMBER

; NOW, REPOSITION THE FILE POINTER

        MOV   AL, 0               ; METHOD 0
        MOV   BX, HANDLE
        MOV   CX, 0               ; SET OFFSET TO ZERO
        MOV   DX, 0
        MOV   AH, 42H              ; MOVE FILE POINTER FUNCTION
        INT   21H

; FINALLY, READ THE FILE INTO BUFFER2

        MOV   CX, OFFSET BUFFER2 -OFFSET BUFFER1
        MOV   BX, HANDLE
        LEA   DX, BUFFER2          ; POINTER TO INPUT BUFFER
        MOV   AH, 3FH              ; READ FUNCTION
        INT   21H
        JC    ERROR               ; CARRY SET=ERROR
        CMP   AX, CX              ; CORRECT NUMBER
        JNE   ERROR               ; NO, ERROR

; NOW, CLOSE THE FILE

        MOV   BX, HANDLE
        MOV   AH, 3EH              ; CLOSE FUNCTION
        INT   21H
        JNC   EXIT

ERROR:  ; NORMALLY, YOU SHOULD PUT AN ERROR-HANDLING ROUTINE
        ; HERE.

EXIT:   MOV   AH, 4CH
        INT   21H                 ; RETURN TO DOS

CODE    ENDS
        END   START
```

As we can see, the use of the ASCIIZ method is straightforward. These functions will return with the carry flag set to indicate an error. A real program should have an error-handling subroutine with more sophistication.

THE EXTENDED FILE CONTROL BLOCK—EFCB

Let's finish the topic of disk access by discussing several of the remaining function calls that relate to directory searches. In Chapter 7, we saw how to access files by using the FCB method. To simplify the presentation, a data structure, called the *extended file control block* or EFCB, was omitted. The EFCB is important because it provides a field for specifying a file-attribute byte. Thus, directories can be searched for files having a particular attribute. Both the FCB-type and the ASCIIZ-type directory search function calls provide this feature.

The EFCB is created by placing seven bytes in front of a standard FCB. The first byte of the EFCB must be 0FFH, followed by five reserved bytes and finally an attribute byte. Lets see how the EFCB is used in a directory search.

FCB-TYPE DIRECTORY SEARCH FUNCTION CALLS

11H—Search for the First Entry. Set DS:DX to point to an unopened file control block. This can be either the standard FCB or the EFCB. The filename can include the global symbol ''?''. The directory is searched and AL indicates the result.

AL = 0FFH   No matching entry was found.

AL = 00   A matching entry was found. The function creates a valid, unopened file control block for the matching file in the DTA. The file control block will be the same as that set up for the function call.

If you have used an EFCB, the function will search for a file with the attribute specified in the EFCB as well as for a matching filename. (See the section on the directory in Chapter 6 for a definition of the attribute byte.)

Function call 12H permits you to keep searching the directory for more matching files.

12H—Search for Next Entry. The setup is the same as for function call 11H. You must not change the reserved areas in the DTA file control block before executing this function (assuming you have already called 11H or 12H). The reserved areas contain information necessary for the ''next search.''

ASCIIZ-TYPE DIRECTORY SEARCHES

The ASCIIZ method provides two function calls (4EH and 4FH) parallel to the two above. They are different, of course, in that you must set DS:DX to point to an ASCIIZ string instead of an FCB. Also, CX must contain the attribute byte to be used in the search. Instead of placing an FCB in the DTA, the DTA will return the following information:

   21 bytes—reserved

    1 byte—attribute

    2 bytes—time

    2 bytes—date

    4 bytes—file size

   13 bytes—ASCIIZ string containing the filename

Example 8-3 Directory Search Using the FCB Method

The following example shows how to search the current directory for ambiguous files, by using the FCB method. To fully appreciate the example, you should make several files on your disk that have filenames beginning with "TEST," such as TEST1.DAT, TEST2.DAT, and TEST3.DAT. It is suggested that you use Debug to observe the FCB created in the DTA. After each directory search, you will see the name of the matching file in this FCB. The DTA is located at the default location—offset 80H in the program segment prefix (PSP). Register ES will be pointing to the PSP.

```
        DATA        SEGMENT

        ; FIRST DEFINE THE EXTENDED FILE-CONTROL BLOCK

        EFCB                    DB    0FFH
                                DB    5    DUP (?)     ; RESERVED
        ATTRIBUTE               DB    0                ; NORMAL
        DRIVE                   DB    1                ; ASSUME DRIVE 1
        PRIMARY_FILENAME        DB    'TEST????'
        FILENAME_EXT            DB    'DAT'
        CURRENT_BLOCK           DW    ?
        RECORD_SIZE             DW    ?
        FILE_SIZE               DW    2 DUP (?)
        DATE                    DW    ?
        TIME                    DW    ?
        RESERVED                DB    8 DUP (?)
        CURRENT_RECORD          DB    ?
        REL_RECORD              DW    2 DUP (?)

        DATA        ENDS

        CODE        SEGMENT
                    ASSUME    CS: CODE, DS: DATA, SS: STACK

        START:      MOV    AX, DATA
                    MOV    DS, AX                   ; INIT DS
```

```
;FIND THE FIRST MATCHING FILE

                LEA   DX,EFCB              ; SET UP POINTER TO EFCB
                MOV   AH,11H               ; SEARCH FOR MATCHING FILE
                INT   21H
                CMP   AL,0FFH              ; ANY FOUND?
                JE    EXIT                 ; NO, EXIT

;NOW SEARCH FOR THE NEXT ONE

NEXT:           LEA   DX,EFCB
                MOV   AH,12H               ; SEARCH FOR NEXT
                INT   21H
                CMP   AH,0FFH              ; ANY MORE?
                JE    EXIT                 ; NO, EXIT
                JMP   NEXT

;RETURN TO DOS

EXIT:           MOV   AH,4CH
                INT   21H

CODE            ENDS
                END        START
```

As the example shows, searching for files is not difficult. The only thing to remember is that you can't change the reserved areas of the FCB formatted in the DTA. If you do, you can't continue the search. We leave the analogous exercise using the ASCIIZ method to the reader. It is easier than the example, because you do not have to set up an FCB.

FUNCTION CALLS NOT DISCUSSED

The last three chapters have rather thoroughly covered disk access. Yet there are several function calls relating to disk access that we have not discussed. These are mainly of utilitarian use: renaming, deleting, and so on. The omitted function calls are listed below for reference.

17H RENAME FILE, FCB METHOD

56H RENAME FILE, ASCIIZ METHOD

13H DELETE FILE, FCB METHOD

41H DELETE FILE, ASCIIZ METHOD

23H FILE SIZE

24H SET RANDOM RECORD FIELD TO MATCH BLOCK RECORD

2FH GET DTA
43H GET/SET FILE ATTRIBUTE
57H GET/SET FILE'S TIME AND DATE
29H PARSE FILENAME
45H DUPLICATE A FILE HANDLE
46H FORCE A DUPLICATE OF A FILE HANDLE

CHAPTER SUMMARY

This chapter completes the topic of logical file access. We saw that one advantage of using relative record numbers (over using the block record approach) is that DOS calculates the required block record numbers for us. The ACSIIZ method takes the further step of avoiding file control blocks altogether, but has the drawback of being byte-, rather than record-, oriented. This drawback is perhaps overcome by its simplicity.

Both the ASCIIZ method and the FCB method provide function calls that search directories. The FCB method must be augmented by an extended file control block to include a file attribute in the search.

Executable Files

The last three chapters were devoted to understanding how the operating system manages and accesses the disk. We are now going to see how DOS manages executable files. We will learn about the two types of executable files, seeing their differences and advantages. In the next chapter, we will see how to use DOS function calls to load and execute files from an application program.

EXECUTABLE FILES—.COM AND .EXE

One main difference between these two types of files really tells the whole story.

.COM   This file must use only one segment.
.EXE   This file can use as many segments as you desire.

Let's discuss the implications of these statements. The fact that a .COM file can use only one logical segment implies the program consists of a CODE segment only. No DATA segments or STACK segments are allowed. If the file is restricted to one segment, it will be completely relocatable. The file can then be directly transferred from the disk to memory and executed.

Why is a file with only one segment a relocatable file? Since in this case data definitions must be within the CODE segment, all data references will use only a 16-bit relative displacement, not an absolute address. Furthermore, all jump and subroutine-call instructions will be of the NEAR type, again requiring only a 16-bit relative displacement.

Thus, there are no absolute references in the program. All that must be done to run the .COM file is to load it into memory, initialize the segment registers, and begin execution at the entry point of the program.

On the other hand, the .EXE file can contain many logical segments. All the example programs presented in the book so far are of the .EXE type. The examples always contain a stack segment, a data segment, and a code segment. We could, if necessary, define more segments, making several data segments and code segments. The example programs, however, have been simple enough that one code, one data, and one stack segment suffice. Why is the .EXE file not relocatable? Consider the following instructions used to initialize the DS register.

```
MOV   AX, DATA
MOV   DS, AX
```

Assume that DATA is the name of the data segment. The first instruction cannot be assembled completely by the assembler. The assembler does not know where the data segment will be, so a number can't be assigned to the label DATA. If you look at an assembler listing you will see this:

```
B8 _ _ _ _        MOV   AX, DATA
```

The B8 in the instruction stands for ''Move the following two bytes into the AX register.'' The following two bytes are blank, indicating that the assembler doesn't know what to put there. The actual location of the data segment isn't determined until the program is loaded. When the .EXE program is loaded, the blanks in the instruction are filled in with the proper segment value. The process of filling in the blanks is called *relocation*. There may be many items that need relocation when the program is loaded. The information about items needing relocation is kept in the file itself, in the ''file header.'' When it loads the .EXE file, DOS refers to the file header to find the items that need relocation.

What overhead is created by the need to perform relocation? The .EXE disk file is larger than the corresponding .COM file because it contains a file header. In addition, loading the .EXE file will take longer because of the relocation process. Which type of file should you use? To create a .COM file, you must first create an .EXE file and convert it to a .COM file with the EXE2BIN utility. Because of this extra step, you may prefer to use .EXE files. The extra file space and loading time required by an .EXE file isn't noticeable on small applications, and you may prefer not to wait for the EXE2BIN file conversion. For large applications, the smaller file-size and load-time features of the .COM file may make them more attractive.

Another possible advantage of the .COM file lies in its relative nature. A relative file is easy to load and move about in memory. You could write a custom ''executive'' program for the .COM files in a fairly straightforward manner.

As we have seen, there are advantages and disadvantages to both types of files. Remember, if your program is larger than 64K bytes you have no choice—you must use the .EXE type, because the .COM type is limited to 64K bytes.

Later in the chapter, we will see an example that shows you how to convert files from .EXE to .COM, but first we must examine a structure that is part of every program—the program segment prefix.

THE PROGRAM SEGMENT PREFIX

Whenever DOS loads a program for execution, it first creates a 256-byte data structure called the *program segment prefix* (hereafter, the PSP). The PSP is located at the first available paragraph of free memory. The program itself is loaded immediately above the PSP. The PSP has these two basic functions:

1. The PSP contains information relevant to the program's environment. This information can be used by the application and is used by DOS to make a correct exit to the program's parent program.
2. The PSP contains space for a "command tail." Information can be passed from the command line to the command tail for processing by the program.

Table 9-1 presents some of the important items in the PSP.

TABLE 9-1   IMPORTANT AREAS IN THE PSP

Offset	Contents
00H	An INT 20H (return to DOS) instruction
02H	Top of memory, in paragraphs
06H	Number of bytes in the segment
0AH	Terminate address (INT 22H)
0EH	Ctrl-Break exit address (INT 23H)
12H	Critical error exit address (INT 24H)
2CH	Address of parent environment
5CH	Formatted FCB1
6CH	Formatted FCB2
80H	Number of characters entered after the command
81H	All characters entered after the command

The area at offset 80H has a second function:

80H	Default DTA, size = default record size of 128 bytes

A few comments are in order. Control will pass to the terminate address when the program is terminated. The Ctrl-Break exit address and the Critical-Error exit address contain respectively the values that interrupt vectors 23H and 24H have when the program is loaded. The application program is free to change the interrupt vectors because they will be restored to the values stored in the PSP when the program is terminated.

The address of the parent environment is a pointer to a sequence of ASCIIZ strings. These strings contain information referred to as the *environment*. The default environment contains an ASCIIZ string telling us where to find the command processor file, COMMAND.COM. It looks like this:

```
"COMSPEC=A:\COMMAND.COM",00
```

If you have used the PATH command to specify a directory search path, you will find the PATH command (as an ASCIIZ string) in the environment. The SET command allows you to insert arbitrary ASCIIZ strings into the environment (see the DOS manual). An application program can use these strings to make decisions.

The command tail consists of the characters in a command that are typed after the filename. You can use the command tail to pass information to a program. The number of characters in the command tail is placed at 80H. If the string contains a valid filename, it will be formatted into an FCB at offset 5CH. A second filename will be formatted into an FCB at offset 6CH. You can easily examine all the features of the PSP by using Debug. Type a command like this:

```
A>DEBUG FILE1.TXT FILE2.TXT
```

After Debug is loaded, use D (DUMP) to examine the PSP. You will see the command tail at 81H and the two FCBs at 5CH and 6CH, respectively. You can also verify other topics mentioned in the preceding discussion—the environment, for example. Note that the area beginning at 80H really has two uses. It contains the command tail and it is used as the default DTA. Be sure to use the information in the command tail before using the area as a DTA.

LOADING EXECUTABLE FILES

We will shortly see an example that shows how to convert an .EXE file to a .COM file. But first we must know a little more about the loading process. As we know, .COM files can be loaded without any relocation process—all memory accesses are relative to the beginning of the code segment. On the contrary, the .EXE files are not relative and contain words that must undergo relocation during the loading process. This leads to a difference in the way the files look in memory.

Let's take care of the simpler case first. When a .COM file is loaded, the following steps take place (refer to Figure 9-1):

1. A PSP is created at the first available paragraph in memory.
2. The .COM file is transferred directly from the disk to the memory immediately after the PSP.
3. All segment registers are set to point to the beginning of the PSP.
4. The SP register is set up so that the stack is located at the end of the segment. A stack of 100H is assumed.
5. The IP register is set to 100H, which means that the program starts at offset 100H in the segment.

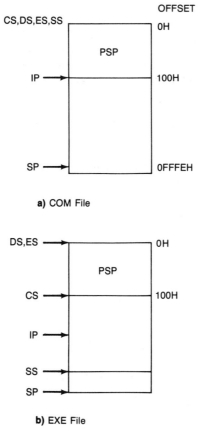

a) COM File

b) EXE File

Figure 9-1 COM and EXE File Types

The loading of the .EXE file is more complicated (because of relocation), but the results can be simply expressed (see Figure 9-1) as follows:

1. A PSP is created at the first available paragraph in memory.
2. The program is loaded into memory and relocated. DOS locates the segments in memory alphabetically.
3. Segment registers ES and DS are set to point to the beginning of the PSP.
4. Registers CS, IP, SS, and SP are determined by values in the .EXE file. If the program was created in assembly language, the CS:IP value is determined by the label on the END statement. The SS:SP values come from the stack definition, "STACK SEGMENT STACK."

Example 9-1 A .COM File to Change the Attribute of a Disk-File

Example 9-1 shows how to make a .COM file. We have seen that the .COM file must contain only one segment. The first instruction to be executed will always be at offset 100H within that segment, so we must put an ORG 100H at the top of the program. The first instruction will typically be a JMP to the "real" entry point of the main code. Data variables and procedures will be defined after the JMP instruction.

The example is designed to illustrate the use of the command tail. We will use the command tail to pass a filename and an attribute to the program. The program will then change the attribute of the designated file to the specified attribute. To change the attribute of a file using this program, we type the following:

A>CHANGE FILENAME.EXT X

In this command, CHANGE is the example program, FILENAME.EXT is the name of the file whose attribute is to be changed, and X is a single character indicating the desired attribute (see the following list):

```
                  N=NORMAL
                  R=READ-ONLY
                  H=HIDDEN
                  S=SYSTEM


CODE          SEGMENT
              ASSUME CS:CODE,DS:CODE,ES:CODE,SS:CODE


              ORG    100H      ;LEAVE ROOM FOR THE PSP


              JMP    START     ;JUMP TO THE BEGINNING


NORMAL            DW    00H
READ_ONLY         DW    01H
HIDDEN            DW    02H
SYSTEM            DW    04H


;FIRST, CHANGE PARAMETER ONE INTO AN ASCIIZ STRING


START:        MOV    BX,82H                  ;POINT TO FIRST PARAMETER


L1:           CMP    BYTE PTR [BX],20H    ;IS THIS THE SPACE?
              JE     YES                  ;YES, STOP LOOKING
              INC    BX                   ;NO, KEEP LOOKING
              JMP    L1


YES:          MOV    BYTE PTR [BX],00     ;MAKE INTO ASCIIZ
              INC    BX                   ;POINT TO SECOND PARAMETER
              CMP    BYTE PTR [BX],'N'    ;NORMAL
              JNE    L2                   ;NO, KEEP LOOKING
              MOV    CX,NORMAL            ;YES
              JMP    SHORT CHANGE
L2:           CMP    BYTE PTR [BX],'R'    ;READ-ONLY
```

```
              JNE   L3                              ; NO, KEEP LOOKING
              MOV   CX, READ_ONLY                   ; YES
              JMP   SHORT CHANGE
    L3:       CMP   BYTE PTR [BX], 'H'              ; HIDDEN
              JNE   L4                              ; NO, KEEP LOOKING
              MOV   CX, HIDDEN                      ; YES
              JMP   SHORT CHANGE
    L4:       CMP   BYTE PTR [BX], 'S'              ; SYSTEM
              JNE   EXIT                            ; NO, EXIT
              MOV   CX, SYSTEM

    ; NOW CHANGE THE ATTRIBUTE

    CHANGE:   MOV   DX, 82H                         ; POINT TO ASCIIZ STRING
              MOV   AL, 01                          ; SET ATTRIBUTE FUNCTION
              MOV   AH, 43H                         ; CHANGE MODE FUNCTION-CALL
              INT   21H

    ; PUT ERROR CHECK HERE

    EXIT:     MOV   AH, 4CH
              INT   21H

    CODE      ENDS
              END   START
```

Notice that the ASSUME statement refers all segment registers to the CODE segment so that default addressing modes will be used. All variables can then be addressed by using the DS register rather than the CS register, avoiding segment-override prefixes. You can observe the absence of the override prefix on the variables NORMAL, READ_ONLY, HIDDEN, and SYSTEM by looking at an assembly listing. The program would have been more efficient if "equates" had been used instead of defining variables. (The variables were defined only to illustrate the absence of the override prefix.) This example is not a finished product, because it contains no error checking. It requires that the command tail be entered with no extra spaces, exactly in the correct format. Nor does it contain messages to indicate to the user that the attribute was changed correctly or that the file was found.

Here are the steps to follow if you want to try the above example:

1. Create a source file.
2. Assemble the source file, creating an .OBJ file.
3. Link the .OBJ file, creating an .EXE file. At this point you will get an error message saying "no stack segment." This is normal.
4. Use the EXE2BIN utility to convert the .EXE file to a .COM file as in this example:

A>EXE2BIN CHANGE.EXE CHANGE.COM

CHAPTER SUMMARY

In this chapter we examined the two types of executable files supported by DOS—.COM and .EXE. We found the basic difference to be that the .COM file is limited to one segment, whereas the .EXE file can include any number of segments. The .COM file is loaded directly, and the .EXE file must undergo relocation as it is loaded. Finally, we discussed the program segment prefix and saw an example of how to create a .COM file. Details of the relocation process can be found in the DOS Technical Reference Manual.

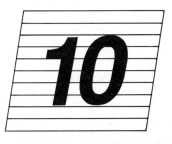

Memory Management
and Executive Functions

This chapter will discuss how to load and execute programs from within an application program. The idea is simple, as the following example shows. Suppose we run a program called PROGA.EXE by typing its name on the command line. Assume that one task of PROGA.EXE is to load and execute PROGX.EXE. Upon termination, PROGX.EXE should return control to PROGA.EXE. (We could complicate the example by adding more levels—PROGX.EXE loads and executes PROGY.EXE, and so forth.) Regardless of the complexity of the example, the basic ingredients are the same.

1. We need some way to load a program file (subprocess) from the disk into an area of "free memory."

2. We need a way to execute the subprocess.

3. We need an orderly way to return to the original program (parent process).

How are these three steps accomplished when you type a program's name on a command line? DOS performs the steps, so we really don't have to think about it. The command-line interpreter looks at the command (the program's name). Since the program is considered by DOS to be an "external" command, DOS uses an executive function that loads and executes the command (program). The DOS loader builds a PSP, performs any necessary relocation, and executes a far jump to the program's entry point. If the program uses a standard method (function call 4CH, for example) to return to DOS, we will see the prompt reappear on the screen when the program is finished.

It turns out that we have access to the same executive function that DOS uses—

function call 4BH (EXEC). By using this function call, we can tell DOS to load and execute a program exactly as if we had typed its name on the command line.

We must bring up the subject of memory management in order to discuss the EXEC function call in detail. Before EXEC can load a program, there must be some "free memory" into which it can be loaded. Some of you may be thinking, "My system has 640K bytes of RAM. Why should EXEC worry about free memory? It is almost all free?" Obviously there must be more to the idea of "free memory" than the simple idea of unused or idle memory. When you invoke a program by typing its name on the command line, the EXEC function call assigns all available memory to that program. How much free memory is then available? None, even though the program is only 100 bytes long and your system contains 640K bytes of RAM. If the invoked program tries to use EXEC to load another program, it will fail because there is no free memory.

MEMORY MANAGEMENT

DOS manages memory by a series of linked structures called *memory control blocks,* as shown in Figure 10-1. The DOS Technical Reference Manual does not document the structure of these control blocks, so the following description might be incomplete. As we will see, understanding the details of the control blocks is not really necessary, because they are accessed via function calls.

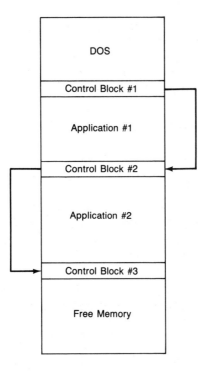

Figure 10-1 DOS Control Block Chain

Each memory control block appears to occupy 16 bytes of memory, although only five bytes seem to be actively used in DOS 2.0 and 2.1. The five bytes can be grouped into three fields:

byte 0   This byte will be either 4DH or 5AH. Only the last control block in the chain will contain a 5AH, all others a 4DH.

bytes 1 and 2   These bytes together contain a word. This word is the segment address of the process that owns the memory block referred to by the control block. If these two bytes contain zeros, then the memory block is free memory.

bytes 3 and 4   These two bytes form a word containing the number of paragraphs in the memory block described by the control block. Recall that a paragraph is 16 bytes long.

Where is the control block located? It is usually directly below the memory block it describes. Before we discuss the chaining of control blocks, let's look at an example to see how it works. Suppose we load an executable file with Debug. We can look at either the DS or ES register to determine where the PSP begins. The beginning of the PSP marks the beginning of memory allocated to the program. Let's suppose the segment address of the PSP is 905H. Where is the control block? It immediately precedes the PSP. If we look at segment address 904H, therefore, we will see the following:

```
0904:0000        5A 05 09 FB 16 ?? ??
```

The first byte is 5A, indicating that this control block is last in the control block chain. The owner's address is segment 905H, the program just loaded. How much memory has been allocated to this program? We see it is 16FBH paragraphs, which happens to be all the available RAM in a 128K-byte system.

905H   beginning segment of this program
  +   memory allocated to this program
16FBH
‾‾‾‾‾

(The example assumed that the system contained 128K bytes of RAM. If we had had a 256K-byte system, the last number would have been 36FBH instead of 16FBH.)

As we see from the example, all available memory is allocated to the program being loaded.

CHAINING OF MEMORY CONTROL BLOCKS

Let's turn now to the chaining process. In Figure 10-2, we see memory divided into three blocks. A memory control block precedes each memory block. How are the control blocks chained together? Each memory block within the chain must be both preceded and succeeded by a memory control block (except for the last one). All we must do is use the

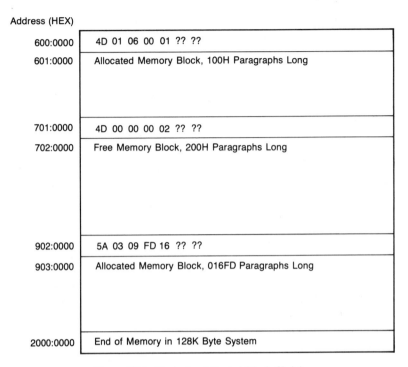

Address (HEX)

600:0000	4D 01 06 00 01 ?? ??
601:0000	Allocated Memory Block, 100H Paragraphs Long
701:0000	4D 00 00 00 02 ?? ??
702:0000	Free Memory Block, 200H Paragraphs Long
902:0000	5A 03 09 FD 16 ?? ??
903:0000	Allocated Memory Block, 016FD Paragraphs Long
2000:0000	End of Memory in 128K Byte System

Figure 10-2   Example of Control Block Chaining

information in a given control block to find the end of the memory block allocated by that control block. At that location we will find another control block. This leads to the following simple algorithm:

1. Add 1 to the segment address of the memory control block. The result is the segment address of the memory block allocated by the control block.
2. Add the size of the allocated memory block (in paragraphs) to the segment address found in 1. The result will now be the segment address of the next memory control block.

(*Note:* The last block in the chain doesn't follow this rule. In that case, the calculation yields the segment address of the first paragraph beyond the system RAM.)

With this algorithm in mind, let's check the addresses in Figure 10-2. The first control block is located at paragraph 600H. The memory controlled by this block is at paragraph 601H. The length of the memory allocated is 100H paragraphs, so the next memory control block is at paragraph 701H. You can do the arithmetic yourself for the second block. Notice that the middle control block describes a free section of memory. The chain can contain free memory intermingled with allocated memory.

MEMORY MANAGEMENT FUNCTION CALLS

Now that you have some idea of the nature of the memory control blocks, let's see how to avoid dealing with them altogether. DOS provides three function calls designed to manipulate the control blocks (and through them, memory allocation).

48H—Allocate Memory.   You must set BX equal to the number of paragraphs of memory desired. DOS will attempt to find a free block of memory at least this size and create a control block for the memory. If the request succeeds, the AX register will contain the paragraph number of the allocated memory. If the request cannot be carried out, BX will contain the maximum number of paragraphs available.

49H—Free Allocated Memory.   Set the ES register equal to the paragraph address of the memory block you wish to free.

4AH—Setblock.   This function might be more aptly named "CHANGE ALLOCATION." Set ES equal to the paragraph address of a previously allocated block, and set BX equal to the new desired size of the block. If the call fails, BX will contain the maximum number of paragraphs available.

As in many of the DOS function calls, the success of the operation is indicated by the fact that the carry flag is zero. If the carry flag is one, then the problem is indicated by the value in AX. Problems relevant to the memory management function calls include the following:

7 Memory control blocks destroyed

8 Insufficient memory

9 Invalid memory block address

By using these three function calls, we can easily allocate memory, change a previously allocated block, and free an allocated block.

FREEING MEMORY

Why do we need to know about memory management before using the EXEC function call? Recall that when EXEC loads a program, it allocates all the available free memory to the loaded program. Before the program can use EXEC to load a subprocess (program), it must first use SETBLOCK to free some memory for the subprocess. In Figure 10-3(a), we see the memory allocation immediately after a program has been loaded. Figure 10-3(b) shows the memory allocation after the loaded program has issued a SETBLOCK function call to reduce the amount of memory allocated to it. The program could now use the EXEC function to load and execute a subprocess in the free memory.

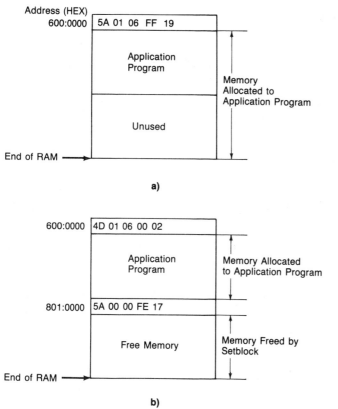

Figure 10-3 Using Setblock

RELOADING THE EXEC LOADER

Before we proceed to an example, we must discuss one more problem. The loader program used by EXEC is part of COMMAND.COM and is normally located at the top of RAM. If the loader portion of COMMAND.COM has not been overwritten, it will be used by EXEC without further ado. If the loader has been overwritten, a new copy will be loaded for use by EXEC. There must be some free memory available for the loader. In DOS 2.1, the loader requires 59 paragraphs of free memory. EXEC will return an "insufficient memory error" unless at least 59 paragraphs of free memory exist—regardless of whether it needs to actually reload the loader! The logic flow seems to be something like this:

1. EXEC function call invoked.
2. Is there enough free memory to reload the EXEC loader?
   a. NO—return "insufficient memory error."
   b. YES—proceed to step 3.

3. Does the EXEC loader need to be reloaded?

  a. NO—go to step 4.

  b. YES—reload and go to step 4.

4. Perform the required function.

The main point is this: Make sure there is enough free memory for both the application program and the loader used by EXEC.

THE EXEC FUNCTION CALL—4BH

This function call has two subfunctions determined by the value in AL. So far, we have been referring to the ability of EXEC to load and execute a program. In addition, EXEC can simply load a program at a desired memory location.

  AL = 0   Load and execute a program.
  AL = 3   Load only.

Function 3, useful for loading overlay programs, will be discussed later in the chapter. Let's concentrate on function 0.

The EXEC Function Call: AL = 0

The DS:DX register pair must point to an ASCIIZ string containing the filename of the program you wish to load and execute. Register pair ES:BX must point to a parameter block that contains information used by EXEC in setting up the PSP for the program to be loaded. The parameter block has the following format:

WORD	Segment address of the environment string. A zero word means that the new process will inherit the environment of the parent (invoking process).
DWORD	Pointer to the "command tail" to be placed at offset 80H in the new PSP.
DWORD	Pointer to the FCB to be placed into the default FCB1 at offset 5CH in the new PSP.
DWORD	Pointer to the FCB to be placed into the default FCB2 at offset 6CH in the new PSP.

EXEC will load the program as discussed in Chapter 9, creating a PSP for the program, performing any relocation necessary, and jumping to the entry point of the program. The items in the parameter block may or may not be important. The actual information placed at offsets 80H, 5CH, and 6CH is important only if the loaded program uses it. For example, if the newly loaded program assumes that the string at 80H is a filename, then you must make sure the pointer points to a filename.

When the subprocess exits (for example, using function call 4CH), control will be returned to the executable statement following the original EXEC function call. All memory allocated to the subprocess by EXEC will be returned to the free memory pool. Recall that EXEC allocates all available memory to the subprocess. If the subprocess wishes to have ''offspring,'' it must first free sufficient memory by using SETBLOCK.

A Final Important Note.   EXEC function 0 will destroy all register contents. It is your responsibility to save any registers you need after EXEC function 0 executes.

Example 10-1 One Program Invoking Another

The following example presents a straightforward use of the SETBLOCK and EXEC function calls. The example contains two programs. PROGA first writes a sign-on message to the console, then after a small calculation shortens the memory allocation through SETBLOCK. (Notice that the calculation leaves room for the stack.) The EXEC function call is then used to load and execute PROGB. PROGB writes a message to the console and exits (returning control to PROGA). PROGA finishes by reinitializing DS, SS, and SP (which were destroyed during the EXEC function call), writing a final message to the console, and exiting to DOS.

```
         PROGA

STACK       SEGMENT    STACK
       DW    128    DUP (?)
TOS         LABEL      WORD
STACK       ENDS


DATA        SEGMENT

MESS1       DB    'PROGRAM 1 HAS STARTED EXECUTING.'
            DB    0AH, 0DH, 0AH, 0DH
MESS2       DB    'NOW LOAD AND EXECUTE PROGRAM 2.'
            DB    0AH, 0DH, 0AH, 0DH, '$'
MESS3       DB    'CONTROL HAS RETURNED TO PROGRAM 1.'
            DB    0AH, 0DH, 0AH, 0DH, '$'


FILE        DB    'EXEC2.EXE', 00       ;FILE TO BE LOADED
;NOW DEFINE THE PARAMETER BLOCK

PARAM       DW          0            ;USE THE PARENT ENVIRONMENT
COM_PTR  DD          FAKE
FCB1_PTR DD          FAKE
FCB2_PTR DD          FAKE


;NOW AN AREA OF SPACES

FAKE        DB    20 DUP (20)
STACK_PTR       DW      ?      ;MUST SAVE STACK PTR
DATA        ENDS
```

```
CODE        SEGMENT
            ASSUME CS:CODE,DS:DATA,SS:STACK

START:  MOV   AX,DATA
        MOV   DS,AX          ;INIT DS

;NOW PRINT THE FIRST MESSAGE USING FUNCTION CALL #9

        LEA   DX,MESS1        ;ADDRESS OF MESS1
        MOV   AH,9
        INT   21H

;NOW CHANGE MEMORY ALLOCATION TO MAKE SPACE FOR PROGRAM 2
        MOV   BX,OFFSET TOS  ;CALCULATE # OF PARAGRAPHS
        MOV   CL,4           ;DIVIDE LAST OFFSET BY 16
        SHR   BX,CL
        ADD   BX,1           ;ROUND RESULT UP
        MOV   AX,SS          ;ADD IN THE SEGMENT ADDRESS
        ADD   BX,AX          ;LAST ADDRESS IN PARAGRAPHS
        MOV   AX,ES          ;ES CONTAINS THE FIRST ADDRESS
        SUB   BX,AX          ;LENGTH OF PROGRAM IN PARAGRAPHS
        MOV   AH,4AH         ;USE SETBLOCK FUNCTION CALL
        INT   21H            ;SHORTEN ALLOCATION


;NOW, LET'S LOAD AND EXECUTE THE OTHER PROGRAM

        LEA   DX,FILE         ;POINT TO ASCIIZ STRING
        PUSH DS
        POP  ES
        LEA   BX,PARAM        ;POINT TO PARAMETER BLOCK
        MOV   AH,4BH
        MOV   AL,00H          ;LOAD AND EXECUTE FUNCTION
        MOV   STACK_PTR,SP    ;SAVE STACK POINTER
        INT   21H            ;DO EXEC FUNCTION CALL

;FINALLY, PRINT MESS3

        MOV   AX,DATA
        MOV   DS,AX          ;RESET DS REGISTER
        MOV   AX,STACK
        MOV   SS,AX          ;RESET SS REGISTER
        MOV   SP,STACK_PTR   ;RESET STACK POINTER
        LEA   DX,MESS3
        MOV   AH,9
        INT   21H

;NOW EXIT TO DOS

        MOV   AH,4CH
        INT   21H
```

```
CODE          ENDS
              END    START
---------------------------------------------------------------

PROGB




STACK         SEGMENT    STACK
              DW            128   DUP (?)
STACK         ENDS

DATA          SEGMENT

MESS1         DB            'PROGRAM 2 IS EXECUTING.'
              DB            0AH, 0DH, 0AH, 0DH, '$'

DATA          ENDS

CODE          SEGMENT
              ASSUME     CS: CODE, DS: DATA, SS: STACK

START:        MOV    AX, DATA
              MOV    DS, AX

              LEA    DX, MESS1          ; SEND MESSAGE
              MOV    AH, 9
              INT    21H

              MOV    AH, 4CH            ; RETURN TO DOS
              INT    21H

CODE          ENDS
              END    START
```

Using EXEC to Issue Commands

It turns out that EXEC can be used by an application program to issue DOS commands. This isn't really a new use of EXEC; it is just an application of the EXEC function, AL = 0, load and execute. We use EXEC to load a copy of COMMAND.COM and then pass a command string to COMMAND.COM via the pointer in the parameter block. When COMMAND.COM executes, it looks at the ''command tail''—the string located at offset 80H in its PSP. If the string is a valid DOS command, COMMAND.COM will perform the command. Control will return to the application program after the command has been carried out.

The format of the data area containing the command string is very specific. The first byte must indicate the number of characters in the command string. The next three characters should be ''/C '', followed by the actual command. It is the ''/C '' that tells COMMAND.COM to interpret the string as a command. For example, if we want the secondary copy of COMMAND.COM to list the directory of the default drive, the following is the correct format:

```
COMMAND          DB        6,'/C DIR'
```

Example 10-2 Using EXEC to Perform the DIR Command

```
STACK       SEGMENT    STACK
      DW     128       DUP (?)
TOS         LABEL      WORD
STACK       ENDS


DATA        SEGMENT

MESS1       DB     'PROGRAM 1 HAS STARTED EXECUTING.'
            DB     0AH,0DH,0AH,0DH
MESS2       DB     'NOW LOAD AND EXECUTE COMMAND.COM.'
            DB     0AH,0DH,0AH,0DH,'$'
MESS3       DB     'CONTROL HAS RETURNED TO PROGRAM 1.'
            DB     0AH,0DH,0AH,0DH,'$'


FILE        DB     'COMMAND.COM',00        ;FILE TO BE LOADED

;NOW DEFINE THE PARAMETER BLOCK

PARAM       DW         0          ;USE THE PARENT ENVIRONMENT
COM_PTR     DD         COMMAND
FCB1_PTR    DD         FAKE
FCB2_PTR    DD         FAKE

;NOW THE COMMAND STRING

COMMAND     DB         6,'/C DIR'
;NOW AN AREA OF SPACES

FAKE        DB     20 DUP(20)
STACK_PTR       DW     ?          ;MUST SAVE STACK PTR
DATA        ENDS

CODE        SEGMENT
            ASSUME CS:CODE,DS:DATA,SS:STACK
```

```
START:      MOV   AX,DATA
            MOV   DS,AX           ; INIT DS

; NOW PRINT THE FIRST MESSAGE USING FUNCTION CALL #9

            LEA   DX,MESS1             ; ADDRESS OF MESS1
            MOV   AH,9
            INT   21H

; NOW CHANGE MEMORY ALLOCATION TO MAKE SPACE FOR PROGRAM 2

            MOV   BX,OFFSET TOS   ; CALCULATE # OF PARAGRAPHS
            MOV   CL,4
            SHR   BX,CL
            ADD   BX,1            ; ROUND RESULT UP
            MOV   AX,SS
            ADD   BX,AX           ; LAST ADDRESS IN PARAGRAPHS
            MOV   AX,ES
            SUB   BX,AX           ; LENGTH OF PROGRAM IN PARAGRAPHS
            MOV   AH,4AH
            INT   21H             ; SHORTEN ALLOCATION

; NOW, LET'S LOAD AND EXECUTE THE OTHER PROGRAM

            LEA   DX,FILE    ; POINT TO ASCIIZ STRING
            PUSH  DS
            POP   ES
            LEA   BX,PARAM   ; POINT TO PARAMETER BLOCK
            MOV   AH,4BH
            MOV   AL,00H      ; LOAD AND EXECUTE FUNCTION
            MOV   STACK_PTR,SP       ; SAVE STACK POINTER
            INT   21H             ; DO EXEC FUNCTION CALL

; FINALLY, PRINT MESS3

            MOV   AX,DATA
            MOV   DS,AX          ; RESET DS REGISTER
            MOV   AX,STACK
            MOV   SS,AX          ; RESET SS REGISTER
            MOV   SP,STACK_PTR        ; RESET STACK POINTER
            LEA   DX,MESS3
            MOV   AH,9
            INT   21H
; NOW EXIT TO DOS

            MOV   AH,4CH
            INT   21H


CODE        ENDS
            END   START
```

The EXEC Function Call: AL = 3

Using the EXEC function with AL = 3 will cause a file to be loaded into memory. That is all it will do. The register pair DS:DX must point to an ASCIIZ string containing the filename of the file to be loaded. The ES:BX register pair must point to a parameter block that contains two words:

> WORD   The paragraph address where the program is to be loaded.
>
> WORD   The relocation factor that is applied to the image (the loaded program).

Remember that relocation occurs during the loading of an .EXE file. When you are loading with function AL = 3, the loader uses the relocation factor from the parameter block during the relocation phase. This relocation factor will typically be the same as the load address (in paragraphs). When you use the "load and execute" function (AL = 0), the loader chooses its own relocation factor, depending on where it decides to put the program.

In contrast to the "load and execute" function (AL = 0), function (AL = 3) results in the following:

- No memory is allocated to the loaded program.
- No PSP is created for the loaded program.
- The loaded program will not execute until your program transfers control directly to it (by a jump or call).
- The loaded program must not use any of the memory-management function calls; it doesn't "own" any memory.

At first glance this EXEC function may seem less useful than the "load and execute" function, but it is actually ideal for loading program overlays. A program that is too large to fit into available memory can often be broken into several pieces, some of which are mutually independent. This scenario is depicted in Figure 10-4. One piece is typically dubbed the *main program,* and the other pieces are called *overlays.* The main program remains resident in memory and swaps the overlays in and out of memory as needed. The overlay programs typically occupy the same memory space.

Example 10-3 Using EXEC for Overlays

> This example illustrates how to do simple overlays. Small programs have been used to save space. Of course, in the real world, little programs like these would never dictate the necessity for overlays. In the example, the main program successively loads and executes two overlay programs. Each overlay prints a message indicating that it has executed.
>
> Let's look at the main program—MAIN. The first thing MAIN does is shrink its own memory allocation, using SETBLOCK. (Remember EXEC will not execute without free memory.) Next, MAIN requests a block of ten paragraphs of memory by using the ALLO-CATE MEMORY function call (48H). If no errors occur, DOS will allocate ten paragraphs of the free memory to MAIN. This block is big enough to hold the overlays. DOS returns the

Main Program with Overlay #1

Main Program with Overlay #2   **Figure 10-4**   Program Overlays

paragraph address of the beginning of the allocated block to MAIN in AX. MAIN stores this in the load-address field of the parameter block. MAIN then loads the first overlay and executes a FAR CALL to the beginning of the overlay. The two overlays are written as FAR PROCEDURES so a RET instruction transfers control back to MAIN. The relocation factor in the parameter block is not used in this example, because neither overlay makes any absolute memory references.

```
;MAIN  This program loads and executes two overlay programs .

STACK      SEGMENT    STACK
           DW     128      DUP  (?)
TOS        LABEL          WORD
STACK      ENDS

DATA       SEGMENT

MESS1      DB     'PROGRAM 1 HAS STARTED EXECUTING. '
           DB     0AH, 0DH, 0AH, 0DH
MESS2      DB     'NOW LOAD AND EXECUTE OVERLAY1'
           DB     0AH, 0DH, 0AH, 0DH, '$'
```

```
MESS3       DB      'CONTROL HAS RETURNED TO PROGRAM 1.'
            DB      0AH,0DH,0AH,0DH,'$'
MESS4       DB      'NOW LOAD AND EXECUTE OVERLAY2'
            DB      0AH,0DH,0AH,0DH,'$'
OVERLAY1    DB      'OVERLAY1.EXE',00    ;NAME OF FIRST OVERLAY
OVERLAY2    DB      'OVERLAY2.EXE',00    ;NAME OF SECOND OVERLAY

;NOW DEFINE THE PARAMETER BLOCK

PARAMETER_BLOCK LABEL    WORD
SEG_ADDRESS     DW    ?
RELOCATION      DW    0               ;NO RELOCATION NEEDED

DATA        ENDS

CODE        SEGMENT
            ASSUME CS:CODE,DS:DATA,SS:STACK

START:      MOV   AX,DATA
            MOV   DS,AX            ;INIT DS

;NOW PRINT THE FIRST MESSAGE USING FUNCTION CALL #9

            LEA   DX,MESS1        ;ADDRESS OF MESS1
            MOV   AH,9
            INT   21H

;NOW CHANGE MEMORY ALLOCATION TO MAKE SPACE FOR PROGRAM 2

            MOV   BX,OFFSET TOS  ;CALCULATE # OF PARAGRAPHS
            MOV   CL,4
            SHR   BX,CL
            ADD   BX,1
            MOV   AX,SS
            ADD   BX,AX           ;LAST ADDRESS IN PARAGRAPHS
            MOV   AX,ES
            SUB   BX,AX           ;LENGTH OF PROGRAM IN PARAGRAPHS
            MOV   AH,4AH
            INT   21H             ;SHORTEN ALLOCATION

;WE MUST ASK FOR SOME MEMORY

            MOV   BX,10H          ;10 PARAGRAPHS SHOULD SUFFICE
            MOV   AH,48H
            INT   21H

;AX NOW POINTS TO THE ALLOTTED SEGMENT, LOAD OVERLAY1
            LEA   DX,MESS2            ;PRINT MESSAGE
```

```
        MOV   AH, 9
        INT   21H
        MOV   SEG_ADDRESS, AX
        PUSH  AX                    ; PUT ADDRESS OF OVERLAY ON STACK
        MOV   AX, 0
        PUSH  AX                    ; PUSH SEGMENT, THEN OFFSET
        LEA   DX, OVERLAY1          ; POINTER TO FILENAME
        PUSH  DS
        POP   ES                    ; POINTER TO PARAMETER_BLOCK
        LEA   BX, PARAMETER_BLOCK
        MOV   AH, 4BH
        MOV   AL, 3                 ; FUNCTION 3, LOAD
        INT   21H

; NOW CALL OVERLAY1, ADDRESS IS ON STACK

        MOV   BP, SP
        CALL        DWORD PTR [BP]
        LEA   DX, MESS3             ; PRINT MESSAGE
        MOV   AH, 9
        INT   21H
; NOW DO OVERLAY #2

        LEA   DX, MESS4             ; PRINT MESSAGE
        MOV   AH, 9
        INT   21H

        LEA   DX, OVERLAY2              ; POINTER TO FILENAME
        LEA   BX, PARAMETER_BLOCK
        MOV   AH, 4BH
        MOV   AL, 3
        INT   21H

; NOW CALL IT, ADDRESS IS STILL ON THE STACK

        MOV   BP, SP
        CALL        DWORD PTR [BP]

; RELEASE ALLOCATED BLOCK
        POP     AX
        POP     AX                  ; CLEAN STACK, AX NOW HAS SEGMENT
                                    ; OF PREVIOUSLY ALLOCATED BLOCK
        MOV   ES, AX
        MOV   AH, 49H               ; FREE ALLOCATED MEMORY
        INT   21H

; FINALLY, PRINT MESS3 AND RETURN TO DOS
```

```
                    LEA    DX, MESS3
                    MOV    AH, 9
                    INT    21H
                    MOV    AH, 4CH
                    INT    21H

        CODE        ENDS
                    END    START
```

`; OVERLAY1—This is the first overlay to be loaded.`

```
        CODE        SEGMENT
                    ASSUME    CS: CODE

        OVERLAY1 PROC        FAR         ; MAKE IT A FAR PROC

                    JMP        BEGIN         ; LEAVE ROOM FOR DATA
        MESS5       DB         'OVERLAY1 IS EXECUTING'
                    DB         0AH, 0DH, 0AH, 0DH, '$'

        BEGIN:      PUSH DS                  ; SAVE DS
                    PUSH CS                  ; MOVE CS TO DS
                    POP  DS                  ; DS: DX IS THE POINTER TO MESS1
                    LEA  DX, MESS5
                    MOV  AH, 9
                    INT  21H
                    POP  DS                  ; RESTORE DS

                    RET                      ; RETURN TO MAIN

        OVERLAY1 ENDP

        CODE        ENDS
                    END
```

`; OVERLAY2—This is the second overlay to be loaded.`

```
        CODE        SEGMENT
                    ASSUME    CS: CODE
        OVERLAY2 PROC        FAR         ; MAKE IT A FAR PROC

                    JMP        BEGIN         ; LEAVE ROOM FOR DATA
```

```
MESS6     DB          'OVERLAY2 IS EXECUTING'
          DB          0AH, 0DH, 0AH, 0DH, '$'

BEGIN:    PUSH DS                 ; SAVE DS
          PUSH CS                 ; MOVE CS TO DS
          POP  DS                 ; DS: DX IS THE POINTER TO MESS1
          LEA  DX, MESS6
          MOV  AH, 9
          INT  21H
          POP  DS                 ; RESTORE DS

          RET                     ; RETURN TO MAIN

OVERLAY2  ENDP

CODE      ENDS
          END
```

You may legitimately wonder why memory must be allocated for the overlays. Why can't we simply load the overlay at some address higher than the highest one in the main program? We can, but unless we know the location of the memory control blocks, we may inadvertently destroy some. For example, when we make the required SETBLOCK function call, DOS creates a memory control block at the paragraph following the memory allocated to the program. Loading an overlay over the control block will cause a "control blocks destroyed" error.

The proper thing to do is officially allocate and deallocate memory as needed, using the function calls. It is not complicated and will possibly save many headaches.

PROGRAM TERMINATION

This chapter will end with a few comments on program termination. To terminate means to return to the invoking (parent) process. This may mean returning to DOS and the command line interpreter or returning to the parent program that invoked the current process (by using EXEC). (Both cases are really the same, the parent in the first case being COMMAND.COM.)

There are two different ways to terminate a program:

1. Terminate so that the memory allocated to the process is returned to the free memory pool.
2. Terminate so that the allocated memory remains allocated. This allows the process to remain resident—to be activated in a special way (by interrupts, for example).

DOS 2.0 and DOS 2.1 supply two function calls that implement these termination methods.

TERMINATION FUNCTION CALLS

4CH—Terminate

Terminate program and return to the parent program. Set AL = return code.

31H—Terminate and Remain Resident

Set DX equal to the number of paragraphs you wish to keep resident. The program will terminate (return to the parent), leaving DX paragraphs in the allocation chain. Set AL = return code.

The advantage these function calls have over earlier methods (INT 20H, INT 27H, function call 0H) is that a parameter may be passed to the parent process. The parameter is called the *return code* and is put into the AL register before terminating. The parent process may look at this return code by issuing function call 4DH. After function call 4DH, AX contains the following information. The return code can also be used during batch processing.

> AL = return code
> AH = 00—normal termination (like 4CH above)
>   01—Ctrl-Brk termination
>   02—critical device error
>   03—termination via function call 31H

We will later find function call 31H very useful for installing hardware drivers.

CHAPTER SUMMARY

This chapter explained the EXEC function call, as well as DOS memory allocation. Memory is allocated in blocks, each controlled by a memory control block. Memory control blocks are chained together. The integrity of the chain must be maintained, or memory allocation errors will occur. We found that DOS provides three function calls that we can use to manage memory without destroying the control block chain. Finally, we saw two example programs that use the EXEC function call. Example 10-1 shows how to use the "load and execute" function, and Example 10-2 illustrates the use of overlays.

Installable
Device Drivers

WHAT IS A DEVICE DRIVER?

The term *device driver* applies to software that provides an interface between the system unit and a peripheral device. As we have seen, BIOS contains device drivers for the printer, the diskette-drives, the keyboard, and the display unit. DOS also contains device drivers for these physical devices. To help explain the meaning of "installable device driver," let's look at the difference between BIOS and DOS device drivers.

We have used the term *low-level* when describing BIOS device drivers to imply that the functions performed are elementary. For example, the BIOS diskette device driver performs the elementary function of reading or writing a sector (or a sequence of up to eight sectors). The BIOS printer device driver performs the elementary function of printing one character.

On the other hand, we refer to the device drivers of DOS as *high-level,* because we use them without reference to the particular physical requirements of the hardware devices. We simply use a command like

```
A>COPY A:LAB1.TXT B:
```

to copy a file called LAB1.TXT from drive A: to drove B: We use a command like.

```
A>COPY A:LAB1.TXT PRN
```

to copy the same file to the printer.

In the first command, the DOS diskette device driver is used for both the source and the destination of the transfer. The DOS driver calls upon the BIOS driver to perform the data transfers to and from appropriate sectors. In the second case, the DOS diskette device driver is used for the source of the transfer, and the DOS printer device driver is used for the destination of the transfer. Both the DOS diskette and the printer device drivers will call upon their respective BIOS counterparts for the actual data transfer.

DEFINING THE INSTALLABLE DEVICE DRIVER

An installable device driver is a software interface to a hardware device that we can use exactly as we use the default DOS device drivers. To make this definition more concrete, consider the following (fairly typical) interfacing problem:

An x-y plotter, complete with an interface card, is to be interfaced to the PC. In the instruction manual, we find examples of assembly-language routines that show how to make the plotter draw alphanumeric characters. Our goal is to be able to print documents with the plotter—that is, to make the plotter act like a printer. How can we do this?

We could write a driver (utilizing the examples in the plotter manual) that prints a specific file on the plotter. We could pass the filename to the driver on the command line (in the command tail), or the driver could prompt the user for the filename. For example, if we used the command tail approach, we would issue a command like

```
A>PLOTPRNT LAB1.TXT
```

to print the file LAB1.TXT. PLOTPRNT is the name of the driver, and LAB1.TXT is the name of the file to be printed. A variation of this approach would be to make the PLOTPRNT program resident (function call 31H), executed via a software interrupt instruction.

Alternatively, we could write and "install" a device driver that conforms to the DOS definition of an installable device driver. After "installation," this driver will be part of DOS, and we will use it in exactly the same manner as we use other DOS device drivers. In the command

```
A>COPY LAB1.TXT PLOTPRNT
```

the diskette driver is used for the source (picking up LAB1.TXT from the diskette) and the driver PLOTPRNT is used for the destination of the transfer.

The two different solutions to this interfacing problem illustrate the difference between "ordinary" and "installed" device drivers. An ordinary device driver is just an interface program. Its definition is completely up to the programmer. The installed device driver is a program that follows a very specific format designed to allow it membership in the chain of DOS device drivers.

WHY USE AN INSTALLED DEVICE DRIVER?

What features of an installed device driver make it desirable?

1. Its use in DOS commands follows the standard DOS rules.

2. It is accessible to assembly language through the DOS file-handling function calls.

3. It is accessible to high-level languages (BASIC, FORTRAN, PASCAL, C) through their file-handling functions.

4. It can replace default DOS device drivers. (For example, ANSI.SYS replaces the default device driver, CON, to provide an enhanced console device driver.)

The major disadvantage of an installed device driver is that the programmer must learn a very specific set of rules to make it work. This disadvantage disappears with practice.

In spite of the advantages of the installed device driver, it may not be the driver of choice for every interfacing application. Consider a stepping motor interface. To drive the stepping motor, the interface program sends to the hardware interface a sequence of bytes containing information about the direction, the speed, and the number of steps to take. We would rarely want to send a sequence of ASCII characters to the hardware interface, so the main advantages of the installed device drivers aren't applicable.

The installed device driver is the best choice when

- the primary function of the hardware device is to transmit and/or receive character data, or when

- the hardware device is a disk drive (diskette or fixed) or the simulation of a disk drive (RAM disk).

TWO TYPES OF INSTALLABLE DRIVERS

Since the remainder of this chapter is devoted to a discussion of installable device drivers, there will be no ambiguity if we refer to installable device drivers simply as *drivers*.

DOS recognizes two types of drivers, the character driver and the block driver.

Character Drivers

The rules for a character driver assume it provides an interface to hardware that is character-oriented. Data is exchanged one character (byte) at a time. Examples of character-oriented devices are

printers
display units

keyboards

serial communications (RS-232, RS-422)

Block Drivers

The rules for a block driver assume that it provides an interface to a disk drive. Data is exchanged in units called *blocks,* each containing many bytes. (The block size for the diskette drives is 512 bytes.) Examples of block-oriented devices are

diskette drives

fixed (hard) disk drives

simulated disk drives (RAM disks)

We note parenthetically that block drivers can be written for character-oriented devices. Suppose a computer is connected over a serial link to a mass storage device. Although the serial link is character-oriented, it may be desirable to hide the character-oriented transfer of data from the user. By installing a block driver, we can make accessing the mass storage device look exactly like accessing a disk drive.

HOW DOES DOS USE A DRIVER?

This book discusses only the character driver in detail. A discussion of the block driver is an order of magnitude more complicated and beyond the scope of the book. (Readers interested in block drivers will find an example in the DOS Technical Reference Manual.) Before we turn to a discussion of the rules for character drivers, let's motivate the rules by examining the events occurring when DOS uses a driver.

For example, if DOS wants the driver to output some characters, the following events take place.

1. DOS makes a far call to the driver, passing a far pointer (two words) in the ES:BX register pair.
2. The driver uses the far pointer (ES:BX) to find a data structure called the *request header*.
3. The driver refers to the request header to find
   a. the desired command (''output characters'' in this example).
   b. the location of the characters to be transferred.
   c. the number of characters to be transferred.
4. The driver carries out the command (outputting the desired number of characters), sets the status word to ''done'' in the request header, and executes a far return to DOS.

This is somewhat simplified but basically correct.

THE LOCATION OF THE DRIVER

How does DOS know where the driver is located? DOS installs the driver in a linked chain of drivers. When the system is booted (power on) or restarted (Ctrl-Alt-Del), DOS searches the default drive for a CONFIG.SYS file. If it is found, DOS reads the file and for each command of the type

```
DEVICE = FILENAME.EXT
```

DOS installs the driver contained in the file.

The linked chain includes all default DOS drivers, as well as all installed drivers (Figure 11-1). Each driver (except the last) contains a link (a far pointer) to the next driver in the chain. When DOS commands refer to a filename, the linked chain of drivers is searched before it is assumed that the filename refers to a file on a disk. DOS tries to find a driver with a name matching the filename. If a match is found, the search ends and the driver is invoked.

The chain link (far pointer) and the driver's name reside (along with several items to be discussed later) in a data structure located at the head of the driver and aptly named the *device header*.

Figure 11-2 summarizes our discussion of the character driver so far.

THE CHARACTER DRIVER—PROGRAM LAYOUT

As we discuss the rules for character drivers, we shall simultaneously construct a simple example. The example driver will simply output characters to the screen. We can use the DOS function call 2H to actually put the character on the screen. This will save us the

Address (HEX)	Driver Name	Link
70:0148	CON	
70:01DD	AUX	
70:01EF	COM1	
70:028E	PRN	
70:02A0	LPT1	
70:0300	CLOCK$	
70:03CC	DISKETTE	
70:06F0	LPT2	
70:0702	LPT3	
70:0714	COM2	
50A:0000	User Driver Number One	

Figure 11-1 Chain of Drivers

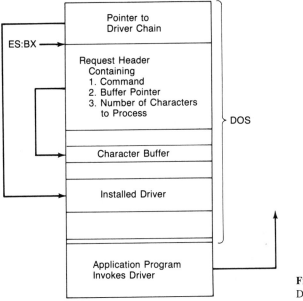

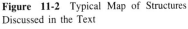

Figure 11-2 Typical Map of Structures Discussed in the Text

work of writing a real output routine. The example will serve as a template for constructing more complicated drivers. For instance, we could replace the DOS function call 2H with a routine outputting a character to a printer. We would then have a printer driver.

The driver, similar to a .COM file, must be written so that it is contained in one segment with no extra-segment references. The driver, in contrast to a .COM file, has no PSP and therefore no ORG 100H at the beginning. The following template illustrates a typical layout for a character driver.

```
CODE        SEGMENT
            ASSUME    CS: CODE

            ORG       00H                          ;NOT REALLY A COM FILE
;THE DEVICE HEADER BEGINS AT OFFSET 00H

;LOCAL DATA CAN BE DEFINED HERE


STRATEGY    PROC    FAR

;CODE FOR THE STRATEGY ROUTINE

STRATEGY    ENDP


INTERRUPT   PROC    FAR
```

```
; CODE TO INTERPRET AND IMPLEMENT THE COMMAND


INTERRUPT      ENDP


CODE           ENDS
               END
```

Whenever DOS uses a driver, it actually makes two far calls to the driver, not one. DOS first calls a routine in the driver named (following the DOS Technical Reference Manual) the *strategy routine*. DOS passes the request header pointer to the strategy routine in the ES:BX register pair. The only function of the strategy routine is to save the pointer for later use by the *interrupt routine*. The strategy routine must make a far return to DOS. Immediately after DOS makes the call to the strategy routine, it makes a far call to the interrupt routine.

The interrupt routine uses the request header pointer saved by the strategy routine to find the request header, to interpret the command, and to perform the desired function. The interrupt routine then executes a far return. Note that while it is called the interrupt routine, it is not an interrupt routine in the usual sense. It is really a far procedure— entered via a far call and exited via a far return. Do not use an IRET instruction to return from the interrupt routine. We will continue to use the name interrupt routine to be consistent with the DOS manual.

THE REQUEST HEADER

Table 11-1 shows the structure of the request header. The request header is 13 bytes long and has the same structure for every command. The data following the 13-byte request header (if any) depends on the specific function requested.

TABLE 11-1   THE REQUEST HEADER

Offset	Size (bytes)	Function
0	1	Total length (request header plus data)
1	1	Used only for block devices
2	1	Command code
3	2	Status word
5	8	Reserved for DOS
13	?	Data (dependent upon the command)

The command code and the status word need some explanation.

THE STATUS WORD

The status word is shown in Table 11-2. DOS initializes the status word to zero before calling the driver. The driver must set the status word before returning. Because a discussion of the ERROR-BIT and the ERROR-CODE occurs later in this chapter, it will suffice here to note that the ERROR-BIT should be zero if no errors occur.

TABLE 11-2 THE STATUS WORD

BIT 15		ERROR BIT (1 = ERROR, 0 = NO ERROR)
BIT 14	!	
BIT 13	!	
BIT 12	!	RESERVED
BIT 11	!	
BIT 10	!	
BIT 9		BUSY BIT
BIT 8		DONE BIT
BIT 7	!	
BIT 6	!	
BIT 5	!	
BIT 4	!	ERROR CODE IF BIT 15 = 1
BIT 3	!	
BIT 2	!	
BIT 1	!	
BIT 0	!	

The DONE-BIT should always be set (= 1) by the interrupt routine.

Setting BUSY will cause DOS to wait. DOS queries the BUSY during the INPUT STATUS, OUTPUT STATUS, and NONDESTRUCTIVE INPUT commands. (See the following for a discussion of commands.) The BUSY bit is discussed further in the section on commands.

COMMAND CODES

There are 13 possible command codes ranging from 0 through 12. Table 11-3 shows the command codes relevant to character drivers. Refer to the DOS Technical Reference Manual for commands related to block drivers.

INIT—COMMAND CODE 0
Required functions:

a. Execute any initialization code—that is, initialize hardware and variables.

b. Set a DWORD pointer pointing to the end of the resident part of the driver.

c. Set the status word in the request header.

TABLE 11-3 COMMAND CODES

Command Code	Desired Function
0	INIT
4	INPUT
5	NONDESTRUCTIVE INPUT (NO WAIT)
6	INPUT STATUS
7	INPUT FLASH
8	OUTPUT
10	OUTPUT STATUS
11	OUTPUT FLUSH

Each command must carry out a specific set of functions.

Request Header for INIT:

Offset	Size (bytes)	Function
0	13	Normal request header
13	1	Used by block driver
14	4	DWORD pointer to ending address

INPUT—COMMAND CODE 4

OUTPUT—COMMAND CODE 8

OUTPUT WITH VERIFY—COMMAND CODE 9

Required functions:

a. Perform the transfer (INPUT or OUTPUT the bytes).

b. Set the actual number of bytes transferred.

c. Set the status word in the request header.

Request header for INPUT, OUTPUT, and OUTPUT WITH VERIFY:

Offset	Size (bytes)	Function
0	13	Normal request header
13	1	Unused
14	4	DWORD pointer to transfer buffer
18	2	WORD containing byte count

An output driver must respond to both the OUTPUT and the OUTPUT WITH VER-IFY commands. The actual command issued by DOS depends on whether the verify flag is off or on.

INPUT STATUS—COMMAND CODE 6

OUTPUT STATUS—COMMAND CODE 10

Required function:

Set the status word in the request header.

The request header for the STATUS commands is the 13-byte normal request header.
DOS uses the STATUS command to determine whether or not the driver is busy.
The following two examples should clarify the use of BUSY in the STATUS command.

Output Example

Before DOS issues an OUTPUT command, it may issue an OUTPUT STATUS command to determine whether or not the driver is busy. The driver could be busy for either of two reasons:

1. The physical device is busy (that is, the printer is executing a carriage return).
2. The driver maintains an output buffer, which is currently full.

In either case, the driver should set BUSY and return. DOS will keep issuing the OUTPUT STATUS command until the driver indicates that it is not busy by resetting BUSY. DOS will then issue the OUTPUT command, sending a character (or characters) to the driver.

Input Example

Before DOS issues an INPUT command, it may issue an INPUT STATUS command to determine whether or not the driver is busy. As in the output example, the driver could be busy for either of two reasons:

1. The physical device is busy (that is, a serial port is collecting a bit stream and is not yet ready).
2. The driver maintains an input buffer, which is currently empty.

In either case, the driver should set BUSY and return. DOS will keep issuing the INPUT STATUS command until the driver indicates that it is not busy by resetting BUSY. DOS will then issue the INPUT command, requesting a character (or characters) from the driver.

In both of these examples, if the driver does not maintain a buffer and is not physically busy, BUSY should be reset to indicate "not busy."

INPUT FLUSH—COMMAND CODE 7

OUTPUT FLUSH—COMMAND CODE 11

Required functions:

a. Flush the input or output queue.
b. Set the status word in the request header.

The request header for the FLUSH commands is the 13-byte normal request header.

Some character drivers maintain queues (buffers) containing characters awaiting transfer. The keyboard type-ahead buffer is an example. Whenever a key is pressed (and released), the ASCII code for the key is placed in the type-ahead buffer. A call to the keyboard driver returns the next character from the buffer rather than the next key pressed. Occasionally, it is desirable to respond to the next key pressed rather than to characters already in the buffer. DOS accomplishes this by requesting that the driver "flush" (empty) the buffer. The next key pressed will be returned. If your driver maintains a queue, you may want to implement this command.

NONDESTRUCTIVE INPUT (NO WAIT)—COMMAND CODE 5

Required functions:

a. Return a byte from the device.
b. Set the status word in the request header.

Request header for NONDESTRUCTIVE INPUT:

Offset	Size (bytes)	Function
0	13	Normal request header
13	1	Returned byte

If a character driver maintains a buffer (see the discussion for the FLUSH command), DOS can use this command to see whether or not the buffer is empty. The response to this command depends on several things:

1. If there is no buffer, always set BUSY = 0 in the status word. DOS waits until BUSY = 0 before sending an INPUT command. Setting BUSY = 1 would make DOS wait forever.

2. If there is a buffer and it is empty, set BUSY = 1 in the status word to indicate an empty buffer. DOS will keep checking until BUSY = 0, indicating that a character is in the buffer.

3. If there is a buffer containing a character, return the character to offset 13 in the request header and set BUSY = 0 to indicate that an INPUT command would find a character in the buffer. Don't remove it from the buffer. Characters should be removed from the buffer only during INPUT or FLUSH commands.

COMMANDS FOR THE EXAMPLE DRIVER

A simple driver that will output characters to the screen must respond to these commands:

INIT   To set up the ending address
OUTPUT   To output the character (VERIFY=OFF)
OUTPUT WITH VERIFY   To output the character (VERIFY=0N)
OUTPUT STATUS   To return status

For simplicity, we will perform the output function by using DOS function call 2H. Once the driver is working correctly, this function call can be replaced by code, which outputs to a real device of your own choice.

THE DEVICE HEADER

The beginning of the driver (see the driver template) contains an area called the *device header*. Table 11-4 shows the field within the device header.

During installation, DOS sets the pointer to the next device header to point to the

TABLE 11-4   THE DEVICE HEADER

Offset	Size (bytes)	Function
0	4	Pointer to next device driver header
4	2	Attribute of device driver
6	2	Pointer (offset) to the strategy routine
8	2	Pointer (offset) to the interrupt routine
10	8	Name of device driver (left-justified with trailing blanks)

next device in the chain of drivers. It is a double-word-pointer because the next driver may be in a different segment. If you intend to have only one driver in a .COM file, this pointer should be set to −1 (0FFFFFFFFH).

It is possible for one .COM file to contain several drivers. In this case, the OFFSET part of the next device pointer should point to the device header of the next driver in the file. Only the last driver in the file should contain a pointer of −1. DOS will fill in the SEGMENT part of the pointers upon installation.

The other two pointers (for the strategy and interrupt routines) are simply offsets, because the driver is contained in one segment.

The name of the device driver should be in CAPITAL letters. We have found that DOS can't find drivers if you use lowercase letters in the name. The driver name should differ from the filename of the .COM file that contains the driver. If the name is the same, later references to the files will be diverted to the driver instead.

THE ATTRIBUTE WORD

The attribute word is shown in Table 11-5. Only fields relevant to character drivers are shown.

Notice that you can make an installed device driver the standard input, standard output, or current clock driver by setting the appropriate bit.

If the IOCTL bit is set, DOS will assume that the driver responds to control strings. Control strings can be sent to a driver via function call 44H. The IOCTL feature allows a

TABLE 11-5   THE ATTRIBUTE WORD

BIT 15	1 =	character device driver
	0 =	block device driver
BIT 14	1 =	IOCTL supported
	0 =	IOCTL not supported
BIT 3	1 =	driver is current clock driver
	0 =	driver is not current clock driver
BIT 1	1 =	current standard output driver
	0 =	not current srandard output driver
BIT 0	1 =	current standard input driver
	0 =	not current standard input driver

driver to distinguish between data and control codes. If the IOCTL bit is reset ($=0$), DOS will return an error to a process attempting to send a control string to the driver.

Two device driver commands, related to I/O control, were omitted from Table 11-3. The study of the IOCTL INPUT and IOCTL OUTPUT commands will be left to the reader. (Refer to the DOS Technical Reference Manual.)

DEVICE DRIVER EXAMPLE

The following is a simple device driver, a pedagogical example. It merely performs output to the display, using function call 2H. However, once you understand this simple driver, you can use it as a template for more complicated examples. We first list the elements necessary for writing the driver.

1. A device header
2. A strategy routine
3. An interrupt routine (implementing the following commands):
   a. INIT
   b. OUTPUT STATUS
   c. OUTPUT
   d. OUTPUT WITH VERIFY

We must

1. write the device driver as a .COM file (without ORG 100H).
2. save and restore all used registers.
3. convert the file to a .BIN, using EXE2BIN.
4. tell DOS to install it (with a CONFIG.SYS file).

Example Driver Program

```
; This is a sample driver that outputs characters to
; the screen using function call 2H.
; The program uses the stack provided by DOS

CODE     SEGMENT
         ASSUME   CS: CODE, DS: CODE

; FIRST, THE DEVICE HEADER

POINTER       DD       -1
ATTRIBUTE     DW       8000H       ; CHARACTER DRIVER
```

```
          STRATEGY_PTR    DW          STRATEGY
          INTERRUPT_PTR   DW          INTERRUPT
          DRIVER_NAME     DB          'DRIVETST'  ;8 CHARACTERS  (BLANKS OK)


;DATA DEFINITIONS

          OFFSET_RH       DW          ?               ;RH POINTER OFFSET
          SEGMENT_RH      DW          ?               ;RH POINTER SEGMENT


          MESSAGES        LABEL       WORD            ;DIAGNOSTIC MESSAGES

          INIT_MESS       DB          'INITIALIZING DRIVETST'
                          DB          0AH,0DH,'$'
          OUTPUT_MESS     DB          'OUTPUTTING'
                          DB          0AH,0DH,'$'
          OUT_VER_MESS    DB          'OUTPUTTING WITH VERIFY'
                          DB          0AH,0DH,'$'
          STATUS_OUT_MESS             DB          'OUTPUT STATUS'
                          DB          0AH,0DH,'$'


;NOW,  THE STRATEGY ROUTINE, WHICH SIMPLY STORES THE
;POINTER TO THE REQUEST HEADER.

          STRATEGY        PROC        FAR
                          MOV         OFFSET_RH,BX    ;SAVE RH POINTER
                          MOV         SEGMENT_RH,ES
                          RET
          STRATEGY        ENDP


;FINALLY,  THE ROUTINE THAT DOES ALL THE WORK,  THE

;INTERRUPT ROUTINE.

          INTERRUPT       PROC        FAR
                          PUSH        AX              ;SAVE REGS
                          PUSH        BX
                          PUSH        CX
                          PUSH        DX
                          PUSH        SI
                          PUSH        DI
                          PUSH        BP
                          PUSH        DS
                          PUSH        ES

;SET UP DS TO ESTABLISH ADDRESSABILITY FOR MESSAGES

                          PUSH        CS
                          POP         DS              ;DS=CS
```

```
                        MOV        BX, OFFSET_RH     ; GET RH POINTER
                        MOV        ES, SEGMENT_RH

; RETRIEVE AND INTERPRET THE COMMAND

                        MOV        AL, ES: [BX + 2]     ; GET COMMAND
                        CMP        AL, 0                ; INIT COMMAND?
                        JE         INIT                 ; YES
                        CMP        AL, 8                ; OUTPUT?
                        JE         OUTPUT               ; YES
                        CMP        AL, 9                ; OUTPUT WITH VERIFY?
                        JE         OUTPUT_VERIFY        ; YES
                        CMP        AL, 10               ; OUTPUT STATUS
                        JE         STATUS_OUTPUT        ; YES
                        JMP        NORMAL_EXIT          ; OTHERWISE RETURN
                                                        ; NO VALID COMMAND
INIT:                   LEA        DX, INIT_MESS
                        MOV        AH, 9
                        INT        21H                  ; SEND MESSAGE

; SET UP ENDING ADDRESS

                        MOV        WORD PTR ES: [BX + 14], OFFSET BOTTOM
                        MOV        ES: [BX + 16], CS
                        JMP        NORMAL_EXIT          ; EXIT


OUTPUT:                 LEA        DX, OUTPUT_MESS
                        MOV        AH, 9
                        INT        21H

; SET UP PARAMETERS FOR OUTPUT

OUTPUT2:                MOV        CX, ES: [BX + 18]    ; COUNT
                        MOV        SI, ES: [BX + 14]    ; BUFFER OFFSET
                        MOV        DS, ES: [BX + 16]    ; BUFFER SEGMENT
OUTPUT1:                MOV        AL, [SI]             ; GET CHARACTER
                        MOV        DL, AL               ; USE FUNCTION CALL 2H
                        MOV        AH, 2
                        INT        21H                  ; SEND CHARACTER
                        INC        SI                   ; POINT TO NEXT
                        LOOP       OUTPUT1
                        SUB        ES: [BX + 18], CX    ; NUMBER TRANSFERRED
                        JMP        NORMAL_EXIT


OUTPUT_VERIFY:          LEA        DX, OUT_VER_MESS
                        MOV        AH, 9
                        INT        21H                  ; SEND MESSAGE
                        JMP        OUTPUT2              ; USE OTHER ROUTINE
```

```
      STATUS_OUTPUT:  LEA    DX, STATUS_OUT_MESS
                      MOV    AH, 9
                      INT    21H                    ; SEND  MESSAGE
                      JMP    NORMAL_EXIT            ; NOT  BUSY

      NORMAL_EXIT:    MOV    WORD PTR ES: [BX+3] ,0100H ; STATUS =D ONE
      INTER_EXIT:     POP    ES
                      POP    DS                     ; RESTORE  REGS
                      POP    BP
                      POP    DI
                      POP    SI
                      POP    DX
                      POP    CX
                      POP    BX
                      POP    AX
                      RET
      INTERRUPT       ENDP
      BOTTOM          LABEL  WORD                   ; USED  TO  FIND  ENDING
      CODE            ENDS                          ; ADDRESS
                      END
```

This driver follows the pattern we have discussed. There is a device header, data definitions, a strategy routine, and an interrupt routine. What are the invariant features of this driver?

The device header shown can be used in any character driver if we simply change the device driver name. The attribute may change if the driver has special characteristics (Table 11-5).

The data area includes space for storing the request-header pointer passed by DOS to the strategy routine. Also in the data area are several messages. Each time DOS issues a command, a corresponding message is displayed on the console. This message feature helps us understand how DOS uses the driver. It would be eliminated from a real driver.

The strategy routine simply stores the request-header pointer, then returns. This strategy routine can be used in any character driver.

The interrupt routine does all the work. It must find and execute the command at offset 2 in the request header. The code that implements each command will most likely vary from driver to driver. For example, a printer driver would replace function call 2H (used in the OUTPUT command) by code that would output a character to the printer. In spite of individual differences in drivers, the structure of the interrupt routine can be used as a template. If a driver responds to more than three or four commands, the use of a jump table is recommended.

Trying the Driver

After creating the source file, follow these steps (assume that the source file is called "DRIVER.ASM"):

1. Assemble the file as usual.

```
A>MASM DRIVER;
```

2. Link the file as usual.

```
A>LINK DRIVER;
```

The LINK program will produce the error message "NO STACK SEGMENT." This is to be expected and is not a fatal error.

3. Convert the file to a .COM type of file.

```
A>EXE2BIN DRIVER.EXE DRIVER.SYS
```

DRIVER.SYS is the file that will be loaded and installed by DOS.

4. Create a CONFIG.SYS file containing the command

```
DEVICE = DRIVER.SYS
```

5. Reboot the system. During the boot process, DOS looks for a CONFIG.SYS file on the default drive. The command "DEVICE = DRIVER.SYS" tells DOS that the file DRIVER.SYS contains a driver to be installed. DOS installs the driver, putting it at the head of the driver chain, and calls the driver with the INIT command.

6. To test the driver, create a small file, TEST.TXT, containing about ten characters, and give the command

```
A>COPY TEST.TXT DRIVETST
```

You should see the file copied to the console along with the diagnostic messages.

DEBUGGING A DRIVER

Debugging an installed device driver is difficult when the driver is invoked by using a command as in item 6 in the previous section. One possible debugging technique is to write a program that invokes the driver, using FCB or ASCIIZ function calls. We can then use Debug to follow program execution from the ASCIIZ function call to the driver. We can also use Debug to set breakpoints in the driver. The location of the driver can be determined by using the Debug search command to search for the driver's name in the device header.

CHAPTER SUMMARY

In this chapter, we learned that the "installable device driver" is a device driver which conforms to a specific set of rules that allows it to become a part of DOS. DOS installs the driver during initialization of the system, giving it the same status as the other DOS drivers. Although there are two types of installable device drivers, the block and the character drivers, we studied only the specifications for the character driver. The driver is written as a .COM file (with no ORG 100H) and is installed via a command in the CONFIG.SYS file. Each driver consists of a device header, a strategy routine, and an interrupt routine. DOS uses data in the device header when installing and invoking the driver. DOS calls the strategy routine to pass a pointer to the request header and calls the interrupt routine to issue a command. The interrupt routine forms the main body of the driver. It is the interrupt routine that actually performs the commands requested by DOS.

IBM PC
Display Adapters

In contrast to most other personal computers, the IBM PC contains display hardware that is not an integral part of the system unit. The display is handled by an adapter card plugged into the I/O channel. When IBM introduced the PC, it offered two different display-adapter cards—the monochrome display adapter and the color/graphics display adapter. IBM has recently introduced two new display cards, the enhanced graphics adapter and the professional graphics adapter. Other companies, encouraged by the open architecture of the IBM PC, also offer a variety of display cards. The monochrome display card made by Hercules has become something of a standard due to its ability to display high-resolution graphics on a monochrome monitor. Other vendors have paid Hercules the compliment of offering "Hercules-compatible display adapters." It is unfortunate that the Hercules and IBM color/graphics cards are not compatible. It is not an easy task to transport graphics programs from one display format to another.

This chapter begins with display fundamentals and continues with detailed discussions of the IBM monochrome and color/graphics display adapters.

MEMORY-MAPPED DISPLAYS

All the displays used with the IBM PC are *memory-mapped*, which means that a portion of the memory address space is used by the display hardware. This memory (referred to as *display memory* or *regen buffer*) can be accessed by the 8088 microprocessor as well as by the display hardware. This fact permits a program to change the display screen by simply changing the contents of the display memory. The display memory is physically located on the display adapter card.

The operation of a memory-mapped display is very different from a typical computer terminal. A terminal is usually connected to a personal computer system via a serial interface. Characters are displayed on the terminal one after another as they are received from the computer. Changing screens on such a terminal is inherently slow (varying from seconds to tenths of seconds, depending on the data transfer rate). In contrast, the entire screen on a memory-mapped display can be rewritten as fast as the processor can transfer 2000 bytes (about 20 ms). Furthermore, if the display memory is large enough to hold two or more screens (pages) simultaneously, we can switch screens between display sweeps.

Memory-mapped displays also make "windowing" relatively manageable. (*Windowing* refers to the technique of splitting the screen into several sections, each individually managed.) Windowing is very useful when we want to view separate processes, menus, and data areas simultaneously.

Memory-mapped displays are not particularly well suited to displaying fast-moving, irregularly shaped objects. The real-time response is slow because a large number of pixels (picture elements) must be manipulated to move the objects. Many so-called game machines, like the Atari 800 and the Commodore 64, contain special hardware for displaying simple objects and moving them rapidly around the screen. The creation of fast-moving, high-resolution graphics for games on the IBM PC is challenging for even the most experienced programmer.

DISPLAY FUNDAMENTALS

A discussion of the detailed design features of the display cards is beyond the scope of this book. We will restrict this discussion to fundamentals.

Both display screens (monochrome and color) consist of scan lines sweeping from left to right, top to bottom, as shown in Figure 12-1. The scan line is created by a beam of electrons striking the screen. If the energy of the electrons is sufficient, light will be emitted by the screen phosphor when the electrons hit the screen.

For the display to draw characters, the energy of the beam must be modulated as the beam is swept across the screen. The modulation, in effect, lights the screen in selected positions. The maximum modulation rate (bandwidth) determines the horizontal resolution of the display. The monochrome display has a horizontal resolution of 720 dots; the color display, 640 dots.

Each character is defined by a dot pattern embedded in a box. For example, Figure 12-2 shows a typical character for the monochrome display—seven dots wide by nine scan lines high, embedded in a 9 by 14 box. The two sets of dots (dark and light) in the box are referred to respectively as the "background" and the "foreground" of the character. As the electron beam sweeps along a scan line, the energy is modulated to light up the foreground dots of each character in the line. After 14 sweeps (scan lines), one row of characters is complete. A reverse-video character is made by reversing the role of foreground and background.

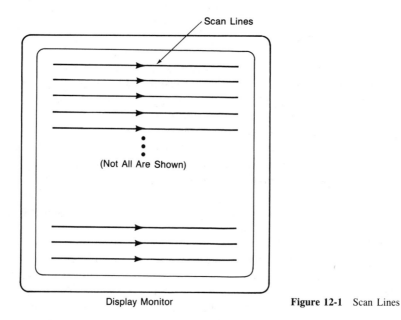

Display Monitor   **Figure 12-1**   Scan Lines

The bookkeeping involved in deciding when to light up the dots to create character patterns is handled by a display chip (the Motorola 6845 Crt Controller) and a character ROM. (The same display chip is used for the monochrome and color/graphics adapters.) The character ROM is simply a ROM that contains bit patterns corresponding to characters. For example, the color/graphics card uses characters in an eight by eight box. Figure 12-3 shows a typical character and the eight bytes that would be stored in a ROM to represent the character. The 6845 is responsible for generating the address of a particular byte

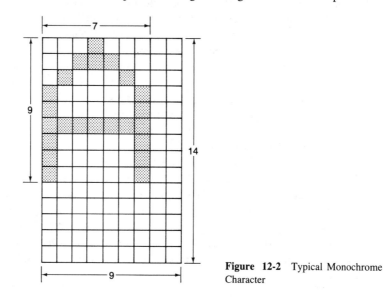

Figure 12-2   Typical Monochrome Character

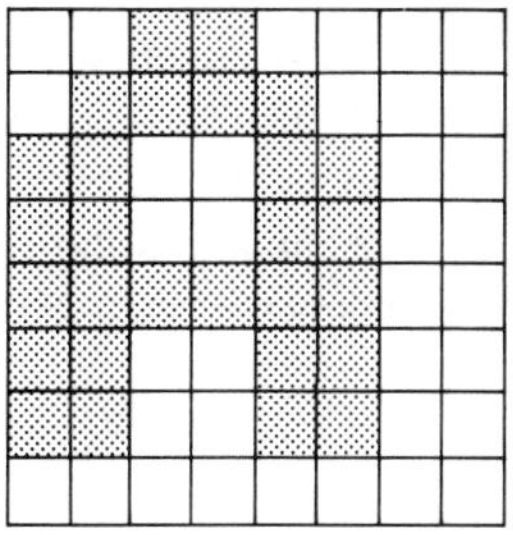

```
0  0  1  1  0  0  0  0
0  1  1  1  1  0  0  0
1  1  0  0  1  1  0  0
1  1  0  0  1  1  0  0
1  1  1  1  1  1  0  0
1  1  0  0  1  1  0  0
1  1  0  0  1  1  0  0
0  0  0  0  0  0  0  0
```

Figure 12-3 Color/Graphics Character and Representation

(scan line) of a character at the right time. The byte is then shifted bit by bit to the scan line modulator to draw one line of the character. To prevent characters from jiggling during successive sweepings of the screen, the 6845 controls the basic timing of the scan line. This creates a precise relationship between the beginning of a scan line and the address generation required for the dot patterns.

To determine which character to display at a particular screen position, the 6845 uses a character code from display memory. The character code for ''A'' is 41H (the ASCII code). The 6845 uses the character code as eight bits of the character ROM address. If each character uses eight bytes in the ROM, ''A'' will begin at address 208H in the character ROM (see Table 12-1). The upper eight bits of the address are the character code, and the lower three bits are generated for the scan lines by the 6845.

In a graphics mode, the bits in a byte of display memory are shifted directly to the scan line modulator rather than being used to decode the character ROM. As we will see, in the high resolution mode each bit in a byte of display memory corresponds directly to one dot. A ''one'' turns the dot on, and a ''zero'' turns it off.

The 6845, a complicated and flexible chip, contains 18 programmable registers that determine its display characteristics. BIOS contains code to initialize these registers to one of eight display modes. With the exception of the cursor-control and page-changing registers, the registers are unchanged after initialization. Those who are interested in programming the 6845 will find the Motorola Microprocessor Data Manual helpful.

THE IBM MONOCHROME DISPLAY ADAPTER

The IBM monochrome display adapter produces an 80-column by 25-row screen of high-quality characters. Each of the 256 characters has a 7×9 dot format within a 9×14 dot box. The 4K-byte display memory is located on the display card and is accessible from

TABLE 12-1 FORMATION OF ROM ADDRESS

A10	A9	A8	A7	A6	A5	A4	A3	A2	A1	A0	
0	1	0	0	0	0	0	1	0	0	0	= 208H

41H = Character code from display memory

3 bits from the 6845 to define the 8 scan lines

both the 8088 microprocessor and the 6845 CRT controller. The display memory is located in the address range: 0B0000H-0B0FFF. The character ROM, also located on the display card, is not accessible to the microprocessor. (There is no way to change the available character patterns short of replacing the ROM.) The BASIC manual and the Hardware Technical Reference Manual contain a table showing the character set.

Display Attributes

Each character can be displayed with several different attributes—normal, reversed, underlined, blinking, and high intensity. Each character code is accompanied by an attribute byte containing attribute information. Thus two bytes of display memory, the character code and the attribute byte, are used for each displayed character. The 80 by 25 character screen contains 2000 characters, requiring 4000 bytes for the display memory. The display memory is organized so that the character code and attribute byte are adjacent, the character code at an even address and the attribute at the next odd address. This particular design of the display memory has the advantage that one can change a character and its attribute with one instruction. It does, however, have the great disadvantage that one cannot easily manipulate text by using the 8088 string instructions.

Table 12-2 shows the format of the attribute byte. To the four basic display modes you can add high-intensity and/or blinking. The attribute for a normal character is 07H.

What happens if the attribute byte isn't one of those listed? The character is displayed anyway with a seemingly unpredictable outcome. Actually, the outcome is predetermined by the display hardware and the results are listed in the Hardware Technical Reference Manual. Knowledge of these unofficial attribute values may be useful when you wish to write an application for the color/graphics display adapter that is compatible with the monochrome display adapter. As we will see shortly, a program written for the monochrome monitor will be displayed in black and white on a color/graphics monitor.

TABLE 12-2   MONOCHROME ATTRIBUTE BYTE

B7	B6	B5	B4	B3	B2	B1	B0	
BL	R	G	B	I	R	G	B	
	R	G	B		R	G	B	
	0	0	0		0	0	0	No display
	0	0	0		0	0	1	Normal-underlined
	0	0	0		1	1	1	Normal
	1	1	1		0	0	0	Reverse

BL   I
1 = Blink   1 = High intensity
0 = No blink   0 = Low intensity

Memory-to-Screen Mapping

Figure 12-4 illustrates the mapping from the display memory to the screen. The first word of display memory is mapped to the upper-left character, the second word to the next character, and so on. Writing directly to display memory gives us a very snappy way to update the screen. The following example program produces a bar graph by directly accessing screen memory. Later in this chapter we will repeat this example, using the functions provided by VIDEO_IO in BIOS.

The program draws nine bars, each three characters wide, with heights specified by the BAR_HEIGHTS table. The ES register is typically used to address screen memory, since DS is normally used to address local data. ES is set to the beginning of screen memory (0B000H), and an index register is used to specify offsets into screen memory. The display "arithmetic" is straightforward. If we label the rows 0–24 and the columns 0–79, then the offset to the memory location corresponding to a character at row R, column C, is

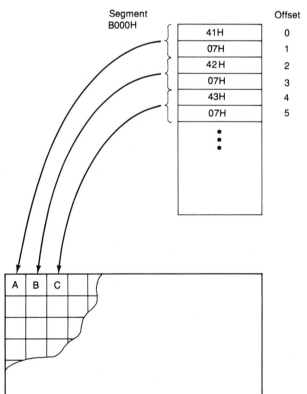

Figure 12-4 Alphanumeric Mode Mapping

$$\text{MEMORY OFFSET} = 2*(80*R + C).$$

This formula is used by the procedure DRAW_BAR to find the memory offset for the bar position.

Example 12-1   A Bar Graph

```
STACK SEGMENT STACK
        DW      100 DUP(?)
STACK   ENDS


DATA    SEGMENT

BAR_HEIGHTS     DB        2,4,6,8,10,12,14,16,18

DATA    ENDS

CODE    SEGMENT
        ASSUME   CS:CODE,DS:DATA

;THIS PROC PRODUCES A BACKGROUND SCREEN AND SETS THE
;ATTRIBUTE TO NORMAL--07H.   ASSUMES ES=0B000H

BACKGROUND_SCREEN     PROC      NEAR
        MOV     CX,2000                 ;# OF CHARACTERS
        MOV     BX,0                    ;USE AS INDEX
CS1:    MOV     WORD PTR ES:[BX],07B0H  ;NORMAL, BACKGROUND
        ADD     BX,2                    ;POINT TO NEXT
        LOOP    CS1                     ;DONE?
        RET
BACKGROUND_SCREEN     ENDP

;THIS PROC IS USED TO DRAW ONE, THREE-CHARACTER-WIDE LINE
;OF A BAR. BX=ADDRESS OF FIRST SCREEN LOCATION
DRAW_3  PROC    NEAR
        PUSH    BX                      ;SAVE FOR LATER
        PUSH    CX
        MOV     CX,3
DR31:   MOV     WORD PTR ES:[BX],07DBH  ;FILL CHARACTER
        ADD     BX,2                    ;POINT TO NEXT
        LOOP    DR31
        POP     CX                      ;RESTORE HEIGHT COUNT
        POP     BX                      ;RESTORE POSITION
        RET
```

```
        DRAW_3   ENDP

; THIS PROC DRAWS A BAR 3 CHARACTERS WIDE.
; HEIGHT = CX
; POSITION (BOTTOM LEFT OF BAR) = BX (COLUMN UNITS)
; ASSUME COLUMNS LABELED 0-79, ROWS 0-24

DRAW_BAR          PROC     NEAR
        PUSH    BX                      ; SAVE POSITION
        SAL     BX, 1                   ; DOUBLE BECAUSE OF ATTR.
        ADD     BX, 24*80*2             ; NUMBER OF BYTES SKIPED IN
                                        ; FIRST 24 ROWS

DRB1:   CALL    DRAW_3                  ; DRAW A ROW
        SUB     BX, 2*80                ; MOVE UP A ROW
        LOOP    DRB1                    ; GO TILL DONE
        POP     BX                      ; RESTORE POSITION
        RET
DRAW_BAR          ENDP

START:  MOV     AX, DATA                ; INITIALIZE THE DS REGISTER
        MOV     DS, AX
        MOV     AX, 0B000H              ; SET UP SEGMENT FOR SCREEN
        MOV     ES, AX
        CALL    BACKGROUND_SCREEN       ; SET UP BACKGROUND

        MOV     DX, 9                   ; NUMBER OF BARS TO DRAW
        MOV     BX, 5                   ; COLUMN # OF FIRST BAR
        XOR     SI, SI                  ; INDEX INTO BAR HEIGHT TABLE
        XOR     CH, CH                  ; HIGH BYTE OF BAR HEIGHT
ST1:    MOV     CL, BAR_HEIGHTS[SI]     ; GET BAR HEIGHT
        CALL    DRAW_BAR                ; DRAW THE BAR
        ADD     BX, 8                   ; NEXT BAR POSITION
        INC     SI                      ; POINT TO NEXT HEIGHT
        DEC     DX
        JNZ     ST1                     ; DO ALL BARS

; LOOK FOR ANY KEY TO EXIT
WAIT:   MOV     AH, 0BH                 ; NONDESTRUCTION INPUT
        INT     21H                     ; FUNCTION CALL
        CMP     AL, 00                  ; KEY PRESSED
        JE      WAIT                    ; NO KEY YET
        MOV     AH, 4CH
        INT     21H                     ; RETURN TO DOS

CODE    ENDS
        END     START
```

THE IBM COLOR/GRAPHICS DISPLAY ADAPTER

The IBM color/graphics display adapter has two basic display modes, the alphanumeric and the APA (All-Points-Addressable). The alphanumeric mode, as the name implies, is a character-oriented mode much like the display of the monochrome display adapter. The APA mode, a graphics mode, treats the screen as a number of individually addressable picture elements (pixels). The color/graphics display adapter has two outputs: direct drive (for an RBG monitor) and composite video (for a composite-video monitor). An rf-modulator connected to the composite video would provide a signal for a color television. The 16K display memory begins at 0B8000H.

The Alphanumeric Mode

Four display formats are available in the alphanumeric mode:

    40 by 25 black and white
    40 by 25 color
    80 by 25 black and white
    80 by 25 color

As in the monochrome display, the character set is contained in a ROM and can only be modified by changing the ROM. One of two different fonts is selected by jumper P3 on the adapter card. The two fonts are as follows:

    7×7 double-dot in an 8×8 box
    5×7 single-dot in an 8×8 box

DISPLAY ATTRIBUTES

The alphanumeric mode parallels the monochrome display, in that a character code and an attribute byte define each displayed character. The character set and character codes are also identical to those of the monochrome display card. (See the IBM Hardware Technical Reference Manual, Appendix C.) The main difference is in the attribute byte. (See Table 12-3.)

The symbols, R, G, and B now take on the meanings

    R = RED
    G = GREEN
    B = BLUE

corresponding to the color guns in a color monitor. Eight colors $(2*2*2)$ can be generated by combining these three colors in all possible ways. These eight colors can be displayed as 16 different colors on a monitor with an intensity control. For example, red turns to

TABLE 12-3 ALPHANUMERIC ATTRIBUTE BYTE

B7	B6	B5	B4	B3	B2	B1	B0
BL	R	G	B	I	R	G	B

BACKGROUND   FOREGROUND COLOR

BL
1 = BLINK
0 = NO BLINK

AVAILABLE COLORS

I	R	G	B	Color
0	0	0	0	Black
0	0	0	1	Blue
0	0	1	0	Green
0	0	1	1	Cyan
0	1	0	0	Red
0	1	0	1	Magenta
0	1	1	0	Brown
0	1	1	1	White
1	0	0	0	Grey
1	0	0	1	Light blue
1	0	1	0	Light green
1	0	1	1	Light cyan
1	1	0	0	Light red
1	1	0	1	Light magenta
1	1	1	0	Yellow
1	1	1	1	White

pink (light red) when displayed in high intensity. Thus the foreground of each character can be displayed in one of 16 colors. The intensity bit for the background is located in the color select register at port 0D9H. (See Table 12-4.) There is but one intensity bit for all characters, so all backgrounds are displayed either in low intensity or high intensity. The 40×25 alphanumeric display is surrounded by a border whose color is also chosen via the color select register.

MONOCHROME AND ALPHANUMERIC MODE COMPATABILITY

By comparing the attribute definitions for the monochrome and color/graphics displays, we find that the monochrome attributes will be displayed in black and white by the color/graphics adapter. All normal characters will be white on a black background. The one real difference is that the monochrome ''underlined'' character will be displayed as a blue

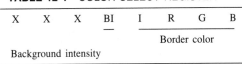

TABLE 12-4 COLOR SELECT REGISTER

X	X	X	BI	I	R	G	B
				Border color			

Background intensity

character by the color/graphics adapter. As this difference is minor, we can conclude that a program written for the monochrome monitor, using the monochrome attributes, would look the same when displayed with the color/graphics adapter. On the other hand, characters with color attributes will usually be visible when displayed with the monochrome display, but the total effect may not be appealing. A character with a grey or black foreground will be blank. Blue or light blue will show up as underlined. Any light color will be high intensity. We may find high-intensity or underlined characters (or both) intermixed with normal characters. The easiest way to prevent such problems is to make the display compatible with the monochrome display adapter from the beginning by using only the defined monochrome attributes.

Most people find the monochrome monitor preferable to the color monitor when viewing textual material for any length of time. The smaller dot size of the monochrome display produces a more readable display.

PAGES

All alphanumeric formats use less than the 16K memory available on the display card. The 40×25 formats use 2000 bytes (40*25*2), and the 80×25 formats use 4000 bytes (80*25*2). We can divide the 16K display memory into pages, eight pages for the 40×25 formats and four pages for the 80×25 formats. One of the registers on the 6845 CRT controller specifies the beginning address of the display memory, effectively allowing us to specify which page will be displayed. We can either program the 6845 register directly or use the BIOS page-switching function in VIDEO_IO. Using the BIOS function is easy. Simply put the desired page number in AL, set AH = 5, and execute the VIDEO_IO interrupt, INT 10H. For example,

```
MOV   AL,1
MOV   AH,5
INT   10H
```

changes the display from the current page to page 1. With paging, one screen can be composed while another is being displayed. This rapid way of changing screens provides interesting possibilities for animation effects. Various incarnations of an object can be located on different pages. Sweeping through the pages gives the illusion of motion.

The Graphics Mode—All-Points-Addressable (APA)

In the alphanumeric mode, the smallest screen element under our control is the character. To be sure, the character is composed of elements (dots), but the dot patterns are predetermined and not programmable. The graphics mode permits us to control the equivalent of the character's dots. The color/graphics display adapter is capable of displaying four different formats in the APA mode, although only three are supported by BIOS. Because the low resolution mode is not supported in BIOS, it is not discussed in this book. The characteristics of the formats are

- low resolution—160×100, 16 colors/pixel, 16,000 bytes/screen, no BIOS support
- medium-resolution color—320×200, four colors/pixel, 16,000 bytes/screen, BIOS support in VIDEO_IO
- medium-resolution black and white—320×200, black/white, 16,000 bytes/screen, BIOS support in VIDEO_IO
- high-resolution black and white—640×200, black/white, 16,000 bytes/screen, BIOS support in VIDEO_IO

MEDIUM-RESOLUTION FORMAT—320×200

In this format, each pixel can be one of four colors. Two bits are needed to specify one of four colors, so we can specify four pixels per one byte of display memory. This format requires 80 bytes per row, or 16,000 bytes, to display an entire screen of 200 rows.

How do we choose the four colors from the 16 available? First, we choose one of the 16 colors to be the background color for all the pixels (Table 12-5). The background

TABLE 12-5   COLOR SELECT REGISTER

B7	B6	B5	B4	B3	B2	B1	B0
X	X	CS	PI	I	R	G	B

BACKGROUND COLOR

PIXEL COLOR INTENSITY

PI = 1 HIGH INTENSITY
   = 0 NORMAL INTENSITY
CS = COLOR SET SELECT (SEE TEXT)

color is one of the four pixel colors. Second, we choose one of two preselected color sets to supply the other three colors. This choice is made with bit 5 in the color select register. The displayed colors are determined by the two pixel bits as follows:

B1	B0	BIT 5=0	BIT 5=1
0	0	BACKGROUND--DETERMINED BY COLOR SELECT	
0	1	GREEN	CYAN
1	0	RED	MAGENTA
1	1	BROWN	WHITE

Once the choice of a background color and a three-color set is made, every pixel on the screen is one of four colors. One can easily change to another set of four colors by writing a new value into the color select register. In the 320×200 black and white format, a pixel is either off (background) or on (foreground).

MEMORY-TO-SCREEN MAPPING

Figure 12-5 shows how the memory is mapped to the pixels on the screen. As we said, each pixel uses two bits of memory, so one byte contains information about four pixels. Byte 0 is mapped to the first four pixels of row 0, byte 1 to the next four, and so on. A

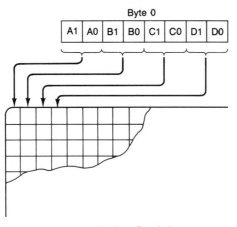

Medium Resolution

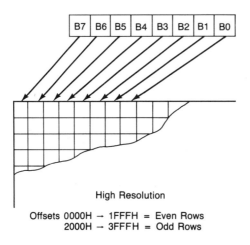

High Resolution

Offsets 0000H → 1FFFH = Even Rows
        2000H → 3FFFH = Odd Rows

Figure 12-5   Graphics Mode Mapping

seemingly strange occurrence takes place between bytes 79 and 80. Byte 79 is mapped to the last four pixels of row 0 as expected, but byte 80 is mapped to the first four pixels on row 2 rather than row 1. This is really not so strange when we realize that the screen is actually being scanned like a TV, in an "interlaced" mode. The even- and odd-numbered lines are written on alternate scans. Because of this, the memory offsets 0000H-1FFFH are mapped to the even rows and offsets 2000H-3FFFH are mapped to the odd rows. The first four pixels of row 1 are contained in the byte at offset 2000H. This makes sense in terms of the display hardware, but it makes graphics programming a little more difficult. An object occupying a local area on the screen will be specified by two widely separated memory areas. BIOS kindly provides several pixel and character manipulation functions in VIDEO_IO. We will discuss these shortly.

HIGH-RESOLUTION FORMAT—640 × 200

A pixel in this format is either off or on (black or white), requiring only one bit per pixel. We need one byte for eight pixels, 80 bytes for one row, and 16,000 bytes for the entire screen. The mapping (Figure 12-5) is similar to that of the medium resolution mode. Byte 0 of the display memory is mapped to the first eight pixels of row 0, byte 1 to the next eight, and so on. Again, byte 80 is mapped to row 2 because of the interlaced scan.

BIOS VIDEO SUPPORT—VIDEO_IO

The VIDEO_IO driver in BIOS provides the 16 video functions illustrated in Table 12-6. We have grouped them under five headings according to function. To use a function, set register AH equal to the function number, initialize any required registers, and execute an INT 10H instruction. The BIOS listing contains detailed information about each function as well as the complete listing for VIDEO_IO.

Some of these functions save us the trouble of learning how to program the 6845. For example, SET MODE initializes all 16 of the 6845 control registers to provide one of the eight different display modes. The cursor is supplied directly by the 6845, and the CURSOR CONTROL group is basically an interface to the cursor-position and cursor-

TABLE 12-6   VIDEO_IO FUNCTIONS

Mode control
0   SET MODE
15 RETURN CURRENT VIDEO STATE

Cursor control
1   SET CURSOR TYPE
2   SET CURSOR POSITION
3   SET CURSOR POSITION

Page control
5   SELECT ACTIVE DISPLAY PAGE
6   SCROLL ACTIVE PAGE UP
7   SCROLL ACTIVE PAGE DOWN

Character handling
8   READ ATTRIBUTE/CHARACTER AT CURSOR
9   WRITE ATTRIBUTE/CHARACTER AT CURSOR
10 WRITE CHARACTER AT CURSOR
14 WRITE TELETYPE

Graphics interface
11 SET COLOR PALETTE
12 WRITE PIXEL
12 READ PIXEL

type registers within the 6845. The SET ACTIVE DISPLAY PAGE function changes the "beginning display address" register in the 6845. With a little work (and the Motorola Microprocessor Data Book), you can manipulate these registers to suit your needs. For example, it is possible to make the display scroll smoothly, instead of a line at a time, by suitable reprogramming of the 6845. The details of this will be left to the reader. Rather than program the 6845 directly, it is probably best to use the services provided by BIOS. The main reason for this is compatibility. If IBM engineers change the hardware on a new version of the PC, they will presumably attempt to make a new BIOS compatible with the old. Your software investment will be preserved if you have not been so clever as to program the 6845 directly.

Character Handling

The remaining VIDEO_IO functions also make life a little easier. The CHARACTER HANDLING functions provide various methods for displaying characters, including displaying characters in the graphics modes. Functions 9 and 10 are useful when you want to display a repeated character starting at the cursor position. Functions 9 and 10 do not, however, move the cursor, so after a character is displayed you must move the cursor to the next position. The WRITE TELETYPE function is superior for displaying text, because it automatically advances the cursor (as a teletype would), supplying the line-feed and carriage-return characters as needed.

In a graphics mode, the CHARACTER HANDLING routines are very useful, because they create a bit pattern in screen memory to match the pattern in the character ROM. The graphics mode character set is divided into two 128-character sets. The character patterns for codes 0–127 are located in BIOS at offset 0FA6EH, and those for codes 128-255 are user-definable. By adding 41H*8 ("A") to 0FA6EH, we can find the eight bytes making an "A". The eight bytes at 0FC76 create an "A" as shown below.

$$30H = 00110000$$
$$78H = 01111000$$
$$CCH = 11001100$$
$$CCH = 11001100$$
$$FCH = 11111100$$
$$CCH = 11001100$$
$$CCH = 11001100$$
$$00H = 00000000$$

You must follow a similar procedure in making the upper half of the character set. Each character is defined by eight bytes. Successive eight-byte blocks represent successive characters. BIOS uses interrupt vector 01FH to find the top half of the graphics mode character set. This vector must be initialized to point to the beginning of the character set you have defined. The first character in the upper half of the character set will be referred to by character code 128, the second character by 129, and so on.

The attribute byte has a different meaning in the graphics mode than in the alphanumeric mode. In the graphics mode, the screen consists of colored pixels, not characters. A character is created by coloring pixels that correspond to the foreground of a character. In the medium resolution graphics mode, the color of the foreground pixels is specified in bits 0 and 1 of the "attribute byte." These two bits specify one of the colors from the preselected three-color set. In the high-resolution graphics mode, the character pattern is moved directly into screen memory, so the attribute byte is almost irrelevant. In all graphics modes, if bit 7 of the attribute byte is set, the character is XORed with the current contents of the memory location.

Graphics Interface

The READ and WRITE DOT functions save us the labor of computing the location in display memory of the bits corresponding to a particular pixel on the screen. For these two functions, a pixel is specified by its row and column coordinates and a color value. For example, for WRITE DOT, $DX = $ row number, $CX = $ column number, and $AL = $ color value. As discussed in the preceding paragraph, bit 7 of the color value causes the color to be XORed with the current contents of the memory location. The main drawback to these functions is the slow performance that becomes noticeable when many pixels are being manipulated. When speed is important, the only recourse is to design routines that take advantage of the topology of the object to be drawn. A subroutine to draw an object should use the fact that all the pixels in an object are relative to one another. Rather than calculate the location in display memory of every pixel in an object, calculate one pixel's location and use the relative information to find the rest.

Graphics Arithmetic

The mapping of display memory to the screen is really fairly straightforward. As an example, we will go through the arithmetic for the medium-resolution graphics mode. The results will merely be presented for the high-resolution graphics mode.

Let's assume that the rows are numbered 0–199 and the columns, 0–319. Given the coordinates of a pixel, we must first decide which half of the screen memory is involved. Even-numbered rows are stored in the first half (0000H–1FFFH) and odd-numbered rows in the second (2000H–3FFFH). If the row number is 6, an even number, the pixel will be in the first half of screen memory. Each row takes 80 bytes of memory, so row 6 will begin with byte 240. Rows 0, 2, and 4 use 80 bytes of the first half—80 + 80 + 80 = 240. The formula for this is

$$80 \times \text{(row number)}/2 = \text{offset of desired row}$$

For odd rows, this formula is modified by subtracting one from the row number and adding 2000H:

$$80 \times (\text{row number} - 1)/2 + 2000H = \text{offset of desired row}$$

If we assume that BX contains the row number, the following code calculates the correct offset. The row number is divided by two by an ROR instruction. The high bit of BX indicates whether the row number is even or odd.

```
          ROR      BX,1       ;DIVIDE BY 2--B15=1 IF ODD
          MOV      AL,80      ;B15=0 IF EVEN
          MUL      BL         ;MULTIPLY ROW BY 80
          TEST     BH,80H     ;EVEN OR ODD?
          JZ       EVEN       ;EVEN
          ADD      AX,2000H   ;ODD
EVEN:     .
          .
```

Each byte corresponds to four pixels, so if we divide the column number by four, we will find the offset of the byte (within the row) that contains the desired pixel. If the column number is 7, $\frac{7}{4} = 1$, so byte 1 will contain the pixel. The remainder indicates the particular pair of the four pairs of two bits that is to be used. With the column number 7, the remainder is 3, so bits 0 and 1 control the pixel. In Table 12-7, XX marks the desired pixel. To summarize: Calculate the row offset, add to that the column offset, and then use the remainder to determine the exact pair of bits.

In the high-resolution format, the calculation is similar. Again, there are 80 bytes per row, so the row offset calculation is identical. To calculate the column offset, divide by 8 instead of 4. Finally, use the remainder to find the desired bit.

Example 12-2   Using VIDEO_IO

The following example parallels Example 12-1, except that instead of directly accessing screen memory, it uses VIDEO_IO functions. Function 10, WRITE CHARACTER, is used instead of Function 14, WRITE TELETYPE, because it allows us to write multiple characters. WRITE CHARACTER doesn't move the cursor, so we use GET CURSOR and SET CURSOR to do so. If you compare the performance of Example 12-1 with Example 12-2, you will find Example 12-1 executes slightly faster. The difference in speed is dramatic when

TABLE 12-7 ARITHMETIC FOR MEDIUM RESOLUTION

	Byte 0								Byte 1							
Bit #	7	6	5	4	3	2	1	0	7	6	5	4	3	2	1	0
	A	A	B	B	C	C	D	D	E	E	F	F	G	G	X	X
Column	0		1		2		3		4		5		6		7	

the WRITE TELETYPE function is used to write a screen of text. The VIDEO_IO functions are useful but slow. Most word processors and commercial programs manage the screen directly, trading possible incompatibility for performance.

```
STACK SEGMENT STACK
        DW       100 DUP(?)
STACK   ENDS


DATA    SEGMENT

BAR_HEIGHTS    DB         2, 4, 6, 8, 10, 12, 14, 16, 18

DATA    ENDS

CODE    SEGMENT
        ASSUME   CS:CODE,DS:DATA

;THIS PROCEDURE CLEARS THE SCREEN BY "SETTING THE MODE"

CLEAR_SCREEN    PROC      NEAR
        MOV      AL,7                 ;80×25 BLACK AND WHITE MODE
        MOV      AH,0                 ;VIDEO FUNCTION "SET MODE"
        INT      10H
        RET
CLEAR_SCREEN    ENDP


;THIS PROC IS USED TO REPOSITION THE CURSOR
;ASSUMES DX = ROW, COLUMN

;THIS PROC FILLS THE SCREEN WITH A BACKGROUND CHARACTER

WRITE_BACKGROUND        PROC      NEAR
        MOV      CX,2000
        MOV      AL,0B0H              ;BACKGROUND CHARACTER
        MOV      AH,10                ;WRITE CHARACTER
        INT      10H
        RET
WRITE_BACKGROUND        ENDP


MOVE_CURSOR     PROC      NEAR
        MOV      BH,0                 ;PAGE
        MOV      AH,2                 ;SET CURSOR POSITION
        PUSH     DX                   ;SAVE POSITION
        INT      10H
        POP      DX                   ;GET POSITION
        RET
MOVE_CURSOR     ENDP
```

```
;THIS PROC IS USED TO DRAW A THREE-CHARACTER-WIDE LINE
;OF A BAR. BX=ADDRESS OF FIRST SCREEN LOCATION

DRAW_3 PROC      NEAR
       PUSH      CX
       MOV       CX,3
       MOV       AL,0DBH         ;CHARACTER TO OUTPUT
       MOV       AH,10           ;WRITE CHARACTER
       INT       10H
       POP       CX              ;RESTORE HEIGHT COUNT
       RET
DRAW_3 ENDP


;THIS PROC DRAWS A BAR 3 CHARACTERS WIDE.
;HEIGHT = CX
;POSITION (BOTTOM LEFT OR BAR) = DL (COLUMN UNITS)
;ASSUME COLUMNS LABELED 0-79, ROWS 0-24

DRAW_BAR       PROC    NEAR
       PUSH      BX              ;SAVE # OF BARS TO DRAW
       PUSH      DX              ;SAVE POSITION OF COLUMN
       MOV       DH,24           ;ROW (DL=COLUMN)
       CALL      MOVE_CURSOR
DRB1:  CALL      DRAW_3          ;DRAW A ROW
       DEC       DH              ;MOVE UP A ROW
       CALL      MOVE_CURSOR     ;MOVE THE CURSOR
       LOOP      DRB1            ;GO TILL DONE
       POP       DX
       POP       BX
       RET
DRAW_BAR       ENDP


START: MOV       AX,DATA         ;INITIALIZE THE DS REGISTER
       MOV       DS,AX
       CALL      CLEAR_SCREEN    ;CLEAR THE SCREEN
       CALL      WRITE_BACKGROUND
       MOV       BX,9            ;NUMBER OF BARS TO DRAW
       MOV       DL,5            ;COLUMN # OF FIRST BAR
       XOR       SI,SI           ;INDEX INTO BAR HEIGHT TABLE
       XOR       CH,CH           ;HIGH BYTE OF BAR HEIGHT
ST1:   MOV       CL,BAR_HEIGHTS[SI] ;GET BAR HEIGHT
       CALL      DRAW_BAR        ;DRAW THE BAR
       ADD       DL,8            ;NEXT BAR POSITION
       INC       SI              ;POINT TO NEXT HEIGHT
       DEC       BX
       JNZ       ST1             ;DO ALL BARS
```

```
                ; LOOK FOR ANY KEY TO EXIT
                WAIT:    MOV      AH, 0BH              ; NON-DESTRUCTION INPUT
                         INT      21H                 ; FUNCTION CALL
                         CMP      AL, 00              ; KEY PRESSED
                         JE       WAIT                ; NO KEY YET
                         MOV      AH, 4CH
                         INT      21H                 ; RETURN TO DOS


                CODE     ENDS
                         END      START
```

CHAPTER SUMMARY

We have examined the two most popular IBM PC display adapters, the monochrome and color/graphics adapter cards. Of the two, the monochrome is most desirable for displaying textual information, but has very limited graphics ability. The monochrome display adapter contains a fixed character set that includes selected graphics symbols for drawing boxes and bar charts. The color/graphics display adapter has several alphanumeric and graphics modes. The alphanumeric modes are similar to the monochrome mode—textual display using a fixed character set. The graphics modes permit individual pixel manipulation. The BIOS VIDEO_IO routines provide a variety of character and pixel handling routines. Of particular importance are the routines that display characters in the graphics modes, making it easy to add text to graphics displays.

The IBM PC Keyboard

This chapter discusses the operation of the IBM PC keyboard, including the keyboard support routines in BIOS. As we shall see, the design of the keyboard interface permits the programmer to redefine the meaning of keys and to implement features like the "hotkey" (a key or a key combination invoking a special task).

KEYBOARD UNIT OPERATION

The keyboard unit is really a separate special-purpose computer. Interfacing a keyboard to a computer always requires overhead—debouncing and buffering keystrokes, checking for hardware errors, and possibly scanning the keyboard. Using the main processor in a system to perform these relatively trivial tasks wastes the power of a microprocessor like the 8088. To ease the burden on the system unit, the IBM PC keyboard contains its own microprocessor, the Intel 8048. Among the functions performed by the 8048 are

- executing a power-on self-test
- scanning the keyboard
- maintaining a 16-byte scan code buffer
- maintaining a typematic (hold-to-repeat) feature
- sending scan codes to the system unit

The 8048 clock signal, coming from the system unit, is enabled by setting bit 6 of port 61H. This bit is set by BIOS during the power-on sequence. (Resetting the clock-enable bit is an easy way to lock up the keyboard. Of course, unless the bit is set again, the only way to interact with the system is via the power-on switch.)

When a key is pressed (or released), the 8048 sends a scan code to the system unit at port 60H. The 8048 then interrupts the system unit to indicate that a scan code is present. The keyboard interrupt routine, KB_INT, reads the scan code at port 60H and acknowledges the interrupt by sending a positive pulse on bit 7 of port 61H. The following code shows how to read the scan code.

```
IN     AL, 60H      ; INPUT THE SCAN CODE
MOV    AH, AL       ; SAVE SCAN CODE IN AH
IN     AL, 61H      ; INPUT CURRENT VALUE
OR     AL, 80H      ; SET BIT 7 (FOR ACKNOWLEDGE)
OUT    61H, AL      ; OUTPUT BIT 7 HIGH
AND    AL, 7FH      ; RESET BIT 7
OUT    61H, AL      ; OUTPUT BIT 7 LOW
```

The scan code is not the ASCII representation of the character on the key. The keyboard has 83 keys numbered from 1 to 83. (Refer to the Hardware Technical Reference Manual.) For example, the "A" key is number 30 and the "S" key is number 31. When a key is pressed, the scan code sent to the system unit is the key number. When a key is released, the scan code is the key number plus 80H. (Bit 7 is set upon release.) Pressing and releasing an "A" results in two scan codes, 30 and 158, being sent. The KB_INT routine is responsible for interpreting the scan codes.

THE KEYBOARD INTERRUPT ROUTINE—KB_INT

The KB_INT routine is entered whenever the keyboard interrupts to the processor. We will discuss interrupts in detail in Chapter 18, but a few short remarks are in order here. The keyboard interrupt type number is 9H, implying that the double word pointer to the interrupt routine (KB_INT) is located at address 0000:0024H (4 × 9H). Knowing the location of this pointer is important if you intend to modify or replace the current KB_INT routine.

The KB_INT routine is responsible for interpreting scan codes and sending appropriate information to system and application programs. Following is a list of some of the functions performed by KB_INT:

1. Translates scan codes into an "extended ASCII" character set (discussed below).
2. Maintains a 15-character type-ahead buffer (independent of the 16 scan code buffer in the keyboard).

3. Implements ''shift'' states for the SHIFT, CTRL, and ALT keys.

4. Implements the ''caps lock'' function for the CAPS LOCK key.

5. Records the state of the SCROLL LOCK key for application programs.

6. Handles the following special key combinations:

    a. CTRL-ALT-DEL = system reset

    b. CTRL-BREAK = causes an INT 1BH to execute. (Refer to Chapter 5 for a discussion of INT 1BH.)

    c. CTRL-NUMLOCK = causes KB_INT to loop, suspending operations such as listing or printing files. Any key (except NUMLOCK) ends the looping.

    d. SHIFT-PRTSC = causes an INT 5H, the print-screen interrupt routine.

7. Suppresses the typematic feature of the following keys: CTRL, SHIFT, ALT, NUM LOCK, SCROLL LOCK, CAPS LOCK, INS.

THE KEYBOARD BUFFER

It is instructive to study the KB_INT program to see exactly how all the above features are implemented. A complete discussion of KB_INT is beyond the scope of this book, but the keyboard buffer provides an interesting example of a ''ring'' or ''circular'' buffer, so we will discuss it. A ring buffer is typically drawn as shown in Figure 13-1. Although shown as a circle, it is really linear memory, 16 words from address 40H:1EH TO 40H:3CH in the PC. The circularity comes about by the way the buffer pointers are managed.

Two pointers, BUFFER-HEAD and BUFFER_TAIL, revolve around the buffer as characters are stored and removed from the buffer. Each character uses two bytes in the buffer, one for the scan code and one for the ASCII code. How is the circular motion achieved? Each time a pointer is incremented, it is checked to see if it has gone beyond the memory allocated to the buffer; that is, it is compared to a variable, BUFFER_END, in the BIOS data area. If the incremented pointer equals BUFFER_END, it is reset to the beginning of the buffer, denoted by the variable BUFFER_START.

BUFFER_TAIL points to the next empty location in the buffer, and BUFFER_HEAD points to the next character to be removed from the buffer, As characters are removed from the buffer (if it is assumed that no characters are entered), BUFFER_HEAD will advance to match BUFFER_TAIL, at which point the buffer will be empty. If characters are entered and not removed, BUFFER_TAIL marches forward until it almost laps BUFFER_HEAD. At this point it must stop, because the buffer is full. In the PC, there is always one empty word between the BUFFER_TAIL and BUFFER_HEAD in the full condition. The maximum number of words in the buffer at any one time, therefore, is 15, even though the buffer is 16 words long.

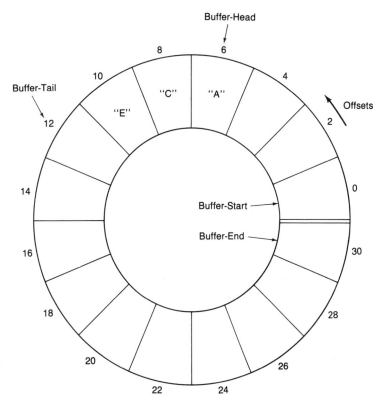

Figure 13-1 Ring Buffer

Example 13-1 Lengthening the Buffer

Many programmers like to enter commands while a program is running. A common example of this is entering the "link" commands during the assembly of a program. The 15-character type-ahead buffer sometimes frustrates this activity. Here we show a very simple way to lengthen the buffer.

There is really no way to lengthen the buffer at the default location. The easiest way to lengthen the buffer is to move it to a location in free memory; that is, to put the buffer in a program and leave the program resident. In doing so, we must make sure that the buffer is still within the BIOS data area, within 64K bytes of the segment begining at paragraph 40H. The reason for this is that BIOS uses word pointers rather than double-word pointers to address the BIOS data area.

Our program first performs a calculation to see whether the buffer is within reach of the BIOS data segment. If it is, the variables are changed and the buffer is left resident. Otherwise, the program returns to DOS. You can change the buffer length by changing the BUFFER_SIZE equate.

```
;THIS EXAMPLE MOVES AND LENGTHENS THE KEYBOARD TYPE-AHEAD
;BUFFER


BUFFER_HEAD        EQU        001AH      ;THESE ARE THE OFFSETS OF
BUFFER_TAIL        EQU        001CH      ;KEYBOARD VARIABLES IN
BUFFER_START       EQU        0080H      ;THE BIOS DATA AREA AT
BUFFER_END         EQU        0082H      ;SEGMENT 40H.


BUFFER_SIZE        EQU        40         ;40 CHARACTERS

STACK SEGMENT STACK
         DW        100 DUP(?)
STACK ENDS


DATA    SEGMENT
GOOD_MESS          DB         'NEW BUFFER INSTALLED'
                   DB         0DH,0AH,'$'
BAD_MESS           DB         "BUFFER CAN'T BE INSTALLED"
                   DB         0DH,0AH,'$'


DATA    ENDS
CODE    SEGMENT
         ASSUME    CS:CODE,DS:DATA


BUFFER DW          BUFFER_SIZE          DUP(5555H)    ;NEW BUFFER


START: CLI                  ;TURN OFF INTERRUPTS

;NOW CHANGE BUFFER_START, BUFFER_END, AND, FINALLY,
;THE BUFFER POINTERS.  THE OFFSETS MUST REFER TO SEGMENT 40H

         MOV       AX,CS              ;SEE IF NEW BUFFER WILL WORK
         CMP       AX,1040H-(2*BUFFER_SIZE/16)-1
         JA        NO_GOOD
         SUB       AX,40H             ;AX=DIFFERENCE IN PARAGRAPHS
         MOV       CL,4
         SAL       AX,CL              ;AX=BUFFER OFFSET IN BYTES
         MOV       BX,40H
         MOV       DS,BX              ;ADDRESS BIOS DATA AREA
         MOV       BX,BUFFER_HEAD     ;CHANGE HEAD,TAIL,START,END
         MOV       [BX],AX
         MOV       BX,BUFFER_TAIL
         MOV       [BX],AX
         MOV       BX,BUFFER_START
         MOV       [BX],AX
         ADD       AX,2*BUFFER_SIZE ;WORDS IN BUFFER
         MOV       BX,BUFFER_END
         MOV       [BX],AX
         STI                          ;REENABLE INTERRUPTS
```

```
          MOV      AX, DATA          ; SEND  SUCCESS  MESSAGE
          MOV      DS, AX
          LEA      DX, GOOD_MESS
          MOV      AH, 09H
          INT      21H


          MOV      DX, CS            ; CALCULATE  #  OF  PARAGRAPHS  TO
          MOV      AX, ES            ; LEAVE  RESIDENT
          SUB      DX, AX
          ADD      DX, (2*BUFFER_SIZE/16) + 1
          MOV      AX, 3100H
          INT      21H               ; TERMINATE  AND  STAY  RESIDENT

NO_GOOD:           MOV     AX, DATA
          MOV      DS, AX
          LEA      DX, BAD_MESS
          MOV      AH, 09H
          INT      21H               ; SEND  FAILURE  MESSAGE
          MOV      AH, 4CH
          INT      21H               ; RETURN  TO  DOS


CODE      ENDS
          END      START
```

THE EXTENDED ASCII CHARACTER SET

The "extended ASCII" character set is an extension to the ASCII character set. It provides character codes for special functions not included in the standard ASCII character set. For example, the special function keys (F1–F10) in combination with the SHIFT, ALT, CTRL keys provide 40 different key combinations with undefined functions. Application programs are free to define these keys as they wish. Each of the 40 combinations is translated into an extended ASCII character, as shown in Table 13-1. How are we to distinguish between these extended ASCII characters and the usual ones? That is, how do we decide whether the number 65 is an ASCII "A" or an extended ASCII "F7"?

The answer at the BIOS level is that the extended ASCII character simply has a different representation in keyboard buffer. Each of the 15 buffer entries consists of two bytes. For a normal ASCII character the representation is

$$\text{low byte} = \text{ASCII character}$$

$$\text{high byte} = \text{scan code}$$

while for an extended ASCII character, the representation becomes

$$\text{low byte} = 00H$$

$$\text{high byte} = \text{extended ASCII character}$$

TABLE 13-1   EXAMPLES OF
EXTENDED ASCII
CHARACTER CODES

Key combinations	Extended ASCII character codes
F1–F10	59–68
SHIFT F1–F10	84–93
CTRL F1–F10	94–103
ALT F1–F10	104–113

The answer at the DOS level is slightly different. When we use function calls 1H, 6H, 7H, or 8H to read a character from the keyboard buffer, DOS notifies us of an extended character by returning a zero byte. We must then make a second function call, during which DOS returns the extended character code. DOS signifies an ''F7'' key by first returning a 00 and then returning the extended code, 65. Note that DOS can't read the normal ASCII NUL character because its code (00H) is used to denote an extended character.

KEYBOARD_IO

In addition to the KB_INT program, BIOS contains a program called KEYBOARD_IO. KEYBOARD_IO provides easy access to the keyboard buffer and the current shift states. Of the two programs, KEYBOARD_IO is more likely to be used by the systems or applications programmer. KEYBOARD_IO is entered via interrupt 16H. The program has three functions:

AH = 0   Return the next word from the keyboard buffer in AX. If the buffer is empty, this function will wait until a character is entered.

AH = 1   Return the ''status'' of the buffer. If ZF = 1 on return, the buffer is empty. If ZF = 0, the buffer is not empty and a word is returned in AX but not removed from the buffer.

AH = 2   Return the current shift states in AL. (Shift states are defined in Table 13-2.)

TABLE 13-2   DEFINITION OF KB_FLAG (SHIFT STATES)

Key	Bit in KB_flag	Meaning (bit = 1)
INS	7	INSERT STATE ACTIVE
CAPS LOCK	6	CAPS LOCK HAS BEEN TOGGLED
NUM LOCK	5	NUM LOCK HAS BEEN TOGGLED
SCROLL LOCK	4	SCROLL LOCK HAS BEEN TOGGLED
ALT	3	ALT KEY DEPRESSED
CTRL	2	CTRL KEY DEPRESSED
LEFT SHIFT	1	LEFT SHIFT KEY DEPRESSED
RIGHT SHIFT	0	RIGHT SHIFT KEY DEPRESSED

The following code will read a word from the buffer:

```
MOV   AH, 0      ; FUNCTION 0
INT   16H        ; KEYBOARD_IO
```

We may want to check the buffer first, rather than waiting for a key to be struck:

```
MOV   AH, 1      ; FUNCTION 1
INT   16H        ; KEYBOARD_IO
JZ    GOAHEAD    ; EMPTY, DO SOMETHING ELSE
MOV   AH, 0
INT   16H        ET BUFFER ENTRY
```

Remember, alternate scan code will be indicated by a 00H in the AL register and the alternate scan code in the AH register. It is not necessary (as when using DOS function calls) to make two reads for the alternate scan-code.

Example 13-2 The "Hot-Key"

The term *hot key* refers to a key (or key combination) that activates a resident program, temporarily suspending any running application. The resident program performs a specific task and returns control to the application. The hot-key behaves somewhat like an interrupt; pressing the key can be thought of as activating an interrupt routine.

Our hot-key program allows a user to display the current time by pressing the "ALT" " + " key combination. (We are referring to the " + " key on the right side of the keyboard.) The time is displayed in the upper right-hand corner of the screen for several seconds. This key combination can be pressed at any time—during editing, during assembly, and during execution of application programs. This particular key combination is not decoded by KB_INT (not put into the buffer) and is therefore unlikely to be used by an application program.

Our goal is to find a way to decode the ALT+ combination without disturbing or changing the operation of KB_INT. One simple and elegant method is to look at all scan codes before KB_INT does. We search the incoming scan codes for an indication that the ALT key was pressed. If the ALT key-press scan code is found, we set a flag (ALT_FLAG) and pass control to KB_INT. We then look for a scan code indicating that the " + " key is pressed before ALT is released. If " + " is found, we display the time before passing control to KB_INT. As we noted, KB_INT doesn't decode ALT+, the combination will have the singular result of displaying the time. All other keys and key combinations will be decoded normally.

Pay particular attention to KEYBOARD_ISR and MAIN. KEYBOARD_ISR is the program that looks at the scan code and determines whether the time should be displayed. It passes control to KB_INT, using an intersegment JMP instruction. MAIN tests the programs that display the time and changes the vector for interrupt type 9H (keyboard interrupt) so it points to KEYBOARD_ISR instead of KB_INT. MAIN then terminates, leaving KEYBOARD_ISR resident.

The program uses INT 1AH to obtain the time rather than function call 2CH (GET TIME), because DOS is not a reentrant operating system. Results would be unpredictable if we issued function call 2CH while DOS happened to be in the middle of a function call. Interested readers can work out the details of the time calculation. Please see the discussion of INT 1AH in the BIOS listing.

```
STACK  SEGMENT  STACK
          DW        100 DUP(?)
STACK   ENDS


CODE      SEGMENT
          ASSUME   CS:CODE,DS:CODE


HOUR     DW        ?
MIN      DW        ?
SEC      DW        ?
ALT_FLAG          DB     0
STORAGE DB        22     DUP(?)        ;FOR SCREEN DATA
TIME     DB        22     DUP(0FH)      ;TIME DATA
KB_INT  DW        0E987H,0F000H   ;ADDRESS OF KB_INT
KEYBOARD_ISR_PTR        DD     KEYBOARD_ISR


;THIS PROCEDURE CONVERTS A NUMBER (<100) IN AX
;TO A TWO DIGIT ASCII REPRESENTATION AND PLACES THE ASCII
;CHARACTERS IN POSITION IN THE ARRAY "TIME"


DISPLAY PROC      NEAR
          MOV       BL,10
          DIV       BL              ;DIVIDE BY 10 TO GET TENS
L2:       ADD       AX,3030H        ;AL=TENS AND AH=ONES
          MOV       TIME[SI],AL     ;MOVE THE TENS DIGIT
          MOV       TIME[SI+2],AH   ;MOVE THE ONES DIGIT
          RET
DISPLAY ENDP


DISPLAY_TIME      PROC     NEAR
          MOV       SI,0            ;INITIALIZE SI FOR "DISPLAY"
          MOV       AX,HOUR
          CMP       AX,12
          JNA       DT1
          SUB       AX,12           ;CONVERT TO 12-HOUR CLOCK
          MOV       TIME+18,'P'     ;ENTER P FOR PM
          JMP       SHORT DT2
DT1:      MOV       TIME+18,'A'     ;ENTER A FOR AM
DT2:      MOV       TIME+20,'M'
          CALL      DISPLAY         ;FORMAT "HOUR"
          MOV       TIME+4,':'
          ADD       SI,6            ;ADVANCE FOR "DISPLAY" PROC
          MOV       AX,MIN
          CALL      DISPLAY         ;FORMAT "MIN"
          MOV       TIME+10,':'
          ADD       SI,6            ;ADVANCE FOR "DISPLAY" PROC
          MOV       AX,SEC
```

```
            CALL     DISPLAY          ;FORMAT SECONDS
            MOV      TIME+16,' '      ;SPACE
;NOW MOVE THE FORMATTED AREA CALLED "TIME" TO THE SCREEN

            MOV      AX,0B000H        ;ADDRESS DISPLAY MEMORY
            MOV      ES,AX
            MOV      DI,138           ;OFFSET TO UPPER RIGHT
            MOV      SI,OFFSET TIME
            MOV      CX,22
REP         MOVSB                     ;MOVE TO SCREEN MEMORY
            RET
DISPLAY_TIME     ENDP


;THIS PROCEDURE CONVERTS THE CURRENT TIME VARIABLE INTO
;HOUR, MIN, AND SEC.

GET_TIME         PROC      NEAR
            MOV      AH,0
            INT      1AH              ;GET THE TIME
            MOV      AX,DX            ;MOVE LOW TIME
            MOV      DX,CX            ;MOVE HIGH TIME
            MOV      CX,32772         ;WE REALLY NEED TO DIVIDE BY
;65543, SO WE DIVIDE BY 32772, THEN DIVIDE BY 2.
            DIV      CX               ;AX = 2*(NUMBER OF HOURS)
            SAR      AX,1             ;AX = NUMBER OF HOURS
            JNC      GT1              ;ADJUST REMAINDER OF C=1
            ADD      DX,32772         ;ADJUST REMAINDER
GT1:        MOV      HOUR,AX          ;SAVE HOUR
            MOV      AX,DX            ;GET REMAINDER
            MOV      DX,00H           ;CLEAR HIGH WORD
            MOV      CX,1092          ;CALCULATE MINUTES
            DIV      CX               ;AX = MIN
            MOV      MIN,AX           ;SAVE MINUTES
            MOV      AX,DX            ;GET REMAINDER
            MOV      CX,10            ;MULTIPLY BY 10 BECAUSE THE
            MUL      CX               ;REAL DIVISOR IS 18.2, NOT
            MOV      CX,182           ;DIVISOR = 18.2*10
            DIV      CX
            MOV      SEC,AX           ;AX = SEC
            RET
GET_TIME         ENDP


;THIS PROCEDURE MOVES THE SCREEN DATA FOR TEMPORARY STORAGE

SAVE_SCREEN      PROC      NEAR
            MOV      AX,0B000H
            MOV      DS,AX            ;SET UP SCREEN ADDRESS
```

```
              MOV     SI,138              ; OFFSET OF UPPER RIGHT
              PUSH    CS
              POP     ES                  ; ES:DI POINTS TO "STORAGE"
              MOV     DI,OFFSET STORAGE
              CLD
              MOV     CX,22
REP           MOVSB                       ; SAVE SCREEN DATA
              PUSH    CS
              POP     DS                  ; RESTORE DS
              RET
SAVE_SCREEN   ENDP

TIME_ON PROC  NEAR
              CALL    GET_TIME
              CALL    SAVE_SCREEN
              CALL    DISPLAY_TIME
              RET
TIME_ON ENDP

; DELAY FOR 2 SECONDS

DELAY   PROC    NEAR
              MOV     CX,10               ; OUTER LOOP
D1:           MOV     DX,CX               ; SAVE OUTER LOOP COUNTER
              MOV     CX,0
D2:           LOOP    D2                  ; DELAY ABOUT 0.2 SECONDS
              MOV     CS,DX               ; GET OUTER LOOP COUNTER
              LOOP    D1                  ; LOOP 10 TIMES
              RET
DELAY   ENDP

; RESTORE ORIGINAL SCREEN

ERASE   PROC    NEAR
              MOV     AX,0B000H
              MOV     ES,AX
              MOV     DI,138
              MOV     SI,OFFSET STORAGE
              CLD
              MOV     CX,22
REP           MOVSB
              RET
ERASE   ENDP

; THIS IS THE KEYBOARD ISR, A PREAMBLE TO THE BIOS KB_INT

KEYBOARD_ISR    PROC    FAR
              STI                         ; ENABLE INTERRUPTS
              PUSH    AX                  ; SAVE REGISTERS
              PUSH    BX
```

```
                    PUSH    CX
                    PUSH    DX
                    PUSH    SI
                    PUSH    DI
                    PUSH    DS
                    PUSH    ES

                    PUSH    CS
                    POP     DS              ; SET UP DS FOR THIS SEG
                    IN      AL, 60H         ; GET SCAN CODE
                    CMP     ALT_FLAG, 0     ; HAS ALT BEEN PRESSED?
                    JNE     KEY2            ; YES
                    CMP     AL, 56          ; ALTERNATE PRESS?
                    JNE     KEY_EXIT        ; NO
                    OR      ALT_FLAG, 01H   ; SET FLAG
                    JMP     SHORT   KEY_EXIT
        KEY2:       CMP     AL, 78          ; IS IT THE + KEY?
                    JNE     KEY3            ; NO
                    CALL    TIME_ON         ; DISPLAY TIME
                    CALL    DELAY           ; WAIT 5 SECONDS
                    CALL    ERASE           ; GO BACK TO NORMAL
                    JMP     SHORT   KEY_EXIT
        KEY3:       CMP     AL, 56 + 128    ; IS IT ALT RELEASE?
                    JNE     KEY_EXIT        ; NO, EXIT
                    MOV     ALT_FLAG, 0     ; CLEAR THE FLAG

     KEY_EXIT:      CLI
                    POP     ES
                    POP     DS
                    POP     DI
                    POP     SI
                    POP     DX
                    POP     CX
                    POP     BX
                    POP     AX
                    JMP     DWORD PTR CS: KB_INT   ; EXIT TO BIOS KB_INT
     KEYBOARD_ISR   ENDP

; MAIN PROGRAM - TEST THE TIME PROGRAM, SET UP THE INTERRUPT
; VECTOR, AND TERMINATE BUT STAY RESIDENT.

     START:  PUSH    CS
             POP     DS

; TEST THE TIME DISPLAY PROGRAM

                    CALL    TIME_ON         ; DISPLAY TIME
                    CALL    DELAY           ; WAIT 5 SECONDS
                    CALL    ERASE           ; GO BACK TO NORMAL
```

```
; SET UP KB_INT VECTOR TO POINT TO OUR PROGRAM
            LDS     DX, KEYBOARD_ISR_PTR    ; DS: DX=ADDRESS
            MOV     AH, 25H                 ; FUNCTION CALL 25H
            MOV     AL, 09H                 ; TYPE 9H
            INT     21H


; RETURN TO DOS, LEAVE TIME PROGRAM RESIDENT

            MOV     DX, OFFSET START
            MOV     CL, 4
            SAR     DX, CL                  ; DIVIDE BY 16
            ADD     DX, 11H                 ; ROUND UP AND ADD 10H FOR PSP
            MOV     AX, 3100H               ; TERMINATE BUT STAY RESIDENT
            INT     21H

CODE        ENDS
            END     START
```

SUPPRESSION OF HOT-KEYS

Instead of adding new hot-keys, you may want to suppress some of those that already exist. For example, you may not want to allow the user of your product to inadvertently press CTRL-NUMLOCK or CTRL-ALT-DEL (however unlikely). A complicated way to prevent this is to write a keyboard driver to replace the one in BIOS. Such a driver could be several hundred bytes long and time-consuming to debug. If but a few features are to be suppressed—for example, the CTRL-ALT-DEL—we can follow the hot-key example, looking for a special key combination. Upon finding CTRL-ALT-DEL, for instance, we simply do not allow "DEL" to go into the keyboard buffer; that is, we return directly from the interrupt without going to KB_INT. We will not include an example, but will suggest that the hot-key example can easily be modified to suppress as well as to implement hot-keys.

CHAPTER SUMMARY

The IBM PC keyboard system is designed with a maximum of flexibility. The keyboard itself contains an 8048 microprocessor that operates the keyboard (self-test, debouncing, buffering, and communication with the system unit). The keyboard interrupts the system unit to pass it scan codes via interrupt type 9H. The KB_INT routine inputs the scan codes from port 60H, interprets them, and buffers them if necessary. The KEYBOARD_IO routine retrieves characters from the keyboard buffer, passing them to system and application programs.

The CPU
and the I/O
Channel

In this chapter we set the stage for a detailed discussion of hardware interfacing as it applies to the IBM PC. We begin by looking at the details of the 8088 microprocessor that are particularly relevant to interfacing. We must understand the design of the 8088 system bus and the types of bus cycles it can execute. We will proceed from a discussion of the 8088 system-bus to a discussion of the I/O channel.

MICROPROCESSOR BUSES

The 8088 is intended to be used in a three-bus system (Figure 14-1). The ADDRESS BUS provides an address to memory and I/O devices. The DATA BUS provides a pathway along which data can flow between the microprocessor and the memory, or I/O devices. The CONTROL BUS provides control signals that control the flow of information along the DATA BUS.

The address bus contains 20 address lines connected to two logical address spaces, the memory address space and the I/O address space. All 20 address lines are active during a memory bus cycle, implying a memory address range from 00000H to 0FFFFFH (1 megabyte). Only 16 lines are active during an I/O bus cycle, which limits the I/O (port) address space to the range 0000H–0FFFFH (64K bytes). In the IBM PC, only the lower ten of these 16 lines are decoded during an I/O instruction, thus further limiting the port space to the range 0000H–03FFH (1K byte). (Any memory reference instruction causes a memory bus cycle, whereas only IN and OUT instructions cause I/O bus cycles.)

The data bus is an eight-bit, bidirectional pathway connected to devices in both address spaces. It is connected to I/O devices as well as memory chips.

The control bus includes signals that correspond to the type of bus cycle being executed. At a minimum, the control bus consists of the following four lines:

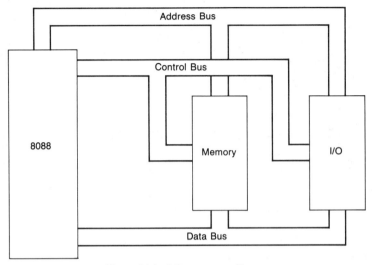

Figure 14-1 Microprocessor Buses

MEMR memory read, active low during memory read

MEMW memory write, active low during memory write

IOR   I/O read, active low during I/O read

IOW   I/O write, active low during I/O write

The MEMR, MEMW lines are connected to the memory chips, and the IOR, IOW lines are connected to the I/O devices. During microprocessor-controlled bus cycles, only one of these lines will be active. During our study of DMA (Direct Memory Access), we will find that DMA cycles require two lines to be simultaneously active, one memory line and one I/O line.

If we look at the pinout of the microprocessor (Figure 14-2), we should be able to identify the three buses. If you can't find everything mentioned above, you needn't be alarmed, as we shall see.

First, the 8088 has a multiplexed address/data bus. The pins labeled AD0–AD7 contain address information during one part of a bus cycle and data information during another. The address and data information must be demultiplexed by external chips.

Second, the MEMR, MEMW, IOR, and IOW pins are missing. This is because the 8088 has two different operating modes—minimum and maximum—determined by the MN/MX pin. The minimum mode is typically used in small systems with no coprocessors. To support the 8087 math coprocessor, the 8088 must operate in the maximum mode. This requires grounding of the MN/MX pin and results in the pinout of Figure 14-2. In the maximum mode another chip, the 8288 bus controller, supplies the control signals.

Figure 14-3 shows a typical 8088 system in the maximum mode. Three 8088 status

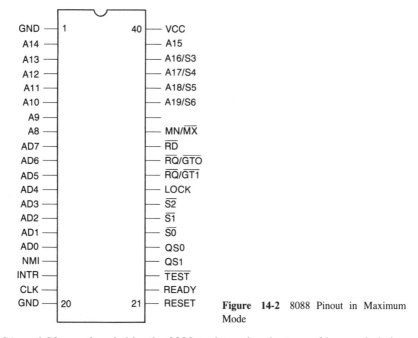

Figure 14-2 8088 Pinout in Maximum Mode

lines, S0, S1, and S2, are decoded by the 8288 to determine the type of bus cycle being run by the 8088. The 8288 responds by activating the appropriate control signals. A 74LS373 transparent latch demultiplexes the address-data bus as follows. The 8088 presents an address during the first part of a bus cycle. Since the 74LS373 is a transparent

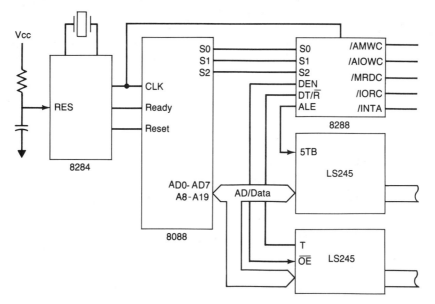

Figure 14-3 8088 Maximum Mode System

latch, the address propagates immediately (15 ns) to the system address bus. The 74LS373 then latches the address on the falling edge of the ALE (address latch enable) signal from the 8288 and holds the address stable until ALE goes high in the next bus cycle. Pins AD0–AD7 are used for data during the remainder of the bus cycle. Note that the 8288 also provides signals to control the bidirectional buffer, 74LS245. The DT/R (data transmit or receive) pin governs the direction of data flowing through the buffer, and DEN (data enable) enables the buffer onto the bus.

Figure 14-3 also shows the 8284 system clock chip. This chip divides the crystal oscillator frequency (14.318 MHz) by three to produce the 2 to 1 duty cycle, 4.77 MHz processor clock. The 8284 divides the processor clock by two to produce the symmetric 2.38-MHz PCLK (peripheral clock). It also provides a buffered version of the 14.318-MHz crystal frequency (OSC). PCLK is used on the system board and OSC is bussed to the I/O channel. The 8284 also has a Schmidt trigger used to provide a good reset signal to the microprocessor during power-on. The final important function of the 8284 is in synchronizing wait-state requests to the processor clock. If this were not done, unpredictable processor operation could occur.

We have reached the point at which we can begin to ignore the detailed connections between the chips in Figure 14-3. We will now emphasize the demultiplexed bus, consisting of the three buses discussed at the beginning of the chapter: the address, the data, and the control buses.

THE I/O CHANNEL

The I/O channel is a set of 62 lines connected to five card-edge connectors on the system board. (There are eight card-edge connectors on the PC-XT.) Nonsystem hardware is added to the PC by simply plugging cards into the I/O channel. Because of its central role in hardware interfacing, we will keep the I/O channel in focus throughout the rest of the book.

The I/O channel lines (see Figure 14-4) can be classified by the function they perform:

ADDRESS—the address bus

DATA—the data bus

CONTROL—the control bus

DMA—lines used to implement DMA functions

INTERRUPT—lines used to implement interrupt functions

CLOCK—14.318 MHz and 4.77 MHz

POWER SUPPLY—power supply and ground

Let's take a closer look.

Address.   Output lines A0–A19 form the address bus. The 74LS373 demultiplexing chip drives these lines as well as the system board address bus.

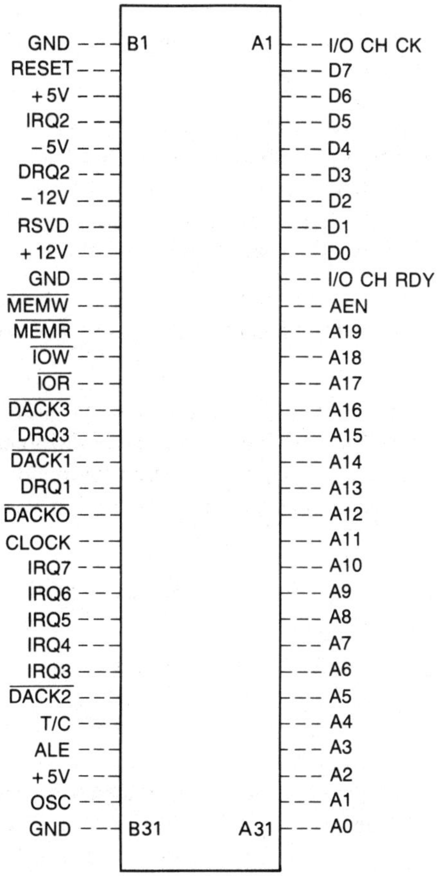

```
        GND  – – –| B1        A1 |– – – I/O CH CK
      RESET  – – –|              |– – – D7
        +5V  – – –|              |– – – D6
       IRQ2  – – –|              |– – – D5
        –5V  – – –|              |– – – D4
       DRQ2  – – –|              |– – – D3
       –12V  – – –|              |– – – D2
       RSVD  – – –|              |– – – D1
       +12V  – – –|              |– – – D0
        GND  – – –|              |– – – I/O CH RDY
       MEMW  – – –|              |– – – AEN
       MEMR  – – –|              |– – – A19
        IOW  – – –|              |– – – A18
        IOR  – – –|              |– – – A17
      DACK3  – – –|              |– – – A16
       DRQ3  – – –|              |– – – A15
      DACK1  – – –|              |– – – A14
       DRQ1  – – –|              |– – – A13
      DACKO  – – –|              |– – – A12
      CLOCK  – – –|              |– – – A11
       IRQ7  – – –|              |– – – A10
       IRQ6  – – –|              |– – – A9
       IRQ5  – – –|              |– – – A8
       IRQ4  – – –|              |– – – A7
       IRQ3  – – –|              |– – – A6
      DACK2  – – –|              |– – – A5
        T/C  – – –|              |– – – A4
        ALE  – – –|              |– – – A3
        +5V  – – –|              |– – – A2
        OSC  – – –|              |– – – A1
        GND  – – –| B31      A31 |– – – A0
```

Figure 14-4 I/O Channel

DATA. Lines D0–D7 form the bidirectional data bus. The data bus is driven by the 74LS245 bidirectional buffer.

CONTROL. In addition to the usual control lines, there are several unrelated lines in this group. First we have the following control lines, which come directly from the 8288 bus controller:

MEMR active-low, output, memory read
MEMW active-low, output, memory write
IOR   active-low, output, I/O read (IN instructions)
IOW   active-low, output, I/O write (OUT instructions)

Other lines in the control group include the following:

ALE—Address Latch Enable. This output signal comes directly from the 8288 bus controller. The main function of this signal is to provide timing information for the

74LS373 demultiplexing latch. ALE can be used in the I/O channel to find the beginning of a bus cycle—to time events that must be synchronized to bus cycles.

AEN—Address Enable. This output signal allows us to distinguish between processor bus cycles and DMA bus cycles. A high on AEN indicates that a DMA cycle is in progress. The high signal is used to "disable" the 8288 bus controller and the address and data bus buffers. The 8237 DMA chip is in control of the address, data, read, and write control lines during AEN high. A low on AEN indicates that the bus cycle is 8088 initiated. This very important signal will be used in almost all of our interfacing examples.

I/O Channel RDY. This normally high input line can be pulled low by a slow device to insert processor wait-states. Insertion of wait states will be discussed in detail in Chapter 16.

I/O Channel Check. This normally high input line is pulled low to indicate a memory or I/O device parity error. The low signal causes an NMI (nonmaskable interrupt, interrupt type 2). This line could be used as a general interrupt line if the type 2 interrupt service routine were rewritten. The routine should query the hardware to determine the source of the interrupt.

Reset DRV. This output signal is active-high during power-on and can be used to reset or initialize I/O devices.

DMA Group. The DMA group consists of the following:

DRQ1–DRQ3. These input lines are connected to the corresponding DMA request pins on the 8237 DMA controller. A DMA request is generated by raising the selected line. The line should be held high until the DMA request is acknowledged on the corresponding DMA acknowledge line (DACK1-3). The DACK signal can be used to reset the DRQ line. Since DMA channel 0 is reserved for memory refreshing (initiated by the 8253-5 system timer), there is no channel 0 request line in the I/O channel. The DMA channels are prioritized with channel 0 highest and channel 3 lowest.

DACK0–DACK3. These four active-low output lines provide "DMA acknowledge" signals for the four DMA channels supported by the 8237 DMA controller. Although DRQ0 is not provided, DACK0 is useful because it indicates that a memory refresh cycle is in progress. Memory in the I/O channel can then be refreshed along with the system board memory.

TC. Terminal Court is an active-high output pulse indicating that some DMA channel has reached terminal count. This signal can be used in conjunction (ANDed) with the DACK signals to determine which channel has completed the transfer.

Interrupt Group. The IRQ2–IRQ7 interrupt request lines are connected directly to the 8259A programmable interrupt controller on the system board. An interrupt request is generated by raising the appropriate IRQ line. The line should be held high until the request is serviced by the appropriate interrupt service routine. The 8259A has eight interrupt inputs. IRQ0 and IRQ1 are used on the system board for the time-of-day and keyboard interrupts and are not available in the I/O channel. We will discuss interrupts and the 8259A in Chapter 18.

Clock Group.   The clock group consists of two clocks that can be used by I/O devices for various timing functions.

OSC.   This output is the 14.318-MHz, buffered crystal oscillator signal coming from the 8284 clock chip.

CLK.   This output is the 4.77-MHz, 2 to 1 duty cycle processor clock coming from the 8284 clock chip.

Power Supply Group.   All of the voltages available on the system board are available in the I/O channel.

+5 Vdc ±5% (located on two pins)
    4 amps available in the I/O channel for the PC.
    11 amps available in the I/O channel for the XT.
−5 Vdc ±10%
    0.3 amp available in the I/O channel.
+12 Vdc ±5%
    2 amps available in the I/O channel for the PC.
    4.2 amps available in the I/O channel for the XT.
−12 Vdc ±10%
    0.25 amp available in the I/O channel.
GND   Ground, located on three pins

I/O CHANNEL, PROCESSOR-INITIATED BUS CYCLES

Designing an interface for an I/O or memory device requires a detailed understanding of bus cycles. Control signals that typically enable or strobe the I/O or memory devices must meet the timing requirements of the devices.

Figure 14-5 shows a typical memory-write bus cycle. The figure is a simplified version of the timing of diagram found in the Intel Microsystem Components Handbook. At the top of the figure, we find the processor clock. The memory-write bus cycle consists of four clock periods, labeled T1, T2, T3, and T4. At the beginning of the bus cycle, during T1, ALE goes high, enabling the 74LS373 demultiplexing latch. Shortly thereafter, the address becomes valid, propagating through the 74LS373 to the system and I/O channel address buses. Near the end of the T1, ALE falls, causing the 74LS373 to latch the address for the rest of the bus cycle. During T2, MEMW goes low, followed by valid data on the data bus. MEMW goes high at the beginning of T4 when both the address and data are still valid. The rising edge of MEMW is often used to strobe data into memory.

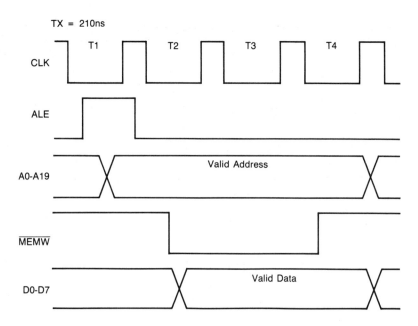

Figure 14-5   Memory-Write Bus Cycle

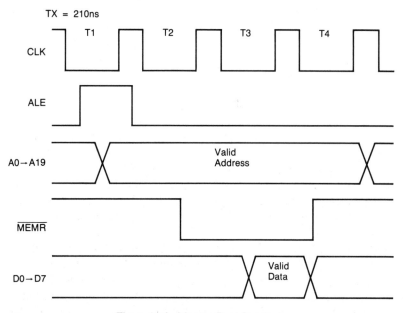

Figure 14-6   Memory-Read Bus Cycle

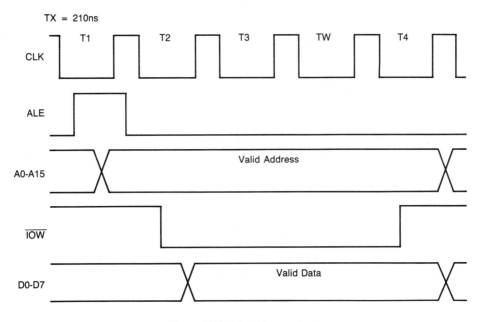

Figure 14-7 I/O Write Bus Cycle

The memory-read bus cycle in Figure 14-6 follows a similar pattern. T1 is essentially the same as for a memory-write bus cycle. The falling edge of MEMR is typically used to enable the device being read. The device responds with the valid data that is strobed into the processor at the beginning of T4.

All memory bus cycles are the same. There are no separate instruction-fetch and memory-fetch cycles as in some eight-bit microprocessors. If the 8088 instruction prefetch queue is not full, a memory-read bus cycle fetches a byte for the queue. If an instruction makes a memory reference, the memory-read bus cycle again fetches a byte, but this time for the instruction operand.

The I/O bus cycles are similar to the memory bus cycles except for the automatic insertion of one wait-state by system board logic. Figures 14-7 and 14-8 show that the I/O bus cycles have one added clock period, TW (T-wait). T1, T2, T3, and T4 are the same as before. The processor is essentially idle during TW. The insertion of the wait-state adds approximately 210 ns to the time available to I/O devices. This long time makes the interfacing task relatively trivial for almost all "microprocessor-compatible" I/O devices.

TIMING REQUIREMENTS

When designing an interface, the designer must determine whether the timing requirements of the particular chip or device are met by the I/O channel signals. To illustrate how this is done, we will see if the processor can read from an Intel 8253-5 counter/timer chip.

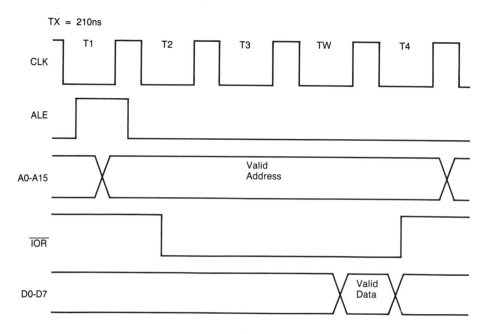

Figure 14-8 I/O Read Bus Cycle

The 8253-5 is typical of Intel microprocessor-compatible peripherals. As shown in Figure 14-9, it contains two address lines (addressing four internal ports), a CS (chip select) line, and RD and WR lines. CS, RD, and WR are active low. CS is normally connected to address decoding circuitry, RD to IOR, and WR to IOW. The 8253-5 also contains eight data lines D0–D7 connected to the data bus. The timing requirements for the 8253-5, shown in the top part of the timing diagram of Figure 14-10, are taken from the Intel data sheet. Only those times relevant to a read cycle are shown. The important facts are these:

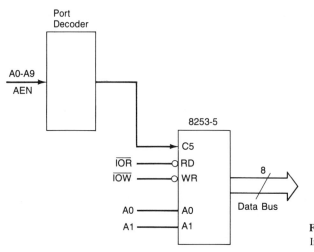

Figure 14-9 8253-5 Programmable Interval Time

1. The falling edge of IOR must be delayed at least 30 ns after a valid address is presented to the 8253-5. This gives the 8253-5 a chance to decode the address.
2. The IOR line must be held low a minimum of 300 ns.
3. The 8253-5 will present valid data at least 200 ns after IOR goes low.

Armed with this information, we look at the bottom half of Figure 14-10, which shows the relevant timing information for the I/O channel I/O-read bus cycle:

1. The address is valid at least 140 ns after the beginning of T1.
2. IOR goes low between 10 and 35 ns after the beginning of T2.

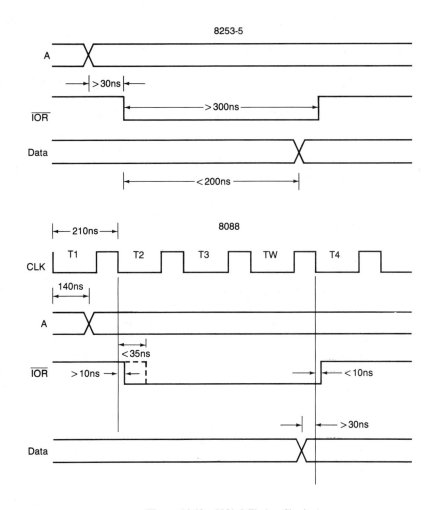

Figure 14-10 8253-5 Timing Check

3. Data must be valid at least 30 ns before the beginning of T4 (referred to as setup time).

4. IOR goes high not more than 10 ns into T4.

Now we can see if the 8253-5 conditions are met. Checking the first condition, we see from the bus cycle that there is a minimum of 80 ns between the valid address and IOR going low (70 ns from T1 and 10 ns from T2). Thus the first condition is certainly met. For condition two, we determine that the IOR line is low for about 3 clock periods, 595 ns to be exact [(3 × 210 ns) − 35 ns). 595 ns is almost twice the 300 ns required by the 8253-5, so condition two is definitely met. Condition three is met because the data will be valid at least 235 ns after the beginning of T2 (200 ns + 35 ns). Thus it will be valid 395 ns before the beginning of T4.

We see that all conditions are easily met, by a factor of two in all cases. This is true of most Intel peripheral chips and of other microprocessor-compatible chips we have used. This fact makes interfacing standard peripheral chips almost as easy as playing with Tinkertoys.

We simplified the timing example by failing to point out various delays inherent in the system. For example, the address-valid time, 140 ns, was taken from the Intel timing diagram and doesn't include the delay of 20 ns encountered when the address passes through the 74LS373 transparent latch. The data is similarly delayed by the 74LS245. These delays are insignificant compared to the factor of two margin we found in the 8253-5 example. However, if the timing requirements are tighter, it may be necessary to consider these and other delays in the calculation.

CHAPTER SUMMARY

Understanding the I/O channel definition and bus cycles is the key to interfacing devices to the IBM PC. We briefly looked at the 8088 microprocessor, mainly to see how the address, data, and control buses are generated. This led to a definition of the I/O channel, from which we learned that DMA and interrupts are supported in addition to the address, data, and control buses. We concluded with a discussion of bus cycles and timing considerations. In the next chapter we will learn how to decode the address bus and will study several examples of interfacing designs.

Interfacing Devices to the I/O Channel

One of the first tasks to be performed when we interface a device to the I/O channel is to design an address decoder. The address decoder monitors the address bus (and possibly other lines) to generate a port select signal (PSEL) when the I/O device is addressed. This chapter illustrates several address decoding techniques and design examples using the Intel 8253-5 Programmable Interval Timer and the Intel 8255A Programmable Peripheral Interface. We will limit our discussion to the interfacing of I/O devices to the I/O address space. The principles illustrated can easily be generalized to other possibilities, for example, I/O devices in the memory address space or memory devices in either space.

I/O ADDRESS SPACE (PORTS)

The 8088 microprocessor is capable of addressing 64K different ports via 16 address lines. However, the IBM PC system board decodes (recognizes) only the lower 10 address lines, restricting the number of available ports to 1024. The lower half of the 1024 ports are reserved for the system board itself, and the upper half is dedicated to the I/O channel. Many of the I/O channel ports are reserved for IBM adapter cards as shown in Table 15-1. Although the space appears crowded, there are several ports available. Ports 300H–31FH are explicitly reserved for a prototype card. They constitute a good starting point. Essentially, any unused ports can be used, even though they are reserved. For instance, if you don't intend to install an SDLC communications card, ports 380H–38CH are available.

If you ran out of ports, you could consider decoding the higher address lines. For

TABLE 15-1   I/O CHANNEL PORT ASSIGNMENTS

Port values (Hex)	Function
200-20F	Game control
210-217	Expansion unit
220-24F	Reserved
278-27F	Reserved
2F0-2F7	Reserved
2F8-2FF	Asynchronous communications (secondary)
300-31F	Prototype card
320-32F	Fixed disk
378-37F	Printer
380-38C	SDLC communications
380-389	Binary synchronous communications (secondary)
3A0-3A9	Binary synchronous communications (primary)
3B0-3BF	IBM monochrome display/printer
3C0-3CF	Reserved
3D0-3DF	Color/graphics
3E0-3F7	Reserved
3F0-3F7	Diskette
3F8-3FF	Asynchronous communications (primary)

example, the system board ignores IN or OUT instructions addressing port 300H. By decoding address lines A10–A15, we could design a decoding scheme that expanded port 300H into 64 different ports.

A15	A14	A13	A12	A11	A10		A9	A8	A7	A6	A5	A4	A3	A2	A1	A0
X	X	X	X	X	X		1	1	0	0	0	0	0	0	0	0
		Ignored by system								Decoded by system						

Thus ports 300H, 700H, 0B00H, 0F00H, 1300H, . . . could be uniquely decoded. This technique should prevent you from running out of ports.

INTRODUCTION TO LOGIC GATES

We provide this introduction for those who are unfamiliar with the subject or notation. Readers experienced in this area should proceed to the next section.

Figure 15-1 shows five elementary gates from which one can build almost anything. Four of the gates have two inputs and one output. The input and output values are restricted to either zeros or ones. The output value of each gate is completely determined by the input values as shown in the "truth tables." A circle present on an input or output indicates the presence of an internal inverter. The OUT shown in the truth table for the NAND (Negative AND) gate is the inverse of the OUT in the truth table for the AND gate due to the inverter. The one gate with a single input merely inverts the input signal.

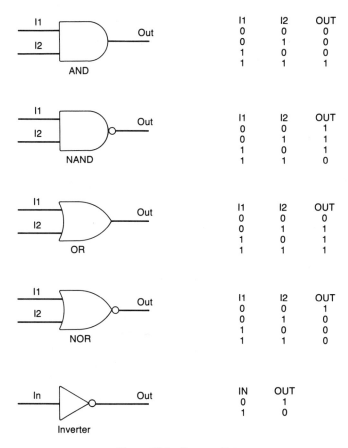

Figure 15-1 Common Gates

Figure 15-2 shows two more widely used gates that turn out to be equivalent to two of the gates in Figure 15-1. Notice that the truth table for the AND with circles on all lines is identical to the truth table for the OR gate. Why are there two symbols representing the same truth table? The answer lies in the way the signals are interpreted. If two active-low signals must both be low to produce an active-low output signal, the logic is really "AND" for negative signals. Thus, the advantage to the AND with circles is that we can see at a glance that all lines are normally high, and the two inputs must both go low to produce a low output.

SIMPLE ADDRESS DECODING

Assume that we want to decode the prototype card address, 300H. The bit pattern is

A9	A8	A7	A6	A5	A4	A3	A2	A1	A0
1	1	0	0	0	0	0	0	0	0

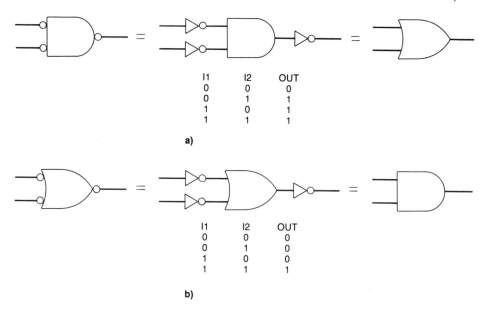

a)

I1	I2	OUT
0	0	0
0	1	1
1	0	1
1	1	1

b)

I1	I2	OUT
0	0	0
0	1	0
1	0	0
1	1	1

Figure 15-2   Alternate Gate Symbols

The CS (chip select) and OE (output enable) pins on most devices are active low. Let's design a circuit to produce an active-low signal we will call PSEL (port select). We must remember to include AEN in the design. AEN must be low; otherwise a DMA cycle is in progress. Figure 15-3 shows a simple circuit to produce the required PSEL. The 74LS30

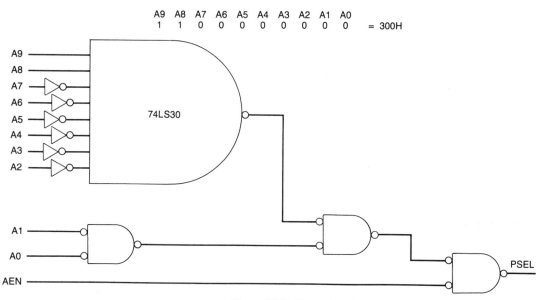

Figure 15-3   Generating PSEL

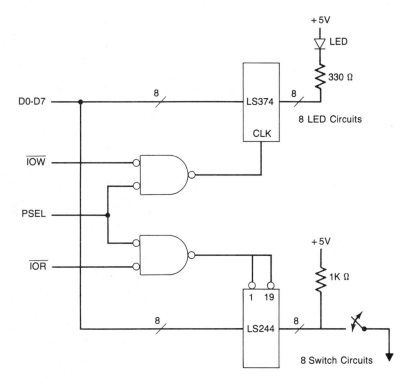

Figure 15-4   Using PSEL

is a multiple input NAND gate: If all eight inputs are high, the output goes low. PSEL will be low only if the address is 300H and AEN is low.

Figure 15-4 shows a simple but practical use of the PSEL signal. The 74LS374 is a latch. The value present on the data bus will be latched on the rising edge of CLK. An OUT instruction to port 300H will cause both PSEL and IOW to go low, thus lowering the CLK. The processor then puts data, which is latched when IOW goes high, on the data bus. One LED (light emitting diode) is connected to each output of the 74LS374 so that a low on the output turns on the LED. This provides an easy way for the processor to communicate information to us. The 74LS244 is a buffer, enabled by low signals at pins 1 and 19. A set of eight switches is connected to the input side of the buffer as shown. An IN instruction from port 300H will cause PSEL and IOR to go low, enabling the buffer and thus the switch values onto the data bus. This way we can read the switches. So we now have a way to get information into the computer (via the switches) and a way to see what the computer says (via the LEDs). What more could we want?

DECODING FOR COMPLEX CHIPS

Many peripheral chips are addressed as more than one port. Here are some examples:

Chip		Number of ports
8253-5	Interval timer	4
8255A	Programmable peripheral interface	4
8259A	Priority interrupt controller	2
8237	DMA controller	16
6845	CRT controller	2

All these chips are microprocessor-compatible, specifically designed to simplify the task of interfacing. As an example, we will design a decoding circuit for the 8253-5. The example can be easily modified for the other chips.

The 8253-5 has many internal registers accessed through four ports. How are these four ports addressed? The 8253-5 contains two address pins, A0 and A1, to which we connect I/O channel address lines A0 and A1. The bit pattern on A0 and A1 selects one of the 8253-5 ports, as follows:

A1	A0	Port
0	0	0—timer 0
0	1	1—timer 1
1	0	2—timer 2
1	1	3—control word

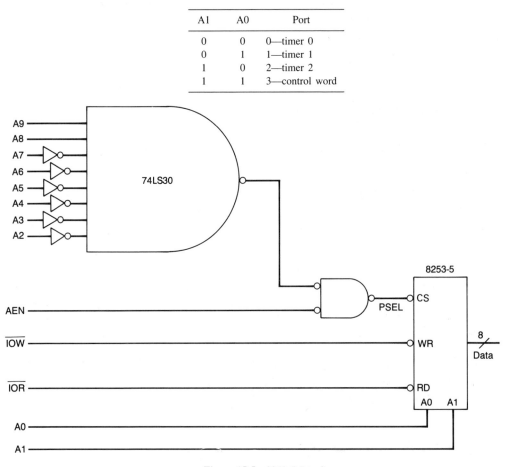

Figure 15-5 8253-5 Interface

Because the port-selection pins A0 and A1 are tied to address lines A0 and A1, the port numbers will be successive, beginning on an integer multiple of four. For example, the system board 8253-5 is addressed as ports 40H, 41H, 42H, and 43H.

The remaining address lines (A2–A9) are decoded to determine the position of the four ports in the I/O channel address space. Figure 15-5 shows the complete circuit to decode the 8253-5 at ports 300H–303H. As in the preceding example, we gate the decoded address with AEN to insure against decoding DMA cycles. The resulting PSEL is connected to CS (chip select) on the 8253-5. CS must be low to enable the 8253-5 onto the bus. IOR and IOW can be connected directly to RD and WR as shown, all being active-low signals. Once D0–D7 are connected to the data bus, the interface is complete.

Programmable interval timers (PITs) are very useful in control applications. With them, one can count events, time events, initiate events, and so on. The next example shows how to connect two PITs to the I/O channel. We have already seen that each 8253-5 has two port select pins, A0 and A1, which we will connect to address lines A0 and A1 as before. We need something new, however, to select one of the PITs. A simple solution to this problem appears in Figure 15-6. Address line A2 is used to select one or another of the PITs. The PITs will be addressed like this:

A2	A1	A0	PIT0—300H–303H
0	0	0	timer 0
0	0	1	timer 1
0	1	0	timer 2
0	1	1	control word
			PIT1—304H–307H
1	0	0	timer 0
1	0	1	timer 1
1	1	0	timer 2
1	1	1	control word

The solution in Figure 15-6 is fine for two PITs, but suppose we want to design the system to be expandable. We may find a future need for more PITs. To be specific, assume that we want four PITs in the system. The two address lines A0 and A1 will be connected to the PITs as before. A2 and A3 can be used to select one of the four PITs. Special "decoding chips" have been designed to facilitate our decoding problem. The 74LS138, three- to eight-line decoder chip will solve our decoding problem very nicely. Figure 15-7 shows the 74LS138. The binary number input on pins B0–B2 selects one of the eight output lines, 00–07. If the output is enabled by G1 = 1, G2 = 0, and G3 = 0, the selected output line will go low. The idea is to use the output lines to select the PITs. Figure 15-8 shows the 74LS138 in the decoding scheme. More PITs could easily be added. In fact, any peripheral chip with four or fewer ports could be added with no changes.

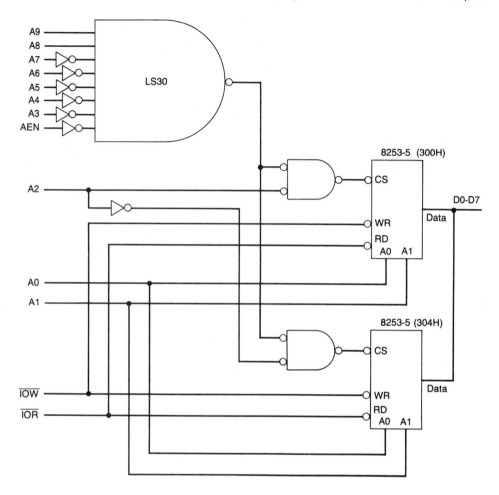

Figure 15-6   Two 8253-5s

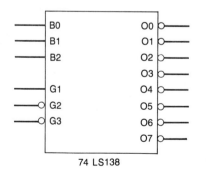

Figure 15-7   The 74LS138 3-8 Line Decoder

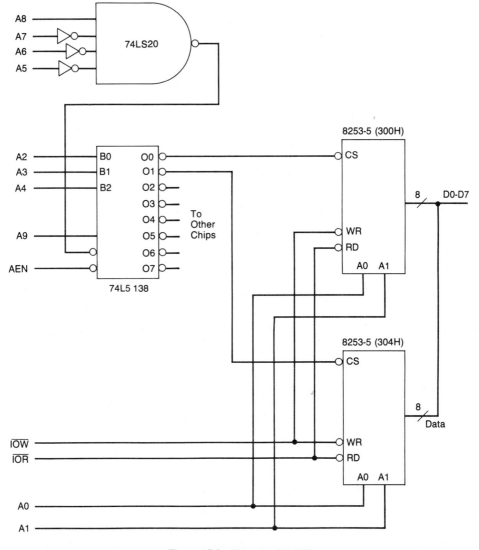

Figure 15-8 Using the 74LS138

SWITCH OR JUMPER SELECTION OF PORTS

In the preceding examples, we have put the PITs in the address space reserved for the prototype card. We may wish to be able to choose the port addresses via switches or jumpers. For example, you may design your board to use the prototype address and then find that the board you purchased uses the same address. One of them must be changed, and it is easier to change switch settings than to rewire. Figures 15-9(a) and 15-9(b) present two

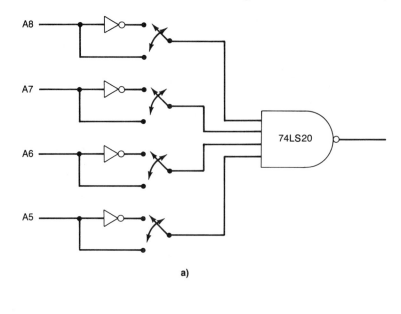

a)

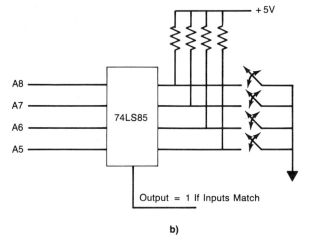

b)

Figure 15-9 Switch Selectable Decoding

simple, switch or jumper selectable decoding schemes. In Figure 15-9(a), we have the
option of inverting each of the address lines A5–A8 (A9 must be high for the I/O channel). Thus, we can select 16 possible base addresses for the 32 consecutive ports decoded
by the 74LS138. Figure 15-9(b) accomplishes the same thing by using a comparator. The
output of the 74LS85 is high only when the inputs on the left match the inputs on the right
(selected by switches). The example in Figure 15-9(b) could easily be made software-
selectable by replacing the resistors and switches with a 74LS374 latch as in the LED
example (Figure 15-4). Of course, we would need to know the port address of the
74LS374 to send it data.

MEMORY-MAPPED I/O

It is possible to put I/O devices in the memory address space. An I/O device in the memory address space has the advantage that it can be addressed with any memory reference instruction. This makes some programming tasks simpler. For example, the TEST instruction can be used to check the state of a bit in the status register of an I/O device. There are several reserved areas in the memory map which make good candidates for memory-mapped I/O. In particular, the areas surrounding video memory aren't used by either the monochrome or color graphics display adapters. The interface design will differ in certain minor details from the examples discussed so far. First, all 20 address lines must be decoded rather than only the lower ten. Second, the MEMR and MEMW lines are used instead of IOR and IOW. Third, and most important, there is no automatic wait-state insertion in microprocessor memory cycles. This last difference makes it important to look at timing diagrams as discussed in Chapter 14.

CHAPTER SUMMARY

We have seen several examples of decoding schemes used to select port addresses in the I/O channel. We illustrated by example exactly what you need to know to interface commonly used peripheral chips to the IBM PC. Intel chips are the easiest to interface, because they are designed to be compatible with the 8088 microprocessor. Peripheral chips from other manufacturers (Motorola, AMD, NEC, Analog Devices, and so forth) are also designed to be ''microprocessor-compatible,'' but they may be referring to a different microprocessor series. Occasionally you will have to exercise a little creativity in the interface design to make them work in the PC. In the next chapter we will see how to extend processor bus cycles for slow devices by inserting wait states.

Inserting
Wait States

Although the I/O bus cycles will easily meet the timing requirements of most microprocessor-compatible peripheral chips, we may occasionally find a chip that needs a little extra time to respond. This is even more likely if we are using memory-mapped I/O, because there is no automatic insertion of wait states in a memory bus cycle. We can lengthen the bus cycle by inserting one or more wait states into the processor bus cycle. Each added wait state will increase the available time by 210 ns.

Wait states are inserted by pulling down on the I/O CH RDY line. The I/O CH RDY signal is passed to the ready-synchronization circuitry on the 8284 clock chip. The 8284 samples the ready input on the rising edge of the 8088 CLK and inactivates the 8088 READY line on the following falling edge. The Intel Microprocessor Data Book specifies very precise timing requirements for the READY line, stating, ''. . . if the timing requirements are not met, unpredictable operation can occur.'' (It doesn't tell us what the 8088 may do!) Specific timing requirements must also be met by the 8284 RDY and AEN inputs to insure that the correct number of wait states are inserted. However, our main concerns are the timing requirements that must be met by the I/O CH RDY line.

These timing requirements are summarized in Figure 16-1. The I/O CH RDY line is normally high and must be pulled low at least 90 ns before the rising edge of the I/O channel CLK in T2 to insert a wait state. To insert just one wait state, it must be raised at least 90 ns before the rising edge in T3. The general rule for ready activation is that I/O CH RDY must be raised at least 90 ns before the rising edge of the clock period preceding the final TW.

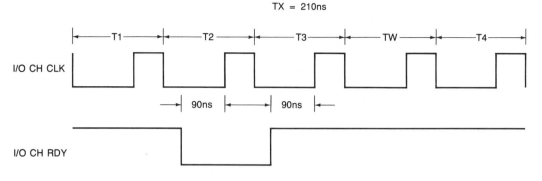

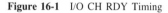

Figure 16-1 I/O CH RDY Timing

EXPLANATION OF I/O CHANNEL TIMING

This section is for readers who aren't satisfied with a simple rule. The rest of you may proceed to the next section.

To insert a wait state, the READY line on the 8088 must go low within 8 ns after the beginning of T3. The READY must not change during T3 or unpredictable operation may occur. To make sure that a particular TW is the last wait state, the READY line must go high 125 ns before the rising edge in the the last TW. That is, it must go high within about 15 ns of the beginning of the last TW.

The 8284 clock chip synchronizes all changes of the processor READY line to the processor clock, CLK88. All changes occur on the falling edge of CLK88. The inputs to the 8284 are sampled on the rising edge of CLK88 and must meet certain setup times to insure that READY changes on the next falling edge of the clock. The 8284 in the IBM PC is used in the "async" mode. As the circuit diagram in the IBM Technical Reference Manual shows, the I/O CH RDY is connected to the preset input on the 74LS74 D-type flip-flop, labeled FF1 in Figure 16-2. The Q1 output of the FF1 is connected to the AEN1 input on the 8284 clock chip. When we pull I/O CH RDY low, the Q1 output is forced high, pulling AEN1 high. If the setup time for AEN1 is met, the following falling edge CLK88 will force READY low. So we need to know the setup time for AEN1 and the delay time through the 74LS74. The 8284 timing diagram shows that AEN1 must be high at least 50 ns before the rising edge of CLK. If we add this to the 20-ns delay through the 74LS74 and the 20-ns delay of CLK behind CLK88, we find that I/O CH RDY must be pulled low at least 90 ns before the beginning of T3 to insure that READY is pulled down at the beginning of T3. Note that the 90-ns figure is with respect to the I/O channel CLK.

The 8284 will hold the 8088 READY line inactive for an integer number of processor clocks, because it changes the 8088 READY only on the falling edge of the clock. To stop wait-state insertion, the 8088 READY line must be raised near the begin-

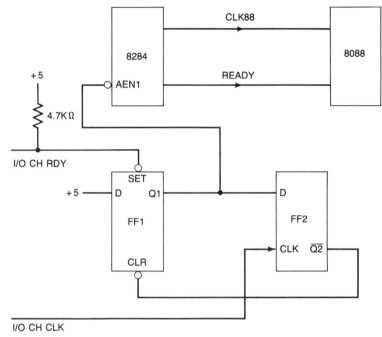

Figure 16-2   Simplified ''Ready'' Circuit

ning of the last desired TW in a bus cycle. This implies that we must raise I/O CH RDY so that AEN1 is low on the rising edge of CLK in the period preceding the last TW. AEN1 must be low at least 50 ns before the rising edge of CLK88. If we add, as above, a 20-ns delay from FF1 and the 20-ns delay of CLK behind CLK88, we obtain this result: We must raise the I/O CH RDY 90 ns before the rising edge of the clock period preceding the last TW. Again, this is with respect to the I/O CH CLK.

This section ends with a final note: Raising I/O CH RDY lowers the line to AEN1 because /Q2 of FF2 is holding CLR low on FF1. Pin /Q2 of FF2 is forced low by CLK immediately after CLK88 latches the AEN1 input.

SIMPLE WAIT-STATE CIRCUITS

To insert one wait state into a memory bus cycle, the I/O CH RDY must be lowered 90 ns before the rising edge in T2 and raised 90 ns before the rising edge in T3. A very simple circuit meeting these requirements is shown in Figure 16-3. In this circuit, FF1 controls the I/O CH RDY line. FF2 is used to reset FF1, allowing one wait state to be inserted. During power-on, RESET DRV goes high, resetting FF1. The resulting low on Q1 enables the I/O CH RDY. When an address decode requires a wait state, the output of the decoder brings the D1 input high. Soon after, near the beginning of T2, MEMR or

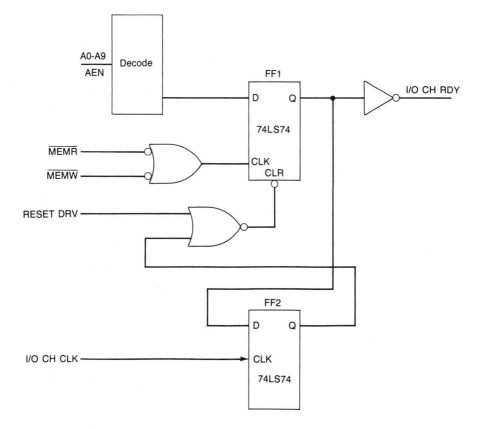

Figure 16-3   Simple Wait-State Circuit

MEMW will go low, forcing the Q1 output high and, consequently, I/O CH RDY low. Since the Q1 output feeds the D2 input on FF2, the rising edge of T2 forces Q2 high, resetting FF1 and again enabling IO CH RDY. This circuit meets the timing requirements for one wait-state insertion.

MULTIPLE WAIT STATES

It may occasionally be necessary to insert more than one wait state into the processor cycle. The circuit of Figure 16-3 can be generalized to an arbitrary number of wait states by simply adding more flip-flops to delay the raising of I/O CH RDY. Figure 16-4 shows a two wait-state generator. This could be used to add two wait states to a memory bus cycle or to add an additional wait state to an I/O bus cycle. (Recall that the system board logic automatically inserts one wait state during an I/O bus cycle. Figure 16-5 shows a 74LS164 eight-bit shift register used to implement a jumper-selectable wait-state generator. The IBM Technical Reference Manual warns us that we should never insert more than ten wait

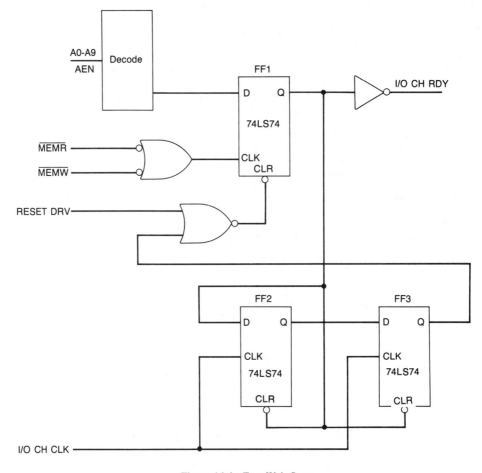

Figure 16-4 Two Wait States

states. During wait states, the DMA controller can't obtain the bus to refresh memory, resulting in delayed memory refresh cycles.

WAIT STATES IN DMA CYCLES

Inserting wait states in DMA cycles is similar to inserting them in processor cycles. The normal DMA cycle consists of five clocks, S0–S4. System board logic automatically inserts one wait state (SW) into DMA cycles on channels one, two, and three. Channel zero, the memory refresh channel, runs normal DMA cycles.

The timing requirements for wait-state insertion in DMA cycles are shown in Figure 16-6. To insert a wait state, the 8237A-5 timing diagram states that DMA-READY must go low at least 60 ns before the falling edge of the clock at the end of S3. It must go high

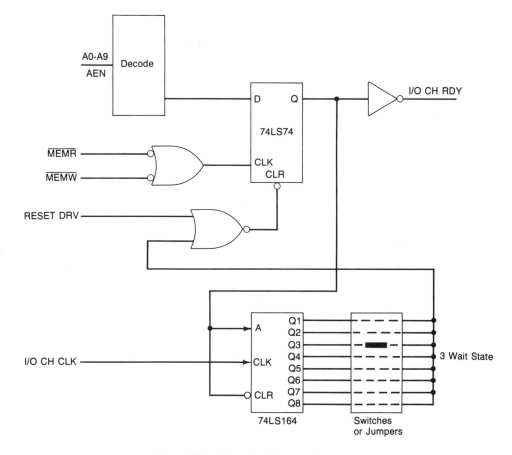

Figure 16-5   Selectable Wait-State Generator

60 ns before the falling edge of S4 to prevent a wait state. The DMA-READY is controlled by the I/O CH RDY in a way similar to the 8284 AEN1 input. Correct times for the I/O CH RDY must include system board delays of about 30 ns. Changes in the I/O CH RDY must occur about 90 ns before the falling edge of S clocks. The S clocks are a more symmetric, slightly delayed version of CLK.

The active DACK that accompanies every DMA cycle is a good signal to use to inactivate the I/O CH RDY. As Figure 16-6 shows, the DACK goes low in the middle of S2. To insert one wait state in a memory refresh cycle, we use the falling edge of S3 to reactivate I/O CH RDY. The system board already inserts one wait state in DMA cycles on channels one, two, and three. To insert an additional wait state, we delay one more clock before asserting I/O CH RDY. We can use the 74LS164 to count clocks as we did in the processor wait-state example.

DMA wait states can be necessary because either the I/O device or the memory is too slow. If the problem is a slow I/O device, DACk can be used to inactivate I/O CH

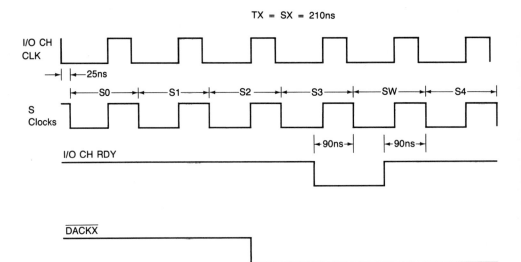

Figure 16-6   Timing for DMA Wait State

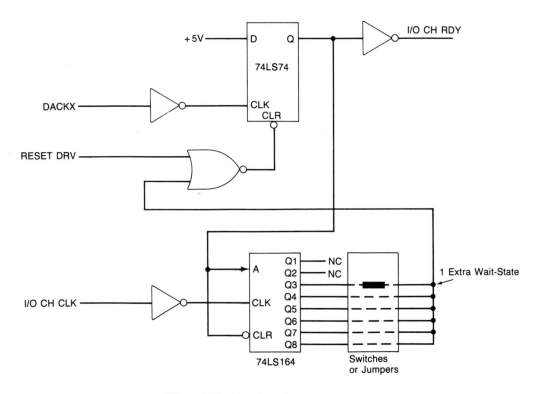

Figure 16-7   DMA Wait State, I/O Device Specific

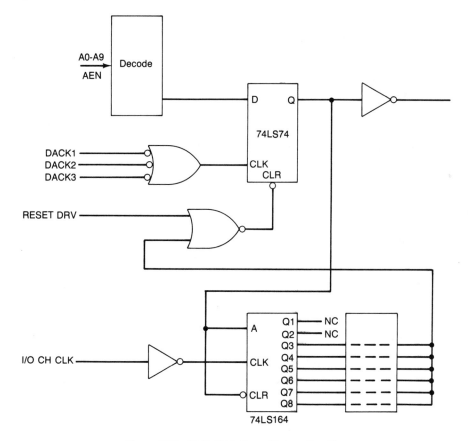

Figure 16-8 DMA Wait State, Memory Specific

RDY as shown in Figure 16-7. If the problem is slow memory, we must decode the memory and gate the decode signal with the three DACK lines as shown in Figure 16-8.

CHAPTER SUMMARY

Inserting wait states in either processor cycles or DMA cycles is straightforward once the timing requirements are stated. Basically, we need a signal to inactivate the I/O CH RDY line soon enough and circuitry to count a specific number of clock states before reasserting I/O CH RDY. For processor wait states, we can use the appropriate control line (MEMR, MEMW, IOR, IOW) to inactivate I/O CH RDY. For DMA wait states, DACK is a good choice. In both cases, a shift register is used to count processor clocks. Since DMA cycles involve both memory and I/O devices, it may be that one or the other (or both) require wait states.

Direct Memory Access (DMA)

It is often imperative to transfer data between an I/O device and memory faster than is possible with the 8088. To complete the transfer at the required rate, it may be necessary for the device to effect the transfer directly by taking over the address, data, and control buses. This type of data transfer is commonly referred to as *direct memory access* (DMA). Indeed, it is so common that special DMA chips have evolved that actually control the transfer rather than the device itself. Even so, projects like video frame buffers, which digitize and store data at video rates, may require the design of a special-purpose DMA controller.

The IBM PC uses the Intel 8237A programmable DMA controller to handle high-speed data transfers. Why is it needed? The diskette data rate is about 250,000 bytes/sec or 1 byte every 32 μs. The 8088 could possibly handle this data rate if it were dedicated to the task. However, it must respond to the timer and the keyboard interrupts, during which time it would lose diskette data. The IBM PC solution is to use the DMA controller to handle the diskette data transfer. The fixed-disk controller is even more of a problem, since it reads the fixed disk at a rate of 650,000 bytes/sec, too fast for the DMA controller. The fixed-disk adapter must interleave sectors during a disk access to slow the data rate below the maximum of the DMA controller.

What is the maximum DMA transfer rate? As we will see, the DMA controller is programmed in a "single transfer mode" to give the 8088 access to the bus after each byte is transferred and to allow a higher-priority DMA channel to interrupt one with a lower priority. This allows the 8088 to operate concurrently with the DMA transfer and ensures the occurrence of DMA-controlled memory refresh cycles. The interleaving of DMA and

206

8088 cycles lowers the DMA transfer rate form a maximum spec of 1.6M bytes/sec to 422K bytes/sec. This is still fast enough for the diskette but requires fixed disk interleaving. This chapter covers programming and interfacing to the DMA controller.

THE 8237A PROGRAMMABLE DMA CONTROLLER (IN THE IBM PC)

Our discussion of the 8237A will be centered around the configuration in the IBM PC. The 8237A has four independent, prioritized transfer channels. Their uses and priorities follow:

Channel	Priority	Use
0	0 (highest)	Memory refresh
1	1	Not used
2	2	Diskette
3	3	Fixed disk

THE DMA SEQUENCE

Each channel has a DMA request pin (DREQ0-3) and a DMA acknowledge pin (DACK0-3). Only I/O to memory and memory to I/O transfers are permitted by the IBM PC design. A typical DMA sequence takes place as follows (refer to Figure 17-1).

1. An I/O device signals a DMA request on one of the DRQX pins.

2. The 8237A prioritizes the request with other pending requests. (Assume for simplicity in the following that only one request is pending.)

3. The 8237A requests the bus from the 8088 by activating the hold request (HRQ) pin.

4. The system-board logic waits for the 8088 to enter an inactive clock period, disengages the processor from the buses, and activates the hold acknowledge (HOLDA) line to the 8237A.

5. The 8237A, having acquired the bus, activates the DACKX line to the device requesting service.

6. The device responds to the DACKX by inactivating the DRQX and preparing for the data transfer.

7. The 8237A activates the appropriate control signals to complete the transfer— MEMR and IOW for a read-transfer, MEMW and IOR for a write-transfer.

8. Finally, the HRQ is inactivated, allowing the processor to continue.

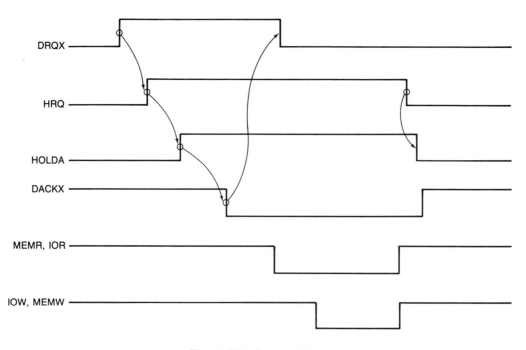

Figure 17-1 Typical DMA Sequence

This description is accurate in broad outline, but some steps need amplification. The timing diagram in Figure 17-2 shows the complete sequence. The symbols used in the diagram correspond to those in the IBM PC Technical Reference Manual. The DMA clock (S clocks) is the same frequency as the processor clock but is more symmetrical and is delayed slightly. The IBM PC designers elected to implement a novel design rather than use the 8088 RQ/GT (request-grant) pins. The activation of the HRQ DMA line enables a gate that scans the processor status lines, looking for an inactive state. An inactive state occurs immediately preceding T4 in every bus cycle.

Upon detecting an inactive state, the HOLDA is activated, and the address and data buffers and the control lines from the bus controller (8288) are tristated (AEN). Thus the 8088 is effectively disconnected from the bus, although it is not in a "hold" state. Furthermore, the RDY1 line on the 8284 clock chip is inactivated (DMA WAIT), so although the processor continues into its next bus cycle, wait states (TW) are inserted after T3. Meanwhile, the DMA controller begins the DMA cycle. The normal DMA cycle consists of five clock cycles, but the system board logic inserts one DMA wait state (RDY TO DMA), making it six. After the DMA cycle is complete, the 8237A inactivates the HRQ DMA line, resulting in the reenabling of the bus buffers and bus controller (AEN). Two more processor wait states are inserted to give the memory and I/O devices time to respond before the processor cycle is completed.

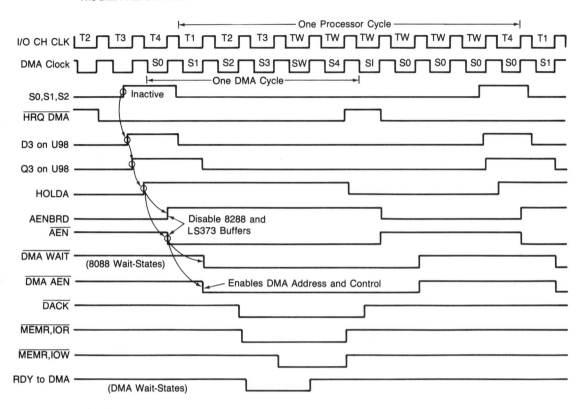

Figure 17-2   DMA Cycle Timing

THE DMA TRANSFER RATE

If the DMA request line (DREQX) is held active, or reactivated, the process will be repeated at the end of the current processor cycle. The processor cycle, consisting of four normal states and six wait states, is ten cycles long. Since one DMA cycle takes place concurrently with each ten-state processor cycle, the maximum DMA transfer rate is 479K bytes/sec. The actual rate will be slightly slower than this because channel 0, with the highest priority, will slip in a memory refresh cycle every 15.2 microseconds. Thus every seven DMA cycles will be followed by one refresh cycle. The total number of clocks to complete seven DMA cycles is $10 \times 7 + 9 = 79$, resulting in a maximum DMA rate of 422K bytes/sec.

Some type of buffering must be used to achieve the maximum DMA rate. For example, suppose we wish to operate an A/D converter at a conversion rate 422K bytes/sec. Without a buffer, the end-of-conversion signal from the A/D converter is used to request a DMA transfer to store the converted value. Occasionally, the request conflicts with a memory refresh request and is delayed. The converted value is read late, and the next conversion is started late. The time between conversions is irregular—most likely an unsatisfactory situation. The solution is to provide two temporary storage buffers. One buffer is filled by the A/D converter while the other is transferred to the main memory by the DMA controller. After the transfer, the role of the buffers is switched. The A/D conversions can take place with a precise frequency, while only the average frequency matters when the buffer is transferred.

As we mentioned in Chapter 2, it appears that the memory refresh time (15.2 μs) may be lengthened without dire consequences. Brave (or foolish) souls may reprogram the 8237A into the block transfer mode to achieve higher DMA rates. This must not be done for long periods, because the higher transfer rate is achieved by locking out the refresh cycles. With the refresh cycles locked out, the highest DMA rate is 793K bytes/sec. If you try this, you should experiment to see how long you can lock out the refresh cycles without crashing the system. Even so, you may be skating on thin ice.

DMA LATENCY

The DMA latency depends on several factors. If a high-priority transfer is in progress, it will be allowed to finish. This could make the latency very large. Even if the higher-priority channel is transferring bytes at the maximum rate, 64K bytes will take about 0.15 sec. If we assume no higher-priority transfers are in progress except memory refresh, then the maximum latency will occur if the request is made simultaneously with the refresh request. In this case, the latency will correspond to length of the refresh, cycle nine clock cycles, or 1.89 μs. If refresh cycles are avoided, the latency is determined by the number of clock cycles needed to reach processor cycle T4.

PROGRAMMING THE 8237A

The 8237A is programmed through 16 ports. Eight of the ports give access to the count and address registers for each of the channels, and the other eight permit more general commands.

Byte-Count and Address Registers

The 8237A data sheet uses the term "WORD COUNT" when referring to the count registers. In keeping with our general use of the term *byte* to refer to eight-bit quantities, we will use the term *byte* rather than *word*.

There is a "byte-count" port and an "address" port for each channel, as shown in Table 17-1. Notice that read and write operations produce different results. Each channel has two byte-count registers and two address registers. One byte-count register, CURRENT, contains the actual count as the transfer is taking place; the other, BASE, retains

TABLE 17-1 BYTE COUNT AND ADDRESS REGISTERS

Channel	Port #	Register	Operation
0	0	Base and current address	Write
		current address	Read
0	1	Base and current byte count	Write
		current byte count	Read
1	2	Base and current address	Write
		current address	Read
1	3	Base and current byte count	Write
		current byte count	Read
2	4	Base and current address	Write
		current address	Read
2	5	Base and current byte count	Write
		current byte count	Read
3	6	Base and current address	Write
		current address	Read
3	7	Base and current byte count	Write
		current byte count	Read

the initial count for autoinitializing a new transfer cycle. The BASE and CURRENT address registers are defined in a similar way. The number of bytes transferred during a DMA operation is always one more than the value programmed into the count registers.

As Table 17-1 shows, writing to the byte-count register really writes to both the BASE and CURRENT byte-count registers, while reading the byte-count register reads only the CURRENT byte-count. There is no way to read the BASE values.

To make matters more complicated, each byte-count and address register is 16 bits, or two bytes, wide. How do we read or write two bytes at an eight-bit port? In succession, of course. To program an address register, we write two bytes to the same port, the low byte followed by the high byte. An internal byte-pointer flip-flop is used to address the high and low bytes of the internal 16-bit registers. The byte-pointer flip-flop is initialized (pointing to the low byte) by writing to port 0CH, after which it is toggled on every read or write. This short code section shows how to initialize the channel one byte-count and address registers.

```
    OUT     0CH,AL              ; CLEAR BYTE-POINTER FF
    MOV     AL,LOW_ADDRESS
    OUT     02H,AL
    MOV     AL,HIGH_ADDRESS
    OUT     02H,AL
    MOV     AL,LOW_COUNT
    OUT     03H,AL
    MOV     AL,HIGH_COUNT
    OUT     03H,AL
```

Once the byte-pointer flip-flop is in a known state, we can ignore it if we always read or write in pairs.

Software Commands

The software commands permit initialization and control via access to several additional internal registers. Table 17-2 lists the software commands. The 8237A has many features and modes that aren't applicable to the IBM PC—for example, memory-to-memory transfer. We will limit the discussion of commands to the operation of the 8237A in the IBM PC environment.

COMMAND REGISTER

The command register determines several features—memory-to-memory disable, fixed priority, sense of DACK and DREQ signals, among others—that should not be changed if the system is to function correctly. For this reason, we will not discuss the specific details of the command register in the IBM PC. It is programmed with a zero byte.

MODE REGISTER

The mode register (Figure 17-3(a)) is one of the most important registers for our purposes. It allows us to specify details of the DMA transfer. The 0 and 1 in bits B7 and B6 select the single-byte transfer mode. This mode permits the 8088 and higher-priority channels access to the bus during the transfer. The HRQ line is released following each byte of the transfer. For a discussion of other uses of the 8237A, see the Intel data sheet.

The following code section illustrates how to program channel one for a read operation, going from low to high in memory, autoinitializing for the next DMA transfer.

```
MOV     AL, 01011001B
OUT     0BH, AL
```

TABLE 17-2   SOFTWARE COMMANDS

Port #	Write operation
8	Write to command register
9	Write to request register
10	Write a single mask register bit
11	Write to mode register
12	Clear byte-pointer flip-flop
13	Master clear
14	Clear mask register
15	Write all mask register bits
	Read operation
8	Read status register
13	Read temporary register

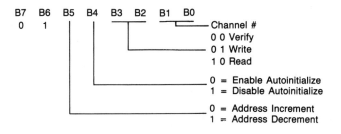

Figure 17-3a   8237A Mode Register-Port 11

Remember that a read-transfer moves data from memory to an I/O device and a write-transfer moves data from an I/O device to memory.

MASK REGISTER

The mask register (Figure 17-3(b)) contains one mask bit for each of the four channels. Three commands permit access to the mask register: command 14 clears all the mask bits, command 15 sets or clears mask bits according to the operand, and command 10 permits setting and resetting selected bits. Note that there is no way to read the mask register. The following code will unmask channel one.

```
MOV        AL, 00000001B      ; SELECT CHANNEL ONE, CLEAR
OUT        10, AL             ; USING COMMAND 10
```

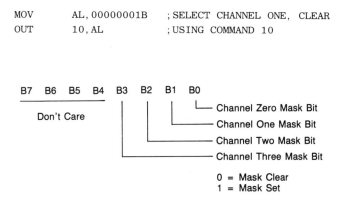

Command 14 — Any Output to Port 14 Clears All Mask Bits

Command 15 — Bits 0-3 of the Output are Transferred to the Mask Register.

Command 10 — Bits 0-1 Select a Mask Bit and Bit 2 Contains the Value to be Written.

Figure 17-3b   Mask Register and Associated Commands

STATUS REGISTER

The status register (Figure 17-3(c)) indicates which channels have a pending request and which have reached terminal count (TC). The bits showing TC are reset when the status register is read. We can use the status register to determine when a DMA transfer is complete. Just poll the status register, as shown here for channel one.

```
L1:     IN      AL, 08H       ; GET STATUS
        TEST    AL, 00000010B ; CHECK BIT FOR CHANNEL ONE
        JZ      L1            ; KEEP CHECKING
```

It is interesting to note that although the diskette uses an interrupt to signal the end of the DMA transfer, the interrupt routine simply sets a "done-flag" and returns. The main DISKETTE_IO routine merely loops, looking at the "done-flag." We can surmise that there must be another reason for the interrupt. If not, the loop could simply look at the status register.

OTHER 8237A REGISTERS

Two other registers, the REQUEST REGISTER and the TEMPORARY REGISTER, are used in 8237A modes that the IBM PC design makes inaccessible.

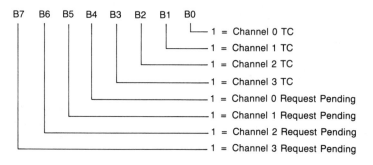

Figure 17-3c   Status Register

PAGE REGISTERS

The 16-bit address and byte-count registers indicate that the 8237A was designed for 16-bit (64K-byte) systems. Since the IBM PC has a 20-bit address bus, a scheme has to be invented to give the DMA chip full access to the 1M-byte memory.

The memory space is divided into 16 64K-byte "pages." The system board contains a four-bit page register for each of the three channels—1, 2, and 3. (The refresh channel needs no page register, because all memory chips are refreshed simultaneously.) The page register defines the page involved in the DMA transfer. The page registers are programmed by writing to the following ports (only bits 0–3 are significant).

    PORT 83H   CHANNEL 1
    PORT 81H   CHANNEL 2, DISKETTE
    PORT 82H   CHANNEL 3, FIXED DISK

Transfers that cross page boundaries must be accompanied by a change in the page register. This means that the transfer must be broken into two parts, with the change of the page register occurring between them. This presents a programming exercise, for the point of the page change must be computed before the transfer takes place. If we assume the transfer goes from low- to high-memory addresses, then if the sum of the base address and the base count is greater than 10000H, the transfer must take place in two parts. (Remember that the actual number of transfers is one greater than the value in the base count register.) In terms of the original base address and base count, the base count for the two transfers is this:

$$\text{BASE COUNT 1} = BC1 = 0FFFFH - \text{original base address}$$
$$\text{BASE COUNT 2} = BC2 = \text{original base count} - BC1 - 1$$

HARDWARE REQUIREMENTS

Figure 17-4 is a simplified timing diagram of the DMA cycle showing only the signals required for the hardware interface. The I/O device must raise the DREQ line and hold it high until an acknowledge is indicated by the corresponding DACK going low. The IOR or IOW signals are active (low) during the DMA cycle and can be used to strobe data onto or off the data bus. Note that the MEMR and IOR signals are low for approximately three clocks (S3, SW, S4), whereas the MEMW and IOW signals are low for only two (SW, S4). The time for two clocks is still about 420 ns, plenty for most chips, but some may require that you add a wait state.

The only address present during the DMA transfer is the address of the memory location. The I/O device is addressed (selected) only by the DACK signal. Because every DMA transfer is preceded by a DREQ, the I/O device that requested the transfer will be looking for the DACK.

The DMA Write Transfer

Figure 17-5 illustrates a circuit to interface an I/O device to DMA channel one for a write transfer. The DREQ requests the transfer and at the same time latches the device data into the 74LS374. The DACK and IOR together enable the data onto the data bus and tell the device to reset the DREQ. The address and MEMW (not shown) strobe the data into the correct memory location.

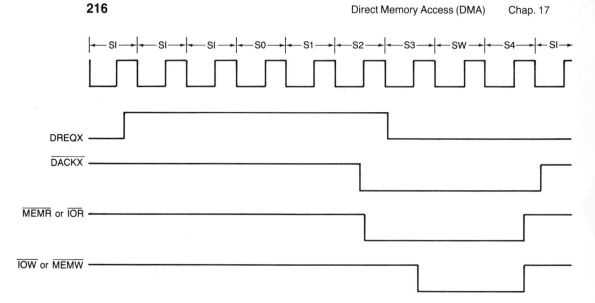

Figure 17-4 DMA Interface Signals

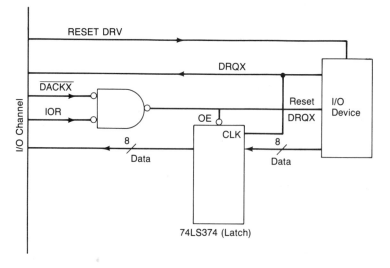

Figure 17-5 DMA Write Transfer

The DMA Read Transfer

The read transfer in Figure 17-6 is similar to the write transfer. The DREQ signals the 8237A. The DACK resets DREQ, and the rising edge of IOW is used to latch the data for the I/O device.

Terminal Count—T/C

Terminal count (T/C) is an active high pulse indicating that one of the DMA channels has reached "terminal count"; that is, its current byte-count register has rolled over to 0FFFFh. T/C can be used to inhibit DMA requests from an I/O device when the required number of transfers has been made. Since there is only one T/C line, it must be gated with the appropriate DACK line to be sure the correct channel has reached terminal count.

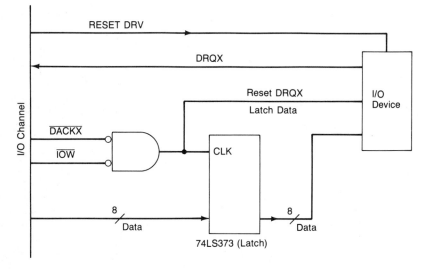

Figure 17-6 DMA Read Cycle

A DMA EXAMPLE—AN A/D CONVERTER

Some microprocessor-compatible chips can be easily interfaced to the 8237A. Figure 17-7 shows an interface to the National ADC804 Analogue to Digital converter. The end-of-conversion signal is used to request the DMA transfer. The DACK signal is connected to CS, and IOR is connected to both RD and WR. The very simple DMA cycle follows:

1. The end-of-conversion signals a DREQ.
2. The request is granted and DACK selects the chip.
3. IOR goes low, strobing the data onto the data bus.
4. IOR also pulls WR low, signaling the beginning of the next conversion.

Steps 1-4 are repeated until terminal count is reached. The only trick is to get the process started. All that is needed is a write cycle to the A/D converter port. (There must be an address decoder not shown that selects the A/D port.)

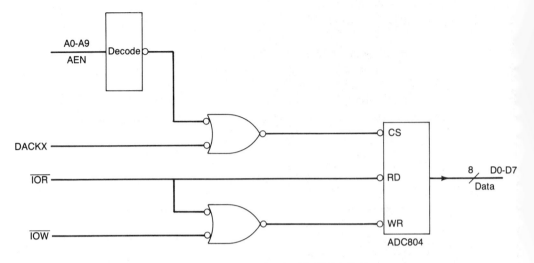

Figure 17-7 DMA Interface for the ADC804 A/D Converter

Example 17-1   Program for the A/D Converter

The following code illustrates how to program channel one of the 8237A to perform a DMA transfer from the A/D converter. We have included the arithmetic necessary to break the transfer into two parts to cross a page boundary. We will transfer 32K bytes (8000H).

```
; SEVERAL EQUATES TO MAKE THE PROGRAM MORE READABLE.

T_COUNT             EQU      8000H      ; NUMBER OF BYTES TO TRANSFER

CH1_ADDRESS         EQU      2          ; 8237A REGISTERS
CH1_COUNT           EQU      3
STATUS              EQU      8
SINGLE_MASK         EQU      10
MODE                EQU      11
FLIP_FLOP           EQU      12

CH1_MODE_VALUE      EQU      01000101B   ; ADDRESS INCREMENT
                                        ; NO AUTOINITIALIZE
                                        ; WRITE TRANSFER
CLR_MASK            EQU      00000001B   ; CHANNEL 1, CLEAR MASK
SET_MASK            EQU      00000101B   ; CHANNEL 1, SET MASK
AD_PORT             EQU      300H        ; A/D PORT NUMBER
STATUS_VALUE        EQU      00000010B   ; CHANNEL 1, TC

DATA      SEGMENT

BUFFER    DB       65536    DUP(5555h)   ; 64K BYTES
```

```
DATA        ENDS

CODE        SEGMENT
            ASSUME   CS: CODE, DS: DATA

DMA_TRANSFER     PROC     NEAR
; CX = BYTE COUNT, BX = PAGE REGISTER, AX = BASE ADDRESS
            OUT      FLIP_FLOP, AL    ; CLEAR BYTE POINTER FF

; PROGRAM ADDRESS, COUNT, AND PAGE REGISTERS

            OUT      CH1_ADDRESS, AL   ; OUTPUT LOW ADDRESS
            XCHG     AH, AL
            OUT      CH1_ADDRESS, AL   ; OUTPUT HIGH ADDRESS
            MOV      AX, CX
            OUT      CH1_COUNT, AL     ; OUTPUT LOW COUNT
            XCHG     AH, AL
            OUT      CH1_COUNT, AL     ; OUTPUT HIGH COUNT
            MOV      AX, BX
            OUT      83H, AL           ; OUTPUT PAGE REG

; PROGRAM THE MODE VALUE AND UNMASK CHANNEL ONE

            MOV      AL, CH1_MODE_VALUE
            OUT      MODE, AL          ; PROGRAM MODE VALUE
            MOV      AL, CLR_MASK
            OUT      SINGLE_MASK, AL   ; CLEAR MASK BIT

; READ STATUS UNTIL DONE

DMA1:       IN       AL, STATUS
            TEST     AL, STATUS_VALUE
            JZ       DMA1                      ; KEEP TESTING

; DONE, NOW MASK CHANNEL ONE AND RETURN

            MOV      AL, SET_MASK
            OUT      SINGLE_MASK, AL    ; SET MASK BIT
            RET
DMA_TRANSFER     ENDP

START:      MOV      AX, DATA
            MOV      DS, AX            ; INIT DS
            MOV      DX, AD_PORT       ; START A/D CONVERTER
            OUT      DX, AL            ; ANY WRITE WILL DO

; CONVERT THE BUFFER ADDRESS TO THE 20 BIT FORMAT
; FIRST SHIFT THE SEGMENT LEFT 4 TIMES
```

```
           MOV     AX, DS              ; AX  =  SEGMENT
           XOR     BX, BX              ; CLEAR  BX
           MOV     CX, 4
ST1:       SAL     AX, 1               ; SHIFT  ONCE
           RCL     BX, 1               ; ROTATE  CARRY  INTO  BX
           LOOP    ST1

; BX: AX CONTAINS THE 20 BIT SEGMENT ADDRESS

           ADD     AX, OFFSET BUFFER      ; ADD  THE  OFFSET
           ADC     BX, 0                  ; INCLUDE  THE  CARRY
           PUSH    BX                     ; SAVE  PAGE  VALUE

; NOW BX HAS THE UPPER FOUR BITS: I.E. , THE PAGE REGISTER
; VALUE AND AX HAS THE BASE ADDRESS VALUE.
; CHECK TO SEE IF A PAGE BOUNDARY WILL BE CROSSED.
           PUSH    AX                  ; SAVE  BASE  ADDRESS
           ADD     AX, T_COUNT-1       ; ADD  BASE  COUNT
           JNC     ONE_TRANSFER        ; CARRY=1  MEANS  TWO
           POP     AX                  ; TWO  TRANSFERS,  GET  BASE
           MOV     CX, 0FFFFH
           SUB     CX, AX              ; GET  BASE  COUNT  FOR
                                       ; FIRST  TRANSFER
           PUSH    CX                  ; SAVE  BC1
           CALL    DMA_TRANSFER        ; DO  FIRST  PART
           POP     BX                  ; GET  BC1  AGAIN
           MOV     CX, T_COUNT-2
           SUB     CX, BX              ; CX=  BC2
           POP     BX                  ; GET  FIRST  PAGE  VALUE
           INC     BX                  ; POINT  TO  NEXT  PAGE
           XOR     AX, AX              ; BASE  ADDRESS  =  0000H
           CALL    DMA_TRANSFER        ; DO  SECOND  PART
           JMP     EXIT

ONE_TRANSFER:  POP     AX             ; GET  BASE  ADDRESS
           POP     BX                  ; GET  PAGE  VALUE
           MOV     CX, T_COUNT-1       ; SET  COUNT
           CALL    DMA_TRANSFER        ; DO  THE  TRANSFER

EXIT:      ; HERE  WE  COULD  PUT  CODE  TO  ANALYZE  OR  SAVE  THE  DATA
           ; BUT  WE  WILL  JUST  EXIT
           MOV     AH, 4CH
           INT     21H

CODE       ENDS
           END     START
```

MULTIPLEXING A DMA CHANNEL

DMA intensive applications may require that several I/O devices use the same DMA channel. Since only one device at a time may access a DMA channel, some provision must be made for enabling a particular I/O device while disabling the others. The easiest solution is to use a digital output port so the I/O devices are software-selectable. It is also likely that we must reprogram the 8237A DMA channel in question each time we select a new I/O device. Figure 17-8 presents one solution to the multiplexing problem. To change devices, we enable the selected device (providing access to DREQ and DACK) and reprogram the DMA channel corresponding to the device.

Although we have concentrated on DMA channel one in the examples, channel two can be used by temporarily disabling the DREQ signal from the diskette adapter. Writing 04H to port 3F2H will disable the DREQ (and interrupts) from the diskette adapter. BIOS will reenable them for us during the next diskette transfer.

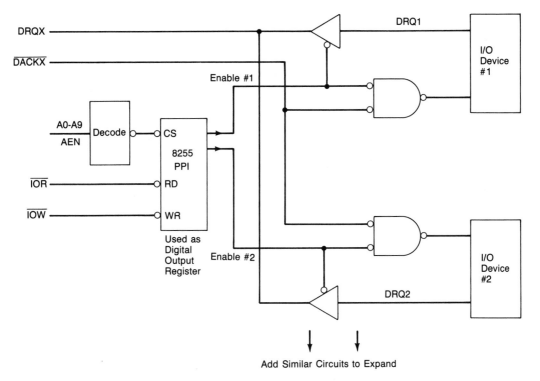

Figure 17-8   Expandable DMA Multiplex Circuit

CHAPTER SUMMARY

We have examined the configuration of the Intel 8237A in the IBM PC, concentrating on the features available in the I/O channel. Of the four 8237A DMA channels, three are available in the I/O channel via the DREQ1-3 and DACK1-3 lines. The three channels permit only I/O-memory transfers, not memory-memory or I/O-I/O transfers. The 8237A is programmed in the single transfer mode to allow the higher-priority memory refresh cycles to occur. The maximum transfer rate per channel is around 422K bytes/sec, if we assume that the only higher-priority channel currently active is the memory refresh channel. The hardware interfacing requirements are straightforward: Raise DREQ and hold it high until DACK goes active, then use IOR or IOW as necessary. T/C can be used to indicate the end of a cycle.

Understanding
and Interfacing
to the Interrupt System

This chapter presents a full description of the Intel 8088 interrupt system, focusing on the IBM PC implementation. We will study the 8259A programmable interrupt controller (PIC) to see how to use the system PIC and how to put additional PICs in the I/O Channel.

THE 8088 INTERRUPT STRUCTURE

The 8088 can field up to 256 different types of interrupts, each specified by an interrupt type number ranging from 0 to 255. An interrupt vector table, containing up to 256 *interrupt vectors,* is used by the 8088 to find the location of each specific interrupt service routine (ISR). Each interrupt vector is a double-word pointer containing the offset and segment address of the associated ISR. Figure 18-1 illustrates the vector table. The table begins at address 0000:0000 and is 1K byte in length (256 vectors, four bytes per vector). Note the order of the offset and segment values. A useful rule to remember is that Intel processors always store the least significant part of multibyte data in the low memory address, that is, least = low.

When an interrupt occurs, the current CS, IP, and the flag word are pushed onto the stack (in that order). IP and CS are then loaded from the interrupt vector table, and the interrupt enable flag (IF) and the trap-single step-flag (TF) are cleared. Thus the ISR is entered with interrupts and single-step disabled. External interrupts can be reenabled during the ISR with the STI (set interrupt enable flag) instruction. The ISR must not change any registers. If it does, the interrupted program will most likely produce errors. At the end of the ISR, the IRET instruction restores the flag word, IP, and CS from the stack.

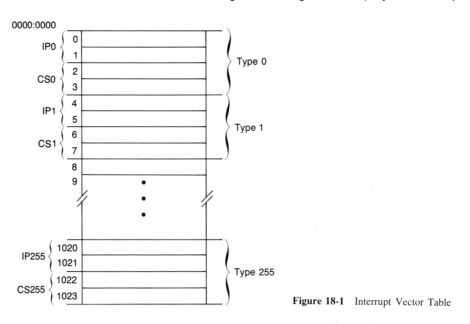

Figure 18-1   Interrupt Vector Table

Execution, therefore, begins at the instruction that was about to be executed before the interrupt occurred.

EXTERNAL INTERRUPTS

The 8088 has two pins that can be used to signal an interrupt. The NMI (nonmaskable interrupt) is positive-edge-triggered and is normally used to signal "catastrophic" events like power failure. Because the type number of NMI is fixed (type 2), NMI doesn't execute interrupt-acknowledge cycles. The IBM PC uses NMI to respond to three different interrupt sources—system board parity error, I/O CH CK, and an 8087 interrupt. The NMI interrupt is externally masked at power-on to prevent interrupts during memory initialization. NMI is enabled by writing 80H to port A0H, disabled by clearing port A0H. The NMI interrupt service routine must determine which of the three sources generated the interrupt and branch to the appropriate program. This check is made at port 62, where bit 6 is set by I/O CH CK and bit 7 is set by a system-board parity error. The NMI ISR must be modified in systems using the 8087 because the current ISR doesn't check for an 8087 interrupt.

The other external interrupt pin is INTR, a high-level triggered interrupt. This interrupt can be masked by clearing IF (CLI instruction) and enabled by setting IF (STI instruction). Interrupts are not latched on INTR, so an interrupt can be missed if a device raises and lowers INTR during the time interrupts are masked. The IBM PC design follows the standard Intel recommendation to connect INTR to an 8259A PIC. Understanding the interrupt sequence on INTR entails understanding the PIC.

Before studying the PIC, we take a brief look at the events taking place when the PIC activates INTR. If INTR is not masked, the processor responds to the interrupt after finishing the currently executing instruction. The processor sends two interrupt-acknowledge pulses (INTA) to the 8259A, which responds by putting an interrupt-type number on the data bus. The processor reads the interrupt-type number, multiplies it by four to get the address of the interrupt vector, and finally executes the corresponding ISR.

INTERNAL INTERRUPTS

Several internal interrupt sources exist. The INT instruction generates an interrupt immediately after its execution. The INT instruction is not maskable; if the instruction executes, the interrupt occurs. Any of the 256 different interrupt types can be executed with INT. INT 3 is unique in that it is a one-byte instruction, whereas all the others are two bytes. For this reason, it is ideally suited for setting software breakpoints. Breakpoints can be set by replacing the first byte of a target instruction by 0CCH, the INT 3 instruction. When a program reaches such a breakpoint, an INT 3 instruction is executed, transferring control to a debugger.

The other internal interrupts are rather special:

DIVIDE-BY-ZERO, interrupt type 0, is executed automatically whenever the result of a DIV or IDIV instruction is too large.

SINGLE-STEP, interrupt type 1, is executed following every instruction if the trap flag (TF) is enabled. The only way to set the trap flag is to push the flags onto the stack, set it, then pop the stack back to the flags. PUSHF and POPF push and pop the flag word.

INTERRUPT-ON-OVERFLOW, interrupt type 4, is executed by the INTO instruction if the overflow flag (OF) is set. This is typically used after an arithmetic instruction that operates on the overflow flag.

All internal interrupts have a higher priority than any external interrupt. For example, if an external interrupt occurs during a DIV instruction, a divide error will cause DIVIDE-BY-ZERO to be processed before the external interrupt. This fact is important in the calculation of interrupt latency (the maximum response time to an external interrupt).

THE 8259A PROGRAMMABLE INTERRUPT CONTROLLER (PIC)

The advantage to using a PIC lies in the PIC's ability to field and prioritize hardware interrupt requests before they are passed to the system's main microprocessor. The 8088 is saved the task of determining the source and priority of the interrupting device. As we will see, we may add a PIC to the I/O channel to save ourselves the trouble of designing interrupt hardware and software.

The 8259A PIC is a very flexible chip, designed by Intel to be used with their 8080 and 8085 processors as well as with the 8086 and 8088 processors. We will discuss only those features of the 8259A that are relevant to the IBM PC (the 8088 features). Intel has written a very thorough application note (AP-59, USING THE 8259A PRO-GRAMMABLE INTERRUPT CONTROLLER) to which the reader may refer for points we have not covered.

8259A OPERATION

The simplified block diagram of the 8259A in Figure 18-2 shows the four blocks needed to explain basic 8259A interrupt processing. (*Note:* We will discuss operational command words, OCWs, later in the chapter.)

IRR—Interrupt Request Register.   This eight-bit register contains one bit corresponding to each of the interrupt request pins, IR0–IR7. A set bit indicates a request on the corresponding pin. This register can be read by an OCW3.

IMR—Interrupt Mask Register.   This eight-bit register contains one bit corresponding to each of the eight interrupt levels. A set bit masks the corresponding level. This register can be read or written via OCW1, providing the ability for selective masking of interrupt levels. Masking a level doesn't remove a pending request. Unmasking a pending request will allow it to be serviced.

PR—Priority Resolver.   The PR determines whether or not an interrupt request has a high enough priority to interrupt an executing interrupt service routine. There are several different priority schemes that are software-configurable.

ISR—In-Service Register.   This eight-bit register contains one bit for each interrupt level. The bit is set to indicate that the corresponding interrupt level is in service. The bits in this register are not reset by the IRET instruction. They must be reset in the interrupt service routine by using an OCW2. This register can be read via an OCW3.

The following sequence of events illustrates how an interrupt request is handled:

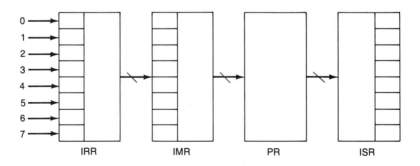

Figure 18-2   8259A Operation

1. Assume that an interrupt request is signaled on IR4.

2. If the request is not masked (IMR4 = 0), it is passed to the PR.

3. The PR decides if the priority is high enough to honor the request. If the priority is high enough, the 8259A raises the INTR line on the 8088.

4. If the 8088 interrupts have been enabled (IF = 1), the 8088 responds with an interrupt acknowledge cycle (two pulses on INTA). During the interrupt-acknowledge cycle, the state of the IRR register is frozen and the PR determines the highest level in the IRR. (IR4 will be the highest unless a higher request came in during the time between INT and INTA.) The interrupt-type number corresponding to IR4 is put on the data bus, and ISR4 is set.

5. The 8088 obtains the type number from the data bus and vectors to the interrupt service routine.

6. Near the end of the interrupt service routine, the programmer must issue an end-of-interrupt (EOI) command via OCW2 to reset bit ISR4. Until this is done, further interrupts on level four will not be accepted.

PROGRAMMING THE 8259A

The programming of the 8259A can be broken into two distinct parts, initialization and operation. Initialization programming determines the basic operating mode of the 8259A, and operation programming allows specific features to be examined and changed during the operation.

Initialization Command Words

We initialize an 8259A by sending it from two to four initialization command words (ICWs). BIOS initializes the system's 8259A in the IBM PC. For this reason, the reader interested in using one of the IRQ2–IRQ7 lines in the I/O channel, but not interested in adding an 8259A to the I/O channel, may skip to the section on operational command words.

Figure 18-3 illustrates the initialization sequence. Once the 8259A is initialized, subsequent changes to ICWs require going through the entire sequence again. Notice that ICW1 and ICW2 are always required; ICW3 and ICW4, only if specified in ICW1. The 8259A requires two port addresses (the 8259A has only one A0 address pin). All ICWs and OCWs are addressed through these two ports. After we begin the initialization sequence, by sending ICW1 to the even port, we must complete it before an OCW can be sent.

Figure 18-4 illustrates the formats for ICW1, ICW2, and ICW4. ICW3 is not shown because it is used only when the 8259A is in the "cascade" mode. The cascade mode is a feature of the 8259A that allows a "slave" 8259A to be connected to each IR pin of a "master" 8259A, expanding the interrupt system to up to 64 levels of interrupts. The

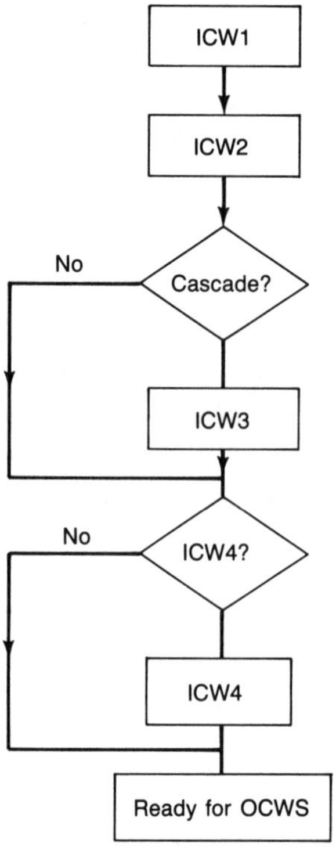

Figure 18-3 Initializing the 8259A

cascade feature cannot be implemented on the IBM PC because the required cascade lines, CAS0-2, and the INT-INTA lines do not exist on the I/O channel.

ICW1

The Xs in Figure 18-4 indicate "don't care" bits when the 8259A is used in the 8088 system with no cascading. We are left with only two decisions to make in ICW1. Bit B3 determines whether the 8259A responds in a level-triggered or edge-triggered mode. In both cases, the interrupt source must bring the IRX pin high and hold it high until the 8088 executes the INTA cycle. The main difference is in the requirement to generate another interrupt. In the level-triggered mode, holding the IRX pin high will cause a second interrupt as soon as the corresponding ISR bit is reset. In the edge-triggered mode, the IRX pin must be brought low before a second interrupt can be generated. The other choice to be made is whether or not an ICW4 is needed. Electing to ignore ICW4 is equivalent to programming a zero byte into ICW4.

In the IBM PC, ICW1 is programmed with the value 00010011B, implying the edge-triggered mode, with ICW4 required. When we discuss putting an 8259A in the I/O channel, we will see that an ICW4 is not needed.

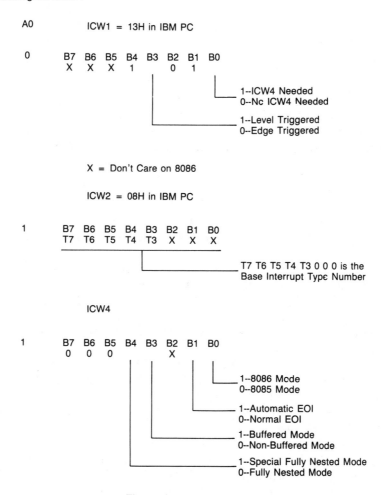

Figure 18-4   ICW1, ICW2, ICW4

ICW2

The five bits B7–B3 of ICW2 (Figure 18-4), determine the most significant five bits, T7–T3, of the eight possible interrupt-type numbers supplied to the 8088 during an INTA cycle. Bits T2–T0 of the type number are determined by the requesting level, as follows:

```
IR0   T7 T6 T5 T4 T3 0 0 0
IR1   T7 T6 T5 T4 T3 0 0 1
IR2   T7 T6 T5 T4 T3 0 1 0
IR3   T7 T6 T5 T4 T3 0 1 1
```

IR4   T7 T6 T5 T4 T3 1 0 0
IR5   T7 T6 T5 T4 T3 1 0 1
IR6   T7 T6 T5 T4 T3 1 1 0
IR7   T7 T6 T5 T4 T3 1 1 1

In the IBM PC, ICW2 is programmed with the value 8H (00001000B), which results in interrupt-type numbers 8–15. When we discuss putting an 8259A in the I/O channel, we will see that the value of ICW2 is irrelevant, although it must be programmed.

ICW4

Several of the choices in ICW4 (Figure 18-4) call for discussion. Bit B0 tells the 8259A which kind of interrupt-acknowledge cycle to expect from the processor, an 8085 type or an 8088 type.

Bit B1 allows us to choose the automatic end-of-interrupt (AEOI) feature, eliminating the need for the interrupt service routine to send an EOI. When in AEOI mode, the appropriate ISR bit is reset at the end of the INTA cycle, even before the interrupt routine is executing. This may not be desirable, because the priority structure of the interrupt system will no longer function correctly. The PR will not be aware of the interrupt levels in service.

In the buffered mode (bit B3), the SP/EN pin will go low whenever the 8259A's data bus output is enabled. Thus SP/EN can be used to selectively enable and disable buffers to give the 8259A exclusive access to the data bus during an INTA cycle. The buffered mode is used in the IBM PC. SP/EN is used to disable the 74LS245 buffer during the INTA cycle.

Although the main use of the special fully nested mode (bit 4) is with a cascaded 8259A system, it may be useful when an 8259A is added to the I/O channel. To explain the special fully nested mode, we need to consider for a moment the 8259A cascade system. In the cascade mode, a "slave" 8259A feeds eight interrupt sources to one IR pin on the "master" 8259A. Suppose a low-priority IR pin on the slave requests and receives service. During the execution of the interrupt service routine, any higher-priority requests on the slave will be ignored when the request is passed to the master, because the ISR bit (for the level connected to the slave) will be set and no further interrupts can be accepted until the ISR bit is reset. However, the special fully nested mode restores the full priority system by allowing multiple interrupts at a given level. Another way of saying this is that the priority rule changes as follows:

Normal fully nested mode.   An incoming request can cause an interrupt if it is at a priority level higher than requests in service.

Special fully nested mode.   An incoming request can cause an interrupt if it is at a priority level equal to or higher than requests in service.

In the IBM PC, ICW4 is programmed with the value 9H (00001001B), resulting in the 8088 mode (8088-type interrupt-acknowledge cycles)

a normal EOI

the buffered mode

the normal fully nested mode

The system's 8259A is located at ports 20H and 21H. The initialization code for the system's 8259A is shown as an example of the simplicity of the initialization procedure once all the hard work is done.

```
MOV   AL, 13H
OUT   20H, AL        ; ICW1
MOV   AL, 08H
OUT   21H, AL        ; ICW2
MOV   AL, 09H
OUT   21H, AL        ; ICW4
```

Operational Command Words

Once the 8259A has been initialized, the operational command words (OCWs) allow us to further customize the priority features and to interrogate various registers.

OCW1   (ODD PORT ADDRESS)

OCW1 allows us to read from and write to the mask register. Setting a bit in the mask register keeps the interrupt request from reaching the PR. BIOS masks all unused interrupts, so you must unmask any level you wish to use in the I/O channel. As an example, the following code unmasks level three of the system's 8259A:

```
IN    AL, 21H           ; GET CURRENT MASK
AND   AL, 11110111B     ; CLEAR BIT3
OUT   21H, AL           ; SET NEW MASK
```

OCW2 (EVEN PORT ADDRESS)

OCW2 provides several ways to send EOI commands and to change the priority structure. When the 8259A is initialized, the priority structure is set to the default.

IR pin	Priority level
IR0	0 (highest)
IR1	1
IR2	2
IR3	3
IR4	4
IR5	5
IR6	6
IR7	7 (lowest)

Each level has a different priority, the highest priority being zero. The priority levels of the IR pins can be "rotated" by specifying the level that is to have the lowest priority. The priority of the remaining levels is determined by their position in the cycle 0–7. For example by setting IR4 to the lowest level, IR4 moves to the bottom, with IR7, IR6, and IR5 cycling back to the top. The new priority structure is as follows:

IR pin	Priority level
IR5	0 (highest)
IR6	1
IR7	2
IR0	3
IR1	4
IR2	5
IR3	6
IR4	7 (lowest)

Your application will dictate the need for priority rotation. In the IBM PC, the priority levels are fixed at the default: The time-of-day interrupt is highest; printer interrupt, lowest. In an application that services several measuring instruments of equal importance, we may rotate the priorities to insure each instrument equal access to the 8088.

The OCW2 provides two ways of sending EOIs without changing the priority structure. The nonspecific EOI always resets the ISR bit of the highest level in service. The nonspecific EOI is sufficient in systems that don't rotate priority levels. The specific EOI resets the ISR of the level selected by bits B0–B2. The specific EOI is necessary when an interrupt service routine has changed the priority levels so that it is no longer the highest priority. The following code sends a nonspecific EOI to the system's 8259A.

```
MOV   AL, 20H       ; 20H = nonspecific EOI
OUT   20H, AL       ; OUTPUT OCW2
```

There are five commands that allow us to rotate the priority levels. The "set priority" command sets the level selected by bits B0–2 to the lowest priority, the others following in cyclic order. We will refer the reader to the Intel literature for discussions of the other rotate commands. Basically, they allow rotation of priority in conjunction with the EOI command.

OCW3 (EVEN PORT ADDRESS)

OCW3 allows us to read IRR and ISR. For example, to read ISR in the IBM PC we do the following:

```
MOV   AL, 00001011B   ; READ ISR ON NEXT RD
OUT   20H, AL         ; SEND OCW3
IN    AL, 20H         ; AL=ISR
```

OCW3 also contains the very important "poll" command. The poll command is provided for systems that don't use the interrupt/interrupt-acknowledge sequence via INT and INTA. This is important if we want to put an 8259A in the I/O channel, where there are no INT or INTA lines. An 8259A in the I/O channel can't provide an interrupt-type number to the 8088 in the same way that the system's 8259A does. We must poll the 8259A in the I/O channel to determine which is the highest level requesting service. The poll command is issued by setting bit B2 in OCW3. The next read from the 8259A is treated like an interrupt acknowledge, and the 8259A puts a byte on the data bus. The byte is not the type number, as one might expect, but is encoded as follows:

```
B7   B6   B5   B4   B3   B2   B1  B0
     X    X    X    X
     B2,  B1,  B0  Type number of highest level requesting service
B7  1  =  Interrupt request pending
    0  =  No interrupt request
```

The interested reader will find a discussion of the "special mask mode" in the Intel literature. This mode allows one to receive interrupts on all levels except the level in service.

INTERRUPT LATENCY

For many devices it is important that the interrupt be serviced promptly. Calculating the worst case interrupt latency involves several factors:

1. The execution time of higher-priority interrupt service routines. For example, the highest-priority INTR interrupt is the TIMER_INT, which takes 147 μs (if the TIMER_TICK interrupt is not being used).

2. The execution time of the longest instruction. The longest instruction is IDIV, using a maximum of 202 clock cycles (43 μs). String instructions are interruptable.

3. The actual interrupt processing time, once the interrupt has been recognized at the 8088. These times are as follows:

INTR	13 μs
NMI	11 μs
INT XX	11 μs
INTO	11 μs
Single step	11 μs

4. The time to save the contents of registers used by the interrupt service routine. The PUSH instruction takes 11 clocks for a register and ten clocks for a segment register. To save AX, BX, CX, DX, SI, DI, DS, and ES takes 86 clocks or 19 μs.

As an example, the shortest possible latency on INTR is 13 µs, if it is assumed that an instruction has just finished and no higher-priority interrupts are executing. The longest latency (if no higher-priority interrupts are executing) is 56 µs (43 µs + 13 µs). Even longer latencies can occur.

USING INTERRUPTS IN THE I/O CHANNEL

The IR2–IR7 pins of the system's 8259A are connected directly to the I/O channel, where they appear as IRQ2–IRQ7. The IBM PC Technical Reference Manual specifies the following uses for these interrupts:

IRQ2   Reserved

IRQ3   Asynchronous Communications (Secondary)
         SDLC Communications
         BSC (Secondary)

IRQ4   Asynchronous Communications (Primary)
         SDLC Communications
         BSC (Primary)

IRQ5   Fixed Disk

IRQ6   Diskette

IRQ7   Printer

Although it appears at first glance that all the IRQ lines are in use, most systems will have several free. IRQ2 is currently not in use although it may be reserved for a future IBM product. IRQ5 is free unless your system has a fixed disk. At any rate, if you wish to service I/O devices on an interrupt basis, you must configure your system so that at least one of the IRQ lines is free.

It should be mentioned in passing that it is possible to connect several interrupting sources to one IRQ line. Connect an inverter to the IRQ line and feed the inverter with open-collector outputs from the various sources. Some provision must be made in the hardware so that the interrupt service routine can determine which device or devices requested the interrupt. Without sophisticated hardware, the software must handle priority resolution. In a later section, we will discuss adding an 8259A to one of the IRQ lines, eliminating the need for special hardware or priority resolving software.

Here, we will restrict our discussion to the simpler problem of connecting just one interrupting source to an unused IRQ line. All that must be done to request an interrupt is for the device to raise the IRQ line and hold it high until the interrupt is acknowledged. Since there is no INTA line in the I/O channel, the interrupt is acknowledged by the corresponding interrupt service routine. The system's 8259A is in the edge-triggered mode, so there is no timing requirement to be met in pulling the line low again. The Intel literature recommends leaving the line high and pulsing it low to request an interrupt.

To prepare the system for the interrupting device, the vector pointing to the interrupt service routine must be loaded into the interrupt vector table and the interrupt must be unmasked in the 8259A's mask register. The following code section indicates the correct procedure (for IRQ3, type 0BH):

```
;Assume that this section is in the CODE segment.

ISR         PROC      FAR

;SAVE REGISTERS USED IN ISR

;THIS IS WHERE THE BODY OF THE INTERRUPT SERVICE ROUTINE
;WOULD BE LOCATED.

             MOV       AL, 20H       ;BEFORE RETURNING
             OUT       20H, AL       ;ISSUE AN EOI

;RESTORE REGISTERS

             IRET                    ;INTERRUPT RETURN
ISR         ENDP

ISR_INITIALIZATION      PROC      NEAR
;DX AND AX ARE DESTROYED BY THIS PROC

             PUSH      DS            ;SAVE DS
             PUSH      CS            ;TRANSFER CS TO DS FOR
             POP       DS            ;SET VECTOR FUNCTION CALL
             LEA       DX, ISR       ;DX=OFFSET OF ISR
             MOV       AL, 0BH       ;INTERRUPT TYPE NUMBER
             MOV       AH, 25H       ;SET VECTOR FUNCTION CALL
             INT       21H
             IN        AL, 21H       ;GET 8259A MASK REG
             AND       AL, 11110111  ;UNMASK LEVEL 3
             OUT       21H, AL       ;SET NEW MASK
             POP       DS
             RET

ISR_INITIALIZATION      ENDP
```

If we now assume that interrupts are not masked on the 8088 INTR pin, interrupt requests will be honored on IRQ3. The ISR routine should make some response to the hardware to provide an acknowledge.

Figure 18-5 shows the eight-bit A/D converter of Chapter 17 connected to IRQ3. The end-of-conversion signal from the A/D converter generates an interrupt request. Reading the A/D converter resets the end-of-conversion signal, and writing to it starts a new conversion. This circuit would require an initial write to the converter to get things

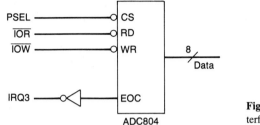

Figure 18-5 A/D-Converter Interrupt Interface

started, after which conversions and interrupts would take place at a speed determined by the A/D converter clock. The ISR could store the conversions in a buffer for later analysis or possibly perform some simple analysis in real time.

ADDING AN 8259A TO THE I/O CHANNEL

Because of the shortage of available IRQ lines, it may be desirable to expand one or more so that they each could handle several interrupt sources. An easy and inexpensive way to expand an IRQ line is to connect it to an 8259A. You can then take advantage of the masking and prioritizing features of the second 8259A. You need build no special hardware, and the hardware interface is straightforward, as shown in Figure 18-6. Figure 18-6 assumes that an address decoder has generated a PSEL signal as discussed in Chapter 15. Otherwise, the figure speaks for itself.

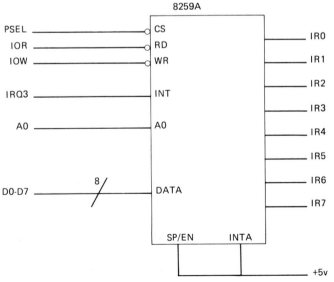

Figure 18-6 Adding an 8259A to IRQ3

As we discussed in the section on OCWs, there is no easy way to take advantage of the natural INT-INTA cycle (short of rewiring the system board), so the added 8259A must be polled. The interrupt service routine must use the poll command to determine the level of the highest priority interrupt request. The interrupt service routine must then jump to the appropriate service code. Remember, there is only one interrupt service routine performing up to eight different services. Since the 8259A treats the poll command as an interrupt acknowledge and sets the ISR bit, we must issue an EOI command to the second 8259A to reset the ISR bit.

The second 8259A can be initialized with two ICWs. Referring to Figure 18-4, we select a suitable trigger mode and "no ICW4 needed." ICW4 will be the same as if we had programmed it with zero, in particular

8085 mode

normal EOI

nonbuffered

fully nested mode

The fact that the 8259A is in the 8085 mode is irrelevant, because it will be operated in the polled mode. ICW2 must be programmed, but its value is again irrelevant because of the polled operation (the type number is not used). If you wish to make use of other features—for example, the special fully nested mode—you must program three ICWs. The following code shows the initialization sequence for the level-triggered mode.

```
MOV   DX, 300H          ; PORT NUMBER TO DX
MOV   AL, 12H           ; EDGE TRIGGERED, NO ICW4
OUT   DX, AL            ; SEND ICW1
INC   DX
OUT   DX, AL            ; SEND ICW2
MOV   AL, MASK          ; MASK UNUSED INTERRUPTS
OUT   DX, AL            ; SEND OCW1
```

Note that we have masked unused interrupts to prevent spurious interrupts from occurring. All interrupts are unmasked after the initialization sequence.

In order to allow high-priority requests to interrupt low-priority interrupt routines in service, some provision must be made to reset the appropriate ISR bit in the system's 8259A. One solution is to allow each individual service in the interrupt routine to issue an EOI command when it is appropriate to allow further interrupts. Other solutions will depend on the reader's creativity and experience.

Let's summarize the sequence of events beginning with an interrupt request at the second 8259A:

1. A request is made on one of the second 8259A IR lines.
2. If unmasked, with a high enough priority, the request is passed to the system's 8259A.

3. Again, if unmasked with a high enough priority, the request is passed to the 8088's INTR pin.

4. If IF = 1, the 8088 runs an interrupt-acknowledge cycle, obtains an interrupt-type number from the system's 8259A, and enters the interrupt service routine.

5. The interrupt service routine sends the poll command to the second 8259A to determine which level requested the service, then branches to the service code.

6. The service code can send an EOI command to the first 8259A, allowing further interrupts from the second 8259A. Interrupts must be enabled at the 8088 as usual by setting IF = 1.

7. At the completion of the service, an EOI must be sent to the second 8259A.

Example 18-1 Interrupt Service Routine for an Added 8259A

This example can be used as a template for an interrupt service routine servicing a second 8259A. Eight possible services are provided, corresponding to the eight IR lines on the second 8259A. Each service can reenable interrupts as shown, if appropriate. The main code section sets the interrupt vector, initializes the 8259A, unmasks the appropriate IRQ line (IRQ3 in the example), and terminates, leaving ISR resident.

```
STACK       SEGMENT STACK
            DW      80H        DUP(5555H)
STACK       ENDS


CODE        SEGMENT
            ASSUME  CS:CODE


ISR         PROC    FAR


SERVICE_TABLE   DW   SER0,SER1,SER2,SER3,SER4,SER5,SER6,SER7


;SER0 IS TYPICAL OF THE EIGHT SERVICES. ONLY SER0 WILL BE
;SHOWN TO KEEP THE EXAMPLE SHORT.
SER0:       MOV     AL,20H       ;SEND EOI TO PERMIT FURTHER
            OUT     20H,AL       ;INTERRUPTS FROM SECOND 8259A
            STI                  ;ENABLE PROCESSOR INTERRUPTS


;ACTUAL SERVICE PERFORMED HERE, CODE NOT SHOWN.


            JMP     ISR_EXIT     ;JUMP TO EXIT


SER1:       ----                 ;SIMILAR TO SER0

  .
                                 ;EIGHT SERVICE ROUTINES IN ALL
  .

  .
SER7:       ----
```

```
ISR_EXIT:
        MOV     DX, PORT_EVEN      ; GIVE EOI TO SECOND 8259A
        MOV     AL, 20H
        OUT     DX, AL
        POP     ES                 ; RESTORE REGISTERS
        POP     DS
        POP     DI
        POP     SI
        POP     DX
        POP     CX
        POP     BX
        POP     AX
        IRET                       ; RETURN

ISR_ENTRY:
        PUSH    AX                 ; SAVE REGISTERS
        PUSH    BX
        PUSH    CX
        PUSH    DX
        PUSH    SI
        PUSH    DI
        PUSH    DS
        PUSH    ES
        MOV     DX, PORT_EVEN      ; 8259A ADDRESS
        MOV     AL, 00001100B      ; SEND THE POLL COMMAND
        OUT     DX, AL
        IN      AL, DX             ; READ THE STATUS
        TEST    AL, 10000000B      ; VALID REQUEST?
        JNZ     ISR1               ; YES
        MOV     AL, 20H            ; OTHERWISE, SEND EOI
        OUT     20H, AL            ; TO MAIN 8259A
        JMP     ISR_EXIT           ; AND RETURN
ISR1:   AND     AL, 01111111B      ; CLEAR HIGH BIT
        SAL     AL, 1              ; DOUBLE AL TO USE AS INDEX
        XOR     AH, AH
        MOV     BX, AX             ; MOVE INDEX TO BX
        JMP     SERVICE_TABLE[BX]  ; INDIRECT JMP TO SERVICE
ISR     ENDP
; NOW, THE MAIN CODE SECTION THAT INSTALLS THE ISR, LEAVING
; IT RESIDENT.

START:  PUSH    CS
        POP     DS                 ; GET READY FOR SET VECTOR F.C.
        LEA     DX, ISR_ENTRY      ; DS: DX = INTERRUPT VECTOR
        MOV     AL, 0BH            ; ASSUME WE USE IRQ3
        MOV     AH, 25H
        INT     21H                ; SET VECTOR
```

```
; INITIALIZE THE SECOND 8259A, MASK UNUSED INTERRUPTS

        MOV     DX, PORT_EVEN   ; PORT NUMBER TO DX
        MOV     AL, 12H         ; EDGE TRIGGERED, NO ICW4
        OUT     DX, AL          ; SEND ICW1
        INC     DX
        OUT     DX, AL          ; SEND ICW2
        MOV     AL, MASK        ; MASK UNUSED INTERRUPTS
        OUT     DX, AL          ; SEND OCW1

; UNMASK IR3 ON FIRST 8259A

        IN      AL, 21H         ; GET CURRENT MASK
        AND     AL, 11110111B   ; CLEAR BIT3
        OUT     21H, AL         ; SET NEW MASK

; NOW, TERMINATE BUT STAY RESIDENT
        MOV     DX, OFFSET START   ; CONVERT OFFSET OF START
        MOV     CL, 4              ; TO PARAGRAPHS
        SAR     DX, CL
        ADD     DX, 11H            ; ROUND UP AND ADD PSP (10H)
        MOV     AX, 3100H          ; TERMINATE-STAY RESIDENT
        INT     21H

CODE    ENDS
        END     START
```

MORE ON 8259As

One could add a third level of 8259As by connecting them to the IR lines on the second level. The third level would be polled in a manner similar to the second level. You could continue to add levels indefinitely.

One could also simply use the 8259A in a noninterrupt fashion by leaving it unconnected to an IRQ line. This approach would require polling the 8259A on a periodic basis to service the devices. The masking and prioritizing features can be used, even though we aren't using it in an interrupt system.

CHAPTER SUMMARY

The 8088 supports 256 different types of interrupts, classified as internal and external. An interrupt vector table located at the beginning of memory contains a four-byte interrupt vector for each implemented interrupt. Internal interrupts have the highest priority and (except for the single-step interrupt) are not maskable. External interrupts consist of two types, nonmaskable (NMI) and maskable (INTR). The INTR interrupts are managed by an 8259A PIC. Six of the eight 8259A IR lines appear in the I/O channel, providing access to the interrupt system. We discussed using one of the available interrupts and adding a second 8259A to the interrupt system.

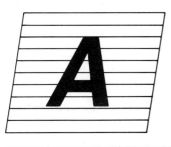

The Pedagogical Board

This appendix examines the hardware teaching aid used in the IBM PC interfacing class upon which this book is based. A discussion of this "pedagogical" hardware, it is hoped, will encourage you to try similar projects by showing you how relatively easy it is to assemble hardware to perform complex tasks. The pedagogical hardware was designed, wire-wrapped (by an inexperienced hand), and debugged in 16 hours.

Building your own circuit board can be a valuable experience. Should you, however, wish to do experiments without going to the trouble of creating hardware yourself, you can purchase the pedagogical board discussed here. See the book insert for details.

ELEMENTS OF THE PEDAGOGICAL BOARD

Figure A-1 shows the circuit for the hardware in block-diagram form. The board was designed to provide a wide variety of experiments using a small number of common interfacing chips. The following are the basic elements of the board:

- an address decoder
- an Intel 8255A Programmable Peripheral Interface
- an Intel 8253-5 Programmable Interval Timer
- a National Semiconductor ADC804 A/D converter
- an Intel 8259A Programmable Interrupt Controller

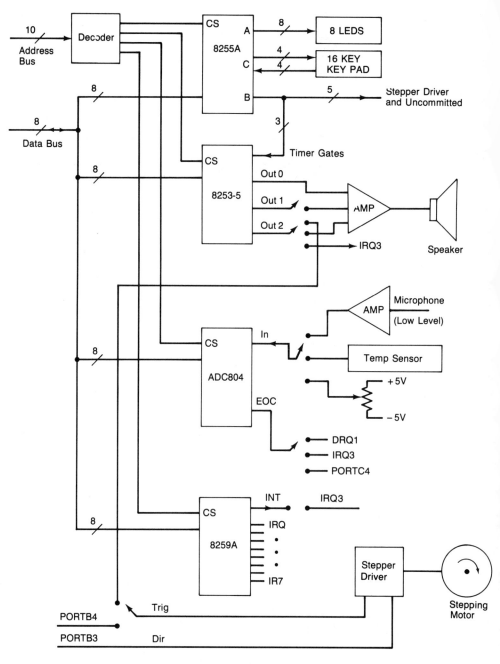

Figure A-1

- a North American Phillips stepping motor and driver
- a set of eight light-emitting diodes (LEDs)
- a numeric keypad
- an audio amplifier and speaker

The Address Decoder

The design of the address decoder follows the examples shown in Chapter 15 using the LS138 three- to eight-line decoder chip. Four chips need decoding (8255A, 8253-5, A/D, 8259A), so four of the eight decoding lines are used. The four extra lines can be used to decode added chips.

The 8255A—a Digital I/O Chip

Hardware interfacing applications usually require some digital I/O, that is, the ability to send and receive TTL-compatible signals. An easy way to provide digital I/O is to use a chip such as the Intel 8255A, which has 24 digital I/O pins, programmable in a variety of ways. The 8255A has three basic operating modes:

- Mode 0   All pins are programmed to be either input or output.
- Mode 1   The 24 pins are divided into two groups of 12 pins. Each group of 12 can be programmed into an eight-bit port (input or output) with three handshaking signals.
- Mode 2   Thirteen pins are used to provide an eight-bit bidirectional bus with five handshaking pins. The remaining pins can be used either in mode 0 or mode 1.

A complete discussion of the 8255A can be found in the Intel technical literature. The hardware we are concerned with here uses the 8255A in mode 0. Eight pins, programmed as output, control the eight LEDs. A second set of eight is programmed with four pins as output and four as input. These eight pins are used to read the numeric keypad. The final set of eight, programmed as output, controls the gates on the counter/timers and can be used to control the stepping motor.

If your project uses most or all of the 24 pins (as does the hardware described in the preceding paragraph), it is a simple matter to add another. Digital I/O can be used in many applications other than those listed above. Controlling DC motors, activating relays, reading on/off light sensors, and reading switches are just a few additional applications.

The 8253-5 Counter/Timer

Most control applications require the use of counting and timing functions. You may want to measure the duration of an event, mark the beginning of an event, or cause an event to take place at regular intervals. Although microprocessors can perform these tasks, relegating the task to another chip frees the microprocessor for more interesting work. The Intel 8253-5 was chosen from the available counter/timer (CT) chips because it is used in the IBM PC and because it is inexpensive (around $4.00) and easy to operate.

The 8253-5 contains three independent 16-bit CTs. Each has an input clock pin, a gate control pin, and an output pin. Each CT may be independently programmed into one of six possible modes. Four of the modes are nonrepetitive and are typically used as "one-shots." The remaining two modes are repetitive, one generating a square wave, and the other, a pulse.

The use of the CTs on the pedagogical board is determined by switches. All three CT outputs can be directed to the amplifier/speaker to produce three-part music. Alternatively, the output from CT1 can be directed to the stepping motor. The stepping motor can be driven at a rate programmed into CT1 by the 8088. Finally, the output from CT2 can be connected to IRQ3 in the I/O channel, providing a CT-driven interrupt.

The Analog-to-Digital Converter

The National Semiconductor ADC804 is an inexpensive, microprocessor-compatible, eight-bit A/D converter. The input circuitry of the pedagogical board was designed to allow a range of input voltages from −5 to +5 volts. A switch permits the selection of four different inputs: an amplifier for microphone input (to digitize sound waves), a temperature sensor, a potentiometer, and an uncommitted input. The National Semiconductor Linear Databook contains many interesting applications for A/D converters.

The ADC804 signals the end of an A/D conversion on an end-of-conversion (EOC) pin. On the pedagogy board, the EOC signal can be used in one of three ways (determined by a switch). The EOC signal can be connected to the following:

- an input pin on the 8255A, allowing the microprocessor to "poll" the EOC signal. In the mode of operation, the 8088 watches the EOC signal until the end-of-conversion is indicated.
- the DRQ1 line in the I/O channel. When a conversion is complete, the EOC signal requests that the DMA controller automatically read and store the result.
- the IRQ3 line in the I/O channel. When a conversion is complete, the EOC activates an interrupt service routine that reads and stores the result.

The 8259A Programmable Interrupt Controller

Chapter 18 covered this chip in great detail. As we learned there, we cannot formally "cascade" an 8259A in the I/O channel. The 8259A on the pedagogy board therefore operates in the polled mode. The interrupt output (INT) can be connected to IRQ3 (in the I/O channel) by a switch. Two of the eight IRQ lines are connected to outputs from the 8255A for testing purposes. The eight inputs can be connected to eight devices to provide an eight-level interrupt system.

The North American Phillips Stepping Motor and Driver

The stepping motor on the board is model K82701, a relatively inexpensive, low-power stepping motor. The resolution is 48 steps per revolution, and the maximum step rate is 300 steps/sec. The main drawback to this motor is that it requires a 12 Vdc supply. Although it may be possible to drive this motor with the IBM PC power supply, the transients generated might make the attempt unwise. North American Phillips makes a single chip driver (SAA 1027) that makes interfacing easy. With the driver chip in place, two signals control the stepper: one, a trigger, determines when a step is taken; the other controls the direction of the step. On the pedagogy board, the trigger input can be controlled either by an output from the 8255A or by the output of CT1.

PEDAGOGICAL-BOARD PLACEMENT

The pedagogical board is connected to the I/O channel via a flat ribbon cable and is thus out in the open to permit ready access to the components. Signals can be observed easily with an oscilloscope; switches can be manipulated; new components can be wired in, and debugging can be performed, all without opening the IBM PC.

EXPERIMENTAL POSSIBILITIES

The following list is intended to give you an idea of the variety of exercises that can be performed with a board such as this:

- Write a keypad driver, displaying the key value on the LEDs.
- Use the keypad to control other equipment, such as the stepping motor or the A/D converter.
- Use the LEDs to display the result of an A/D conversion, for example, the temperature.
- Write a program that allows the A/D converter to request DMA service.
- Write a program that allows the A/D converter to invoke an interrupt service routine.
- Wire the outputs of the 8253-5 to the 8259A IRQ line permitting three timer-controlled interrupts.
- Write three-part music.
- Program the 8253-5 to cause interrupts on IRQ3. For example, the interrupt service routine could read the keypad to control the stepping motor. All this would be done in the "background"; that is, the 8088 could be doing something else (analyzing data) at the same time.
- Program the 8253-5 to control the stepping-motor rate.

- Write a device-driver (the formal kind) that copies characters from the A/D converter to a disk-file.

This is a partial list of possibilities. By adding a few more components to the board (D/A converters, sensors, relays, DC motors), the possibilities for education and entertainment become unlimited.

We hope that the discussion of the pedagogy board will encourage you to build devices to meet your own needs. Expert knowledge is required only for high-speed and high-precision applications. You can do many interesting things with a board of your own devising.

A diskette containing the program examples in this book is available for $19.95. (Price subject to change.)

To Order, Mail your check to
Royer Associates
206 Santa Margarita Avenue
Menlo Park, CA 94025

(California residents add $1.30 for the 6.5% sales tax.)

Information about the pedagogical board discussed in the Appendix, about other PC boards, and about the course on which this book is based can be obtained by writing to the above address

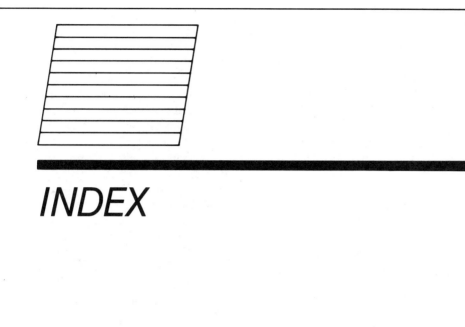

INDEX